I0102572

Proceedings of the Grand Lodge of the District of Columbia 1898

Also from Westphalia Press

westphaliapress.org

The Idea of the
Digital University

Bulwarks Against
Poverty in America

Treasures of London

Avate Garde Politician

L'Enfant and the Freemasons

Spring or Cruel Winter?: The
Evolution of the Arab Revolutions

Making Trouble for Muslims

Philippine Masonic
Directory ~ 1918

Paddle Your Own Canoe

Opportunity and Horatio Alger

Careers in the Face of Challenge

Bookplates of the Kings

The Boy Chums Cruising in
Florida Waters

Freemasonry in Old Buffalo

Original Cables from the Pearl
Harbor Attack

Social Satire and the
Modern Novel

The Essence of Harvard

The Genius of Freemasonry

A Definitive Commentary
on Bookplates

James Martineau and
Rebuilding Theology

On Foreign Service

Baghdad and Points East

Mexico: Wonderland of the South

Anti-Masonry and the
Murder of Morgan

Understanding Art

Spies I Knew

Lodge "Himalayan
Brotherhood" No. 459 C.E.

Ancient Masonic Mysteries

Collecting Old Books

Masonic Secret Signs and Passwords

Death Valley in '49

Lariats and Lassos

Mr. Garfield of Ohio

The Wisdom of Thomas
Starr King

The French Foreign Legion

War in Syria

Naturism Comes to the
United States

New Sources on Women and
Freemasonry

Designing, Adapting, Strategizing in
Online Education

Gunboat and Gun-runner

Meeting Minutes of Naval Lodge
No. 4 F.A.A.M ~ 1812 & 1813

Proceedings of the Grand Lodge of the District of Columbia

1898

by John P. Sheiry

Introduced by Paul Rich

WESTPHALIA PRESS
An imprint of Policy Studies Organization

Proceedings of the Grand Lodge of the District of Columbia ~ 1898
All Rights Reserved © 2014 by Policy Studies Organization

Westphalia Press
An imprint of Policy Studies Organization
1527 New Hampshire Ave., NW
Washington, D.C. 20036
info@ipsonet.org

ISBN-13: 978-1633910430
ISBN-10: 1633910431

Cover design by Taillefer Long at Illuminated Stories:
www.illuminatedstories.com

Daniel Gutierrez-Sandoval, Executive Director
PSO and Westphalia Press

Devin Proctor, Director of Media and Publications
PSO and Westphalia Press

Updated material and comments on this edition
can be found at the Westphalia Press website:
www.westphaliapress.org

MASONIC WASHINGTON IN THE GILDED AGE:

With the Proceedings of the Grand Lodge for 1898

Masonry at the End of the Nineteenth Century

The Proceedings of the Grand Lodge of the District of Columbia, which are included in this volume, provide a detailed view of the progress Masonry had made in the capitol since the Civil War. One would think that a bitter war dividing the country would be devastating for Freemasonry, yet the society not only survived the Civil War but also started on a period of great growth. Washington D.C. was no exception. Brother Mark Twain called the later part of the nineteenth century the Gilded Age, and so it proved for Masonry.[1]

While the fratricidal conflict destroyed many institutions, the Masons in the capital succeeded remarkably in keeping brotherhood alive, and the war did not slow the growth of Masonry in the District. In 1863 there were 1233 Masons. By 1865 there were 1720. New lodges were founded, including Harmony Lodge Number 17 in 1863, Acacia Lodge Number 18 and Lafayette Lodge Number 19 in 1863. Columbia Lodge revived and its charter was returned in 1865. This trend in growth as it did elsewhere in the country continued with the urbanization of the last part of the nineteenth century.

During the Civil War, Masonry's cable tow had extended to families searching for loved ones, even to extent of the Grand Lodge in the District supporting Masonic doctors who provided a service "for the purpose of embalming and preserving the bodies of such brother Masons, citizens or soldiers who may be so unfortunate as to die or be killed, while at the seat of war and away from their families and friends, a service was free of charge to Masons."[2] Washington lodges provided travel money for stranded brothers and paid for clothes for brethren who were prisoners of war in the South. This help continued long after the end of the war: In 1869 Masons in the District obtained a congressional charter for the Masonic Mutual Relief Association of the District of Columbia to help widows and orphans. This eventually became the mega company known as Acacia Life Insurance.[3]

Creation of military lodges was another response.[4] Washington Masons were staunch Unionists and many enlisted In fact, in 1862 Naval Lodge presented Bro. Robert Clarke, its past master and an active officer, with a sword, belt, and revolver.[5] The first military lodge to be chartered was for the Seventh Regiment of the National Guard of the State of New York, followed by a lodge for the Third Regiment Pennsylvania Reserve Corps, known as the Potomac Watch. Then the 59th Regiment New York State Volunteers was given dispensation for a lodge, followed by a dispensation for the Third Brigade of the First Division of the Fifth Army Corps Army of the Potomac, to be known as the Lodge of the Union.[6] These traditions of supporting those in service were reaffirmed in 2006 with the organization of Freedom Military Lodge No.1775 for brethren in the military.[7]

The social diversity of the membership of Washington lodges, which had marked the earlier founding period, initially continued although by the end of the century it would wane. It was retrospectively singled out when the 140th anniversary of the founding of Harmony in 1863 was commemorated: "... recall Brothers C. Cammack, Sr.; E. C. Eckloff; G. Alfred Hall; J. E. F. Holmead; J. W. D. Gray; William Blair Lord; Y. P. Page; William H. Rohrer; and W. Morris Smith. These were nine men who lived, worked, laughed, loved, suffered, and served Masonry 140 years ago. We know little about them as men except that their very names indicate their national origins as English, Eastern European, Scottish, German. Of such was our union of states created."[8]

The same categorization of varied membership describes the charter members of Anacostia Lodge No.21 in 1868: "The Master, a clerk; the Senior Warden, a bricklayer; the Junior Warden, a clerk; the Secretary, a lawyer...[members] Hotel–keeper, Tin-smith, Blacksmith, Watchmaker, Merchant, Druggist, Carpenter, Gardener, Grocer, Farmer, Musician, Wood-dealer, Cigar-maker, Barber ...".[9] This diversity was all the more noteworthy because as mentioned earlier, lodge fees in this era could exceed a month's wages.[10]

After the war was over, lodges were quick to extend a hand to the former rebels; when Lebanon Lodge received a request in 1866 from brethren in Columbia, South Carolina, for a donation towards rebuilding their temple, it was met. However while others might be helped, the Grand Lodge itself lacked an adequate headquarters. Over the years it has not been as lucky in its real estate as in its opportunities to lay cornerstones.

The loss of the original headquarters during the Anti-Masonic agitation already has been recounted.

At long last, in 1868 Masonry showed its renewed strength by erecting a magnificent temple at Ninth and F Streets N.W. which still stands, restored at great expense in the 1990s to its former glory for, among other things, a seafood restaurant. Brother Adolf Cluss, the architect, also designed the Smithsonian's Arts and Industries Building and the Eastern Market on Capital Hill. He was a staunch member of Lafayette Lodge and the architect as well of the Lafayette School. The ballroom during Grand Lodge occupancy became a favored venue for the city's important social events.

When the cornerstone was laid in May 1868, President Andrew Johnson, a Master Mason, excused all members of the Executive Branch who were Masons to march with him in the parade to the site.[11] The building served well, but an even more impressive new headquarters opened on 13th Street in 1908. In 1983 this was purchased from the Masons for what is now the National Museum of Women in the Arts. While a Masonic center, the building for a time housed the George Washington University Law School, and the edifice is on the National Register of Historic Places, The exterior retains its beautifully crafted Masonic symbols, as well as the remarkable interior features such as the sweeping marble staircases.[12]

The New Grand Lodge in 1870

The Ninth Street building was a credit to the growth of Washington Freemasonry and to Grand Master Benjamin B. French. This was a period of many prominent Masons, but Brother French was such an exceptional one that he requires special notice.[13] He knew every president from Andrew Jackson (1833) to Andrew Johnson (1867), organizing Lincoln's Inaugural, and the Gettysburg memorial dedication. He oversaw the completion of the Capitol with its new dome, and President Lincoln's funeral, visiting him on his deathbed. His house was on the site of the present Jefferson building of the Library of Congress. Commissioner of Public Buildings in Washington, he lost the job because of his anti-slavery views and then was reappointed by Lincoln. He chaired the Board of Alderman of the District, headed the Telegraph Company, and chaired the District relief committee to support families of soldiers during the Civil War. [14]

The former 1870 Grand Lodge building today

Initiated in 1826 in New Hampshire and courageously serving there as master during the Anti-Masonic period, he was also an officer of the Grand Lodge of New Hampshire. After moving to Washington, he was Grand Master of the Grand Lodge from 1847 to 1853, and in 1868 became Grand Master again after much persuasion. He was active in many other bodies.

In his diary French describes an early encounter with Albert Pike on Wednesday, January 12, 1853: "... passed the day at my office and the Capitol, and in the evening attended a meeting of the Encampment of Knights Templars, and conferred the orders on Albert Pike, Esq. of Arkansas. He is a scholar and a poet. Was an officer in the Mexican War and a man I am disposed to hold in High estimation." Then, on February 6, 1853: "Thursday evening, Washington Encampment met and we conferred the orders of Knighthood on General Sam Houston. We had a full encampment, and everything went off admirably."[15] In 1851 French had received the degrees of the Scottish Rite and on Dec 12, 1859 Albert Pike as Sovereign Grand Commander of the Southern Jurisdiction, conferred upon him the 33°.[16] In 1870, he was made Lieutenant Grand Commander of the Supreme Council Southern Jurisdiction.[17]

Arguably no Mason has been associated with more public Masonic functions over a longer period in the District than French.[18] As recounted, when Grand Master he laid the cornerstone of the Smithsonian Institution in 1847. In 1848 in a grand ceremony, he laid the cornerstone of the Washington Monument in Washington D.C. In 1850, accompanied by President Zachary Taylor, he laid the cornerstone of the Washington Monument in Richmond, Virginia. Again as Grand Master, wearing the original apron used by Washington, French laid the cornerstone of the Capitol extension on July 4, 1851, following which a pilgrimage was made to Washington's tomb with an address given by French. Nearly twenty years later, in 1867, he accompanied President Andrew Johnson to Boston for a national meeting of the Masonic Knights Templar, of which French had also been Grand Master. On April 15, 1868 he presided over the dedication of Washington's first statue of Abraham Lincoln.[19]

Reminiscent of the raising to Master Mason by Potomac Lodge of the great, great, great, great grandson of Valentine Reintzel, it happily fell to Benjamin B. French Lodge to raise Peter French, great grandson of Benjamin French. The family has deposited a treasure of papers in the Library of Congress that are waiting to be researched by Masonic scholars.

Benjamin French exemplifies the strength of Masonry in Washington at this critical time. The period after the war was marked by an enormous increase in American wealth, by waves of immigrants, and for Masons in the District as in many parts of the country, a time of unprecedented prosperity. Steven Bullock observes that in the twenty years after 1855, more men joined than in the 125 previous years, and that "By 1884, Masonry had experience extraordinary growth. Its membership rolls far exceeded their pre-1826 peak." [20]

This era continued for the lodges to be marked by a diversity in nationalities and a diversity in the social standing of members, with a good representation of men who had taken advantage of the public schools for their education and were not the beneficiaries of silver spoon childhoods.[21] Members who were trade folk sat in lodge next to lawyers and doctors.[22] The grand masters held respectable but hardly stellar positions; they were renowned more as grand masters than in their professions, with exceptions like Benjamin French.

French was not the only unforgettable figure enlivening Washington Freemasonry in the nineteenth century, and even he could hardly match the activities of Albert Pike.[23] It would be a great mistake to think that Pike's leadership of the Scottish Rite kept him from participating in the Grand Lodge or that he arrived on the scene only after the Civil War. Pike was a visitor to Washington long before the Civil War, as his early encounters with French make clear, and in fact was admitted to the Supreme Court Bar in 1842.[24] Moreover, he was a good citizen. When he noticed after establishing the Supreme Council in Washington that the public was asking to use its library, he formalized the arrangement by establishing the first free general library in Washington, housed in the Supreme Council headquarters.[25]

There could hardly be a better example of an Enlightenment figure than Pike. "That Masonry is in some sense the product of the Enlightenment is beyond dispute. Because Albert Pike was a great Freemason, and a great scholar of the Craft," writes Bro. Peter Paul Fuchs, "then we would expect him in some way to be an Enlightenment product." Given Pike's hundreds of books and articles, that is easily demonstrated.[26] Pike was indeed extraordinary and stories about him are not only extraordinary but also often true. Typically in his larger than life character, he attended his own funeral wake in Washington in 1859 when a rumor that he was dead caused his grieving friends to organize a farewell banquet. Since all was in place for the wake, news that he might indeed be alive did not keep the event from going ahead and Pike appeared dramatically after a number of libations had been consumed. Rather than annoyed, he thought the experience useful: "I am wiser than before, and know men better. I know them better, and therefore love them more, and would fain do the world and my fellows some service before I die."[27]

Pike still intrigues those not only Masons but also those outside the Craft. Craig Parshall in the novel, *The Rose Conspiracy*, describes Pike's colorful career as a focal point for his Washington thriller: "A man who bragged of being conversant in numerous languages, well-read in the world religions and philosophies, and an international leader among the Freemasons, Albert Pike met, and was most certainly captivated by, Vinnie Ream, the pretty, coquettish sculptor who had wooed Washington's high society. During their long relationship, Pike arranged for Ream to ceremonially receive Masonic degrees, despite the fact that women were generally forbidden from joining the Masons."[28]

The Scottish Rite in the District remained small compared to the York Rite for most of the nineteenth century,[29] but Pike displayed a genius for re-packaging fraternal rites as theatrical experiences.[30] He established an impressive center in the first House of the Temple, a row of brownstones that he connected and converted at Third and E Streets, N.W., used as the Scottish Rite headquarters in 1870-1900. He conferred the Scottish Rite degrees in the White House itself on President Andrew Johnson in 1867 and, befriending James Garfield before his brief presidency, gave him the fourteenth degree in 1872.

The capitol and Albert Pike went together like the proverbial horse and carriage, and he continues to be an enormous influence; his challenge to Masons still relevant: "Masonry in our day cannot forsake the Broadway of life. She must journey on in the open street, appear in the crowded square, and teach men by her deeds, her life more eloquent than any lips."[31]

Pike was not so preoccupied with the Scottish Rite that he had no time for the Grand Lodge. This contradicts claims that he was indifferent to the blue lodge because he joined the Scottish Rite only four years after being raised.[32] He was for a time a member of Pentalpha Lodge No. 23, and was the Representative of the Grand Lodge of Louisiana near the Grand Lodge of the District of Columbia from November 21, 1870 to 1891. He was also the Grand Representative of the Grand Lodge of Lower California (Mexico) near the Grand Lodge of the District of Columbia, and a Regent of the American Masonic Home for widows and orphans in the city.[33] There were increasing numbers of new Masons for his degrees as by

President Andrew Johnson as a Scottish Rite Mason

1884 Masonic membership in the District exceeded 3000. [34]

The election in 1882 of Brother James A. Garfield as President was greeted with jubilation, but he was assassinated after only two months in office. Active in the Craft for many years while a congressman, like Pike he was a member of Pentalpha Lodge Number 23 (now Osiris-Pentalpha) and took the degrees in the York Rite bodies in Washington.[35] The Scottish Rite's Mithras Lodge of Sorrow in 1881 reminded the mourners that "…all his life he accepted the emblems of our order, significant of deep religion, high morality and well organized strength of purpose, rectitude, equality, brotherly love – the keystone of the arch, the plumb, the level, the trowel – the pot of incense as the emblem of a pure heart."[36]

The final dedication of the Washington Monument was on February 21, 1885.[37] Brother John Philip Sousa conducted a brief band concert, drowned out by the stamping of feet to keep warm. Grand Master Myron M. Parker did the honors with corn, wine, and oil. Treasures related to George Washington that the Masons safeguard were again in evidence. The Washington Gavel and the Washington Trowel were used along with the Bible on which Washington was obligated in his Mother Lodge, Fredericksburg No. 4, Fredericksburg, Virginia. The Bible belonging to St. John's Lodge No. 1, New York City, the very Bible on which Washington took his first oath of office as President, was on display along with the Masonic apron given to him by the Marquis de Lafayette, and made by

Madame Lafayette. The Grand Lodge of Massachusetts displayed their golden urn containing a lock of Washington's hair. The stones given by various Masonic bodies provide an interesting sight if one takes the stairs down from the top. That of the Grand Lodge is on the Third Landing, adjacent to one given by Naval Lodge.[38]

This post Civil War era was a period when there were Masonic scholars in the city with international reputations. One of these who should be more remembered, and who is awaiting a modern biography, as well as adequate republication of his many works, is William R. Singleton, the Grand Secretary of the Grand Lodge of the District of Columbia, from 1875 until his death in 1900. He collaborated with the famous Masonic scholar Bro. Dr. Albert Gallatin Mackey, but on his own authored at least 57 publications, including *Organization of the Grand Lodge of England*, *Freemasonry in Asia, An Introduction to The Symbolism of Freemasonry*, *The Astrologers and Freemasons*, and *The Legend of Hiram Abif.* An enduring mystery is the disappearance of the manuscript he prepared on the history of the Grand Lodge and of Freemasonry in the District, which was known to exist, and never published, but could not be found after his death in 1905.

Scholars like Brother Singleton were a resource for the Grand Lodge because of the need to determine which other jurisdictions it should recognize. Over many years the Proceedings contain discussions about the pros and cons of answering requests for recognition by other grand lodges.[39] These requests continue to be made and given careful attention.

While the Victorian era was noteworthy for the fraternity, by the end of the nineteenth century membership no longer displayed all the social diversity and cosmopolitan origins that it had earlier. Social stratification was a late nineteenth century trend in society, and a trend that lodges reflected. A generalization, which has been challenged, is that "This was the era when capital and labor fought their first pitched battles on a national scale, and capital won. Wealth became far more concentrated, the super-rich turned their backs callously on the poor, lavishing millions on banquets and ball gowns."[40]

Part of the reason given for the social changes is the influence of large-scale immigration: "A great gulf was opening between a predominantly native plutocracy and a predominantly foreign working class. The United States was becoming two nations separated by language and religion, residence, and ... the outcome was nativism."[41] This hardening in attitude was not only true of Masonry: "Americans basked in the 'romance of reunion' between North and South, at the expense of African-Americans, but the celebration of an Anglo culture required the repression of some memories. Nativists also clamored for restrictions on foreign immigration and demanded Anglo-conformity from immigrants already arrived."[42] So a case can be made that Masonry was becoming as the century drew to a close more of "a homogeneous group: white, Anglo-Saxon, Protestant, and Republican."[43] While Washington was growing in population, its neighborhoods became more defined by social class: "When the Constitution was ratified in 1788 only about 5 percent of the residents of the new nation lived in cities. Today, about 80 percent of the population lives in places defined as urban. …The later third of the nineteenth century – years when the interrelated process of urbanization, industrialization, and immigration reached high tide – was a key period in that transition."[44]

While earlier assimilation of various groups had not always been without incident, it had not presented the challenges that new waves of emigrants did, challenges which would take a long time to be addressed,[45] and only after debating alternatives of heterogeneous and homogenous membership and ritual.[46] This was despite the tradition of Masonic Diversity. Albert Mackay, the great Masonic scholar, thought that the values of this diversity were inherent in the colors identified with different degrees,[47] which he held can be mined for ideas from the past which revitalize the fraternity: "… Not only are we challenged by the different symbols we see, and the ritual we observe, but most importantly, we learn that diversity and individual interpretation, is the norm in Masonry, it is fundamental to the Craft, and to us, as individuals in promoting our daily advancement in Masonic knowledge."[48] A vision statement by Justice-Columbia Lodge sums up the case that was made for appreciating a variety of Masonic styles:

Freemasonry, like a priceless tapestry of truths and beliefs, draws its beauty from varying shades, tints and patterns that come together under the hands of an ever-caring Architect. Its beauty comes from the diversity of the brethren, as is the strength of the individual mason who grows through contact with brethren of other countries, religions, professions and backgrounds. Only through exposure to others can one grow. Similarly, only through the brotherly fray of different views can a spontaneous order of ideas emerge in an optimal way. [49]

If partly lost as the century ended, cosmopolitanism would, like a certain word about which much of Masonic ritual revolves, be found again.[50] In fact, despite being nearly 200 years old, the Grand Lodge in the twenty-first century would become possibly the most cosmopolitan grand lodge anywhere in terms of membership and rituals.

Paul Rich

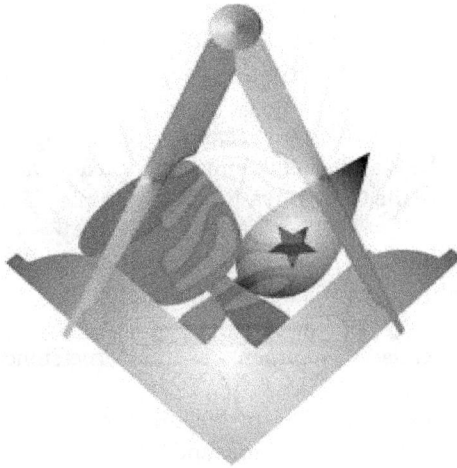

[1]   Twain's satire, *The Gilded Age*, appeared in 1873. Possibly a triple pun was intended on gilt, guilt, and guilds (in the sense of interest groups). Sean Dennis Cashman, *America in the Gilded Age*, 3rd ed., New York University Press, New York, 3. Also, Louis j. Budd, introduction, Mark Twain and Charles Dudley Warner, *The Gilded Age*, Penguin Books, New York, 1001, xiv-xv.

[2]   Allen E. Roberts, "Masonry Under Two Flags", Jack Buta ed., *Fiat Lux, Vol. I: 1956-1986*, Philalethes Society, Sebring (Ohio), 2009, 48.

[3]   "Masonic insurance", http://www.masonic-lodge-of-education.com/masonic-

insurance.html, ac.12 Sept. 2011.

4   For an excellent discussion of military lodges of the era see Michael A. Halleran, *The Better Angels of Our Nature: Freemasonry in the American Civil War,* The University of Alabama Press, Tuscaloosa (Alabama), 2010, 140-158.

5   Walter L. Fowler, *History of Naval Lodge No.4, F.A.A.M., June A.D. 1905-June A.D. 1955,* Naval Lodge No.4, 1955, 334. Fowler provides mini biographies of all masters from Naval's inception.

6   African-American freemasonry allegedly using its secret ways of recognition contributed to the "Underground Railroad" that enabled escaping slaves to find their way to Canada. See "Prince Hall Masonry and Harriet Powers" at http://ugrrquilt.hartcottagequilts.com/rr5.htm, ac.23 March 2011.

7   Military lodges chartered by northern grand lodges were regarded as clandestine by the Grand Lodge of Virginia, as were other activities such as those of the Grand Lodge of the District of Columbia during the war. See *Report of the Committee under the Resolutions of 1862,* Grand Lodge of Virginia, Richmond, 1865, esp. 38. Prince Hall grand lodges continue to charter military lodges to this day.

8   Charles L. Overman, *140 Years of Harmony,* Harmony Lodge No. 17, n.d., Washington D.C. Address at the 140th anniversary celebration of the Lodge on Friday, June 20, 2003, in the George Washington Masonic National Memorial in Alexandria, Virginia.

9   Walter L. Fowler, *History of Anacostia Lodge No.21 - F.A.A.M.,* December 1868 to December 1961, Anacostia Lodge, Washington D.C., 1962, 19.

10   Ibid, 21.

11   Staff Report, "Architect's Comments at the Cornerstone Ceremony", *The Voice of Freemasonry,* Vol.23 No.2, 6.

12   Christopher Weeks, *AIA Guide to the Architecture of Washington, D.C.,* Johns Hopkins University Press, Baltimore and London, 1974,113-114. Weeks is incorrect in stating that the 13th Street building was given up because it was too small; the loss of the building was because of decreased income.

13   See Ralph H. Gauker, *History of the Scottish Rite Bodies in the District of Columbia,* Centennial Edition, Mithra Lodge of Perfection, Washington, D.C., 1970, 1-74.

14   Donald B. Cole, John J. McDonough eds., *Benjamin Brown French, Witness to the Young Republic: A Yankee's Journal, 1828-1870,* University Press of New England, Hanover and London, 1989, 165, 189-1909, 211, 303.

15   John Vergalia, "Benjamin B. French", *Voice of Freemasonry,* Vol.20 No.3, 13.

16   Bro. French was a close friend of Albert Pike and worked incessantly to get him a pardon after the Civil War. Fred W. Allsopp, *Albert Pike,* Parke-Harper Company, Little Rock, Arkansas, 1928, 180, 220.

17   Vergalia, "Benjamin B. French", 13.

18   Bro. French may have been the only Grand Master of the Grand Lodge to

be impersonated after his death: Grand Master Renah Camalier costumed and made himself up as French for the 100th anniversary observation of Washington Centennial Lodge No.14. Robert F. Ensslin, *Centennial Celebration: Washington Centennial Lodge*, Gibson Brothers, Washington, 1953, 6. Bro. Camalier, who while in the Navy during World War II was assigned to be stenographer for President Franklin Roosevelt, gave the Japanese Pagoda by the Tidal Basin. A personal gift to him in 1957, he donated it to the city. "Japanese Pagoda", http://citywalkingguide.com/westnationalmall/japanese-pagoda, ac.3 Dec 2010. Bro. Camalier deposited his FD memorabilia in the National Archives: ARC Identifier 558734 / Local Identifier DM-CAMAL-M103. Chief Rabban of Alamas Temple, he was successful in involving President Truman in Shriner charities.

[19]   Vergalia, "Benjamin B. French", op cit.

[20]   Steven C. Bullock, *Revolutionary Brotherhood: Freemasonry and the Transformation of the American Social Order, 1730-1840*, University of North Carolina Press, Chapel Hill & London, 1996, 316. Bullock hypothesizes that anti-Masonry changed Masonry itself, forcing it to be more acceptable to the public.

[21]   For an overview of Victorian Freemasonry see Mark C. Phillips, "The Influence of Victorian Progress on Scottish Rite Freemasonry", *Heredom*, Vol. 16, 2008, 101 ff.

[22]   Fowler, *History of Anacostia Lodge No.21*, 129.

[23]   The literature about Pike is voluminous, but a short useful description of his genius at ritual is seen in Jim Tresner, *Vested in Glory*, Scottish Rite Research Society, Washington DC, 2000, with it paintings by Robert H. White.

[24]   Robert Lipscomb Duncan, *Reluctant General: The Life and Times of Albert Pike*, E.P. Dutton, New York, 1961, 110.

[25]   William L.Fox, *Lodge of the Double-Headed Eagle: Two Centuries of Scottish Rite Freemasonry in America's Southern Jurisdiction*, University of Arkansas Press, Fayetteville, 1997, 101. James D. Carter, History of The Supreme Council, 33o, 1861-1891, The Supreme Council, 33o, Washington DC, 1967, 259, 338, 344, 365-366. In 1890, the library had 15,000 volumes. ibid, 367.

[26]   Peter Paul Fuch, "Incense to the Intellect: Implications of the Albert Pike Library", *Heredom*, Vol.17, 2009, 78.

[27]   Duncan, *Reluctant General*, 150.

[28]   Craig Parshall, *The Rose Conspiracy*, Harvest House, Eugene (Oregon), 2009, 79.

[29]   However, it benefited being in the right place at the right time as an urban phenomenon and enjoyed steady growth.

[30]   Robert G. Davis, "Freemasonry and the Theatre Tradition", *Transactions*, American Lodge of Research, New York, Vol. XXXVII, 2010, 46-47.

[31]   Qtd. H.L.Hayward, Symbolical Masonry, 1923, at http://www.sacred-texts.com/mas/syma/syma06.htm, ac.17 Jan 2011.

[32] David A. Roach, *God Loves Masons, Too: The First Defenders of Human Rights*, BookSurge, Charleston (South Carolina), 2006, passim.

[33] Albert Pike supported the York Rite in the District, affiliating with Lafayette Chapter No. 5 about 1872. He was Grand Representative of the Grand Chapter of Mississippi near the Grand Chapter of the District of Columbia as well as Grand Representative of the Grand Chapter of Nevada near the Grand Chapter of the District of Columbia and Grand Representative of the Grand Chapter of Oregon near the Grand Chapter of the District of Columbia. (He represented the Grand Chapter of the District of Columbia at the General Grand Chapter of the United States, Buffalo, N.Y., 1877.) Pike received his Cryptic and Commandery degrees in Washington – the Commandery degrees received in the presence, as noted, of French. He was President of the Masonic Veteran Association of the District of Columbia from its organization in 1879 to the time of his death 1891. He was also Supreme Magus of the Rosicrucian Society, whose "See" was established by him at Washington on May 17, 1880. Arturo de Hoyos, *Masonic Formulas and Rituals*, Scottish Rite Research Society, Washington DC, 2010, 53-57.

[34] *Proceedings of the Grand Lodge of Washington, D.C.*, 1884.

[35] William R. Denslow, *10,000 Famous Freemasons, Vol.II*, Cornerstone, Lafayette (Louisiana), 2007, 106.

[36] George Bailey Lording, "Address at the Mithras Lodge of Sorrow, Washington, November, 10, 1881: In memory of James A. Garfield", Library of Congress reprint service, original publisher unknown.

[37] For an account of the building of the Monument with much detail not recounted elsewhere, Louis Torres, *The United States Army Corps of Engineers and the Construction of the Washington Monument*, University Press of the Pacific, Honolulu, 2001.

[38] A history of the Monument and list of the stones of donors and the inscriptions appears in a Library of Congress reprint of Rudolf De Zapp, *The Washington Monument: An authentic history of its origin and construction, and a complete description of its memorial tablets*, Caroline Publishing, Washington, D.C., 1900. See also "The Melodies of the Washington Monument", http://www. greatdreams.com/washmnmt.htm, ac.22 Feb 2011.

[39] The Grand Lodge in the 1880s recognized Mexican grand lodges in Mexico City, Jalisco, Morelos, Oaxaca, Vera Cruz, Guerrero, Lower California, and Tamaulipas, while wondering whether it should recognize others such as Puebla, Tabasco, Durango, and Campeche.

[40] Rebecca Edwards, "Politics, Social Movements , and the Periodization of U.S. History", *The Journal of the Gilded Age and Progressive Era*, Vol.8 No.4, October 2009, 464. But, "…political commentators who argue that we now live in a 'New Gilded Age' would have to confront the fact that social and economic inequality, selfish use of wealth, and indifference to the poor have characterized –most eras of U.S. history, not just the first three decades after the Civil War." ibid, 473.

[41]   Sean Dennis Cashman, *America in the Gilded Age: From the Death of Lincoln to the Rise of Theodore Roosevelt*, 3rd ed., New York University Press, New York and London, 1993 (1984), 96.

[42]   Ruth C. Crocker, "Cultural and Intellectual Life in the Gilded Age", Charles W. Calhoun ed., *The Gilded Age: Perspectives on the Origins of Modern America*, Rowman & Littlefield Publishers, Lanham (Maryland), 2007, 230.

[43]   Alan Trachtenberg, *The Incorporation of America: Culture and Society in the Gilded Age*, Hill and Wang, New York, 2007 (1982), 79.

[44]   Robert G. Barrows, "Urbanizing America", Calhoun, ed. *The Gilded Age*, 102.

[45]   See Barrows, "Urbanizing America", Calhoun ed., The Gilded Age, 101-118. Cf. James W. Russell, *After the Fifth Sun: Class and Race in North America*, Prentice Hall, Englewood Cliffs (New Jersey), 1994, 110=111.

[46]   See Johannes Quack and William S. Sax, "The Efficacy of Rituals", *Journal of Ritual Studies*, Vol.24 No.1, 2010, 5-12.

[47]   See Mackay's fascinating entry on "Masonic colors" in the *Encyclopedia of Freemasonry, Vol.1* (1909). A 2003 reprint is available from The Masonic History Company.

[48] J.J.P. Goody, "Diversity in Freemasonry", Lecture at Godolphin Lodge No.7790, Cornwall, United Kingdom, 18 Aug 2005, http://web.mit.edu/dryfoo/Masonry/Essays/diversity.html, ac.8 Mar 2011.

[49] "About JC3", http://www.thethirdlodge.org/, ac. 8 Mar 2011.

[50] The 1924 National Origins Act restricting immigration can be seen as the culmination of this trend. Hasia Diner, "The Encounter between Jews and America in the Gilded Age and Progressive Era, *The Journal of the Gilded Age and Progressive Era*, Vol.11 No.1, January 2012, 4-5.

PROCEEDINGS

OF THE

GRAND LODGE

OF

Free and Accepted Masons

OF THE

District of Columbia

FOR THE YEAR

...1898...

EIGHTY-EIGHTH ANNUAL REPORT.

John F. Sheiry, Printer, Washington, D. C.
1899.

PROCEEDINGS

OF THE

GRAND LODGE

OF

Free and Accepted Masons

OF THE

DISTRICT OF COLUMBIA

FOR THE YEAR 1898.

———o———

Eighty-Eighth Annual Report.

———o———

JOHN F. SHEIRY, PRINTER, WASHINGTON, D. C.
1899.

PROCEEDINGS

OF THE

GRAND LODGE, F. A. A. M.,

OF THE

DISTRICT OF COLUMBIA

FOR 1898.

———✦———

SPECIAL COMMUNICATION.

———

WASHINGTON, D. C., *March* 30, 1898.

A Special Communication of the Grand Lodge, F. A. A. M., was held in Masonic Temple at 7 o'clock p. m.

PRESENT.

Bro. SAMUEL C. PALMER . M. W. Grand Master.
Bro. WM. G. HENDERSON . R. W. Senior Grand Warden.
Bro. CHARLES BECKER . as R. W. Junior Grand Warden.
Bro. WM. R. SINGLETON . R. W. Grand Secretary.
Bro. WM. A. GATLEY . . R. W. Asst. Grand Secretary.
Bro. CHAS. C. DUNCANSON . R. W. Grand Treasurer.
Bro. JOSEPH HAMACHER . W. Grand Lecturer.
Bro. CLAUDIUS B. SMITH . Rev. and W. Grand Chaplain.
Bro. MALCOLM SEATON . . W. Grand Marshal.
Bro. JOSEPH JOUY . . as W. Senior Grand Deacon.
Bro. JAMES A. WETMORE . W. Junior Grand Deacon.
Bro. LURTIN R. GINN . . W. Grand Sword Bearer.
Bro. FRANCIS J. WOODMAN . W. Senior Grand Steward.
Bro. A. B. COOLIDGE . . W. Junior Grand Steward.
Bro. JOHN N. BIRCKHEAD . Grand Tiler.

Past Grand Masters R. B. Donaldson and Matthew Trimble.

Representatives and Past Masters of Lodges Nos. 1, 3, 4, 5, 7, 9, 10, 11, 12, 14, 15, 16, 17, 18, 19, 20, 21, 22, 23, 24, 25, 26, 27, 28, 29.

The Grand Lodge was opened in ample form. Prayer by the Rev. and W. Grand Chaplain.

The Grand Master stated that the Special Communication was called for the purpose of the exemplification of the work of the several degrees and the reception of reports from the Committees of Jurisprudence and on Proposed Removal of the Grand Lodge Library.

The M. W. Grand Master caused a letter from R. W. Deputy Grand Master John H. Small, Jr., to be read, explaining his absence. Bro. George H. Walker, W. Senior Grand Deacon, was also unavoidably absent.

The Committee on Proposed Removal of the Grand Lodge Library reported, that, owing to conditions beyond their control they were unable to make a satisfactory report, and asked for an extension of time to the May Semi-Annual Communication, which request was granted.

The Committee on Jurisprudence made the following report:

REPORT OF COMMITTEE ON JURISPRUDENCE.

WASHINGTON, *March* 30, 1898.
To The Grand Lodge, F. A. A. M., of the District of Columbia:

The M. W. Grand Master has referred to your Committee on Jurisprudence a communication from the W. M. of Hiram Lodge, No. 10, and also one from the W. M. of Potomac Lodge, No. 5, each of which relates to the construction of the recent amendments to Sections 8 and 9 of Article XX of the Grand Lodge Constitution, together with a copy of his decision in the matter referred to in the communication of Hiram Lodge.

It appears that there is some uncertainty as to whether these amendments are intended to apply to cases of rejection, whether by ballot, or by objection, which occurred previous to their adoption, or only to those occurring subsequent thereto—or, in other words, whether the amended law is retroactive in its effect.

Your committee would report:

That in recommending the adoption of the amendments in question it was clearly the intention of the committee to have them apply to all cases of rejection then standing upon the records of our lodges, as well as to those occurring after their adoption, and they recommend that such construction is to be put upon said amendments.

The following decision in this connection was recently made by the M. W. Grand Master:

"WASHINGTON, D. C., *February* 12, 1898.
"MR. W. F. R. PHILLIPS,
     " *W. M. Hiram Lodge, No. 10, F. A. A. M.*
     " DEAR SIR AND BROTHER : Your communication of 5th inst., in reference to the reception of petition of Mr. Frank Hibl for the degrees of Masonry in your lodge, has been received and duly considered and in reply thereto I answer:

"(1) 'Whether the lapsing of a period of five years from the date of the rejection of a petition, constitutes a waiver of jurisdiction on the part of the lodge having original jurisdiction,' and (2) 'whether such a petition can be received by another lodge without the consent of two-thirds of the members of the lodge having original jurisdiction, it being still in existence,' in the affirmative; and therefore decide, (3) that the petition of Mr. Frank Hibl, who states that he was rejected by Pentalpha Lodge, No. 23, F. A. A. M. of D. C., in 1892, can be legally received by your lodge without waiver of jurisdiction by said Pentalpha Lodge, your lodge first being informed definitely of the date of such rejection.
"Truly and fraternally,
     [SEAL]   "SAMUEL C. PALMER,
                                        " *Grand Master.*
"Enclosure,
"Mr. Frank Hibl's petition."

Your committee would further recommend that the above quoted decision be confirmed by the Grand Lodge.
     Respectfully submitted.

R. B. DONALDSON,
Committee on Jurisprudence.

On motion of Past Grand Master Matthew Trimble the report was adopted.

A request was presented from Arminius Lodge, No. 25, for permission to permanently occupy the lodge room now used by it, which request, on motion of Past Grand Master Matthew Trimble, was unanimously granted.

On motion of the R. W. Grand Secretary it was ordered that the letter containing said request be spread in full upon the records of the Grand Lodge, but not to be included in the printed proceedings.

The R. W. Grand Secretary offered the following resolution, which, after amendment by Past Grand Master R. B. Donaldson, was unanimously adopted.

Resolved, That in consequence of the invitation to all the lodges in the District of Columbia from the Fair Committee to visit the Fair at Convention Hall on the 12th of April, such lodges as have the stated communication that night may select any night, prior or subsequent thereto, transact their regular business and work as provided for in their by-laws, and give due notice thereof to all their members in the District.

The Most Worshipful Grand Master stated that he had received a communication from Bro. John H. Small, Jr., President of the Board of Control of the proposed National Masonic Fair and Exposition, requesting that the Most Worshipful Grand Master, and the other officers of the Grand Lodge should attend the fair, in full regalia, on its initial night, April 11th, and in connection with Bro. William McKinley, President of the United States, formally open the same. Also that the Most Worshipful Grand Master had been solicited to request the constituent lodges to meet him and the other Grand Officers, at the Masonic Temple, on the evening of April 12th, at 7.30 o'clock, to escort him and the other Grand Officers to the fair, said evening having been designated as "Blue Lodge" night. He stated that he had accepted both invitations and had caused a circular letter to be addressed to the Worshipful Masters requesting them to cause their lodges to assemble at Masonic Temple on the 12th inst., as duly organized lodges; members to wear dark clothing, black hats, and regalia.

The R. W. Assistant Grand Secretary presented the credentials of Bro. Past Grand Master George W. Baird, and Bro. Past Master James A. Wetmore, of Benjamin B. French Lodge, No. 15, as representatives of the Grand Lodges of Nevada and South Carolina, respectively, near the Grand Lodge of the District of Columbia, and moved that they be received and acknowledged as such. Carried.

The Most Worshipful Grand Master invited the Grand Lecturer to assume the East, who then, under the supervision of the Committee on Work and Lectures, proceeded to exemplify the degrees of Entered Apprentice, Fellow Craft, and Master Mason, consecutively, with the assistance of the following named brethren, viz: Benjamin S. Graves, of No. 19, as Senior Warden; John A. Moyer, of No. 27, Junior Warden; William A. Gatley, of No. 15, as Secretary; Robert V. Godman, of No. 9, as Treasurer; John D. Hinternesch, of No. 20, as Senior Deacon; John S. Beach, of No. 11, as Junior Deacon.

At the conclusion of the exemplification of the degrees, the Most Worshipful Grand Master resumed his station.

The Grand Lodge was closed in ample form. Prayer by the Rev. and W. Grand Chaplain.

WM. R. SINGLETON,
Grand Secretary.

SEMI-ANNUAL COMMUNICATION.

WASHINGTON, D. C., *May* 11, 1898.

The Semi-Annual Communication of the Grand Lodge, F. A. A. M., of the District of Columbia was held at the Masonic Temple at 6 o'clock p. m.

PRESENT.

Bro. SAMUEL C. PALMER . M. W. Grand Master.
Bro. JOHN H. SMALL, JR. . R. W. Deputy Grand Master.
Bro. WM. G. HENDERSON . R. W. Senior Grand Warden.
Bro. HARRY STANDIFORD . R. W. Junior Grand Warden.
Bro. WM. R. SINGLETON . R. W. Grand Secretary.
Bro. WM. A. GATLEY . . R. W. Asst. Grand Secretary.
Bro. C. C. DUNCANSON . . R. W. Grand Treasurer.
Bro. JOS. HAMACHER . . W. Grand Lecturer.
Bro. C. B. SMITH . . . . Rev. and W. Grand Chaplain.
Bro. MALCOLM SEATON . W. Grand Marshal.
Bro. GEORGE H. WALKER . W. Senior Grand Deacon.
Bro. JAMES A. WETMORE . W. Junior Grand Deacon.
Bro. LURTIN R. GINN . . W. Grand Sword Bearer.
Bro. WALTER A. BROWN . W. Grand Pursuivant.
Bro. THOMAS H. YOUNG as W. Senior Grand Steward.
Bro. A. B. COOLIDGE . . W. Junior Grand Steward.
Bro. JOHN N. BIRCKHEAD . Grand Tiler.

Past Grand Masters: Thomas F. Gibbs, E. G. Davis, H. Dingman, R. B. Donaldson, M. Trimble, George W. Baird.

Past Deputy Grand Master J. H. Jochum.

Past Junior Grand Warden George E. Corson.

Visitor: William M. Somerville, P. M., Dalhousie Lodge, Canada.

REPRESENTATIVES:

LODGES.	W. MASTERS.	S. WARDENS.	J. WARDENS.
Federal, No. 1................	....	*G. Z. Colison, P....*	....
Columbia, No. 3...........	....	J. C. Keiper...........	L. F. Speer...........
Lebanon, No. 7............	*George Spransy,P.*	....	....
New Jerusalem, No. 9..	....	Edw. Matthews...	....
Hiram, No. 10...............	W. F. R. Phillips..	....	John T. Meany....
St. John's, No. 11..........	W. T. Jones.........	....	....
National, No. 12..........	Joseph E. Falk....	....	Abner P. Wilde....
Wash'n Centen'l, No. 14	J. H. Davis...........	Edson Phillips....	....
B. B. French, No. 15.....	....	....	E.St.C.Thompson
Dawson, No. 16............	E. G. Harbaugh...	Ed.S. Holmes, Jr.	....
Acacia, No. 18...............	....	*J. M. Brous, Prox.*	....
La Fayette, No. 19........	Thos. P. Morgan..	....	....
Hope, No. 20.................	C. C. Van Horn...	....	....
Geo. C. Whiting, No. 22	....	....	Jas. H. Taylor.....
Pentalpha, No. 23.........	G.Tauberschmidt	Wm. J. Wallace...	Wm. L. Price.......
Stansbury, No. 24........	....	Henry Yost, Jr....	....
Arminius, No. 25........	W. F. Meyers.......	*M. Glaeser, Proxy.*	....
M. M. Parker, No. 27....	....	J. M. McCoy.........	*W.R.Carver, Prox.*

Past Masters: No. 1, George Colison, W. S. Jenks; No. 3, A. M. Muzzy, W. S. Macgill, W. H. Decker; No. 4, K. N. Harper; No. 7, Thomas H. Young, H. K. Simpson; No. 9, R. V. Godman; No. 10, Joseph Jouy, G. W. Uline; No. 12, Joseph M. Eggleston, W. E. Handy; No. 14, H. P. Marshall, E. C. Elmore, E. C. C. Winter, F. W. Harper, C. K. Berryman; No. 15, H. M. Gillman; No. 16, F. A. Sebring, John N. Birckhead; No. 17, Samuel Baxter, W. Ham. Smith, O. S. Firmin, A. W. Johnston, Charles F. Heilbrun; No. 19, W. H. Olcott; No. 20, W. A. Craig, F. P. Hays; No. 22, W. H. Griffin; No. 23, William J. Naylor; No. 24, W. S. Nalley, J. W. Ray, T. M. F. Dowling, Thomas Calver, Angus Lamond; No. 25, Moritz Glaeser; No. 26, William Oscar Roome.

Grand Representatives: Canada, Joseph H. Jochum; Connecticut, George E. Corson; Georgia, Harrison Dingman; Idaho, E. G. Davis; Illinois, L. C. Williamson; Indiana, James A. Sample; Louisiana, M. Seaton; Mississippi, R. B. Donaldson; Nevada, George W. Baird; New Zealand, Samuel C. Palmer; Nova Scotia, W. A. Craig; North Dakota, William A. Gatley; Prince Edward Island, M. Trimble;

Quebec, Harrison Dingman; South Australia, W. G. Henderson; South Carolina, James A. Wetmore; Texas, Thomas F. Gibbs; Utah, William Oscar Roome; Victoria. R. B. Donaldson; Wisconsin, John H. Small, Jr.; Arizona, Cuba, Federal District of Mexico, Hidalgo, Jacob de Molay, Jalisco, Lower California, Missouri, Morelas, New South Wales, Vera Cruz, Vincente Guerrero, William R. Singleton.

The Grand Lodge was opened in ample form. Prayer by the Rev. and W. Grand Chaplain.

On motion of the Grand Secretary the reading of the minutes of the Installation Communication held December 27, 1897, were dispensed with, as they had been printed and circulated.

The minutes of the special communication held March 30, 1898, were read and approved.

The following report from the Committee on Jurisprudence was presented through its chairman, Past Grand Master R. B. Donaldson, viz:

REPORT OF COMMITTEE ON JURISPRUDENCE.

WASHINGTON, D. C., *May* 11, 1898.
To the Grand Lodge, F. A. A. M., of the District of Columbia:

At the last November Communication of the Grand Lodge a letter was read from Bro. F. L. Crosby, the Grand Representative of this Grand Lodge near the Grand Lodge of Peru, in reference to the condition of Masonry in Peru, and tendering his resignation as our Grand Representative. On motion the resignation was accepted, and the letter was referred to your Committee on Jurisprudence "to ascertain the facts and *status* of Masonry in the Grand Lodge of Peru."

Having discharged the duty thus assigned them, so far as circumstances permitted, your committee would respectfully report:

That the resignation of Bro. Crosby as our Grand Representative was in consequence of a decree issued June 13, 1897, by Grand Master Christian Dam, which decree was sanctioned by the Grand Lodge of Peru at its regular session of September 13, 1897, and was as follows:

"I decree that on all Masonic altars the 'Bible' shall be removed and replaced by the constitutions of the order of Freemasonry; and that in our rituals the word 'Bible' shall be struck out, and the words 'the constitution of the Grand Lodge of Peru' be put in its place.

"For the better and full observance of this decree, let it be noted in the books of this Grand Lodge, and signed and sealed with our grand seal of the Grand Lodge, in ample session, this 13th day of June, Vulgar Era 1897.

[Signed] "CHRISTIAN DAM,
"M. I. CACERES, "Grand Master.
"Grand Secretary."

This decree was prefaced by the announcement of the Grand Master's reasons for its issuance, from which we quote as follows:

"That, according to Catholicism, the Bible is a sacred book, in which the revealed word is deposited, and, as such, cannot be freely examined and criticised—without which the spirit cannot progress or be perfected, nor the truth found."

* * * * * * * * * * * * * *

"That the Bible cannot be considered as a fountain of scientific knowledge or history, nor as a basis of morality."

We learn, also, from the letter of Bro. Crosby, that at the same communication of the Grand Lodge "the formation of female lodges was authorized."

From an article in "El Libre Pensimicuto" (The Free Thinker)—official organ of the Grand Lodge of Peru, of October 2, 1897, we learn that after the report of the Grand Master containing the decree, it had been "passed to a special committee named by the Deputy Grand Master," who "approved the report in full." The report of this committee "was approved by the Grand Lodge, and ordered it to be printed." "When this was done a copy was sent to each lodge by the Grand Secretary, in obedience to order from the Grand Master, requesting that it should be read in all the lodges in the jurisdiction, that everybody might know its contents and the proposed reforms."

Three months later, at the quarterly meeting on June 13th, when all of the lodges had acknowledged the receipt of the Grand Master's report and made no remarks on same, the Grand Lodge of Peru discussed and approved by an unanimous vote "the decree of the Grand Master." It appears, however, that after this "unanimous vote," "Lodge No. 7 presented a petition for the reconsideration of the decree, which was not admitted."

This fact would indicate that some members of the constituent lodges in Peru are "Masons at heart."

Such your committee find to be the "facts and the *status* of Masonry in the Grand Lodge of Peru," and it is with profound regret that we have found a Grand Lodge with which we have heretofore held fraternal relations voluntarily taking action which, in our opinion, places it and the members of its constituent lodges who do not repudiate it on account of this action entirely without the pale of Masonry.

When we consider what the "Great Light" in Masonry is to the institution—the fact that it is in reality the basis upon which the whole superstructure rests; that the whole plan and design of the institution has evidently been drawn from the inspired volume, as the outlines of every degree in Ancient Craft Masonry may be found in its wonderful pages—is it not pitiable to find a body of men claiming to be Masons, an organization claiming to be Masonic, so far departing from the teachings of Masonry as to seek to throw discredit upon the sacred volume which is so generally recognized among enlightened nations and peoples as containing the WORD OF GOD, and as His best gift to man? It seems difficult to believe such infatuation possible in this age of the world and among professedly Christian people.

Remove this Book from our altars; cease to regard it as a basis of morality; ignore the lessons of virtue which Masonry draws from its pages and dispenses to her initiates through lectures, charges, and symbolic teachings, and Masonry would be poor indeed.

Put out the "Great Light" and all the lesser lights will become extinguished; the stars will fall, one by one, from our moral firmament, and decay and final death to Masonry will, sooner or later, be sure to follow!

Can the Grand Lodge of the District of Columbia recognize as Masons any body of men—any organization—that strikes a blow at the very foundation of our beloved institution? With entire confidence your committee leave this question to be answered by a vote of its members upon the following resolutions submitted for their action:

WHEREAS it has come to the knowledge of this Grand Lodge that the Grand Lodge of Peru has sanctioned and sustained a decree issued by the Grand Master, Dr. Christian Dam, as follows:

"I DECREE, That on all Masonic Altars the 'Bible' shall be removed and replaced by the constitutions of the order of Freemasonry; and that in our ritual the word 'Bible' shall be struck out and the words 'the constitution of the Grand Lodge of Peru' be put in its place.

"For the better and full observance of this decree, let it be noted in the books of this Grand Lodge, and signed and sealed with our grand seal of the Grand Lodge, in ample session, this 13th day of June, Vulgar Era 1897.

(Signed) "CHRISTIAN DAM,
"M. I. CACERES, "*Grand Master.*
"*Grand Secretary.*"

Therefore resolved, That the Grand Lodge of the District of Columbia strongly condemns this action of the Grand Lodge of Peru, and sees in it just and proper cause for declining to hold further Masonic intercourse with that body;

That the fraternal relations heretofore existing between the Grand Lodge of the District of Columbia and the Grand Lodge of Peru are hereby suspended;

That the Grand Representative of the Grand Lodge of Peru near this Grand Lodge be no longer recognized as such;

That the constituent lodges and individual Masons of this jurisdiction are hereby forbidden to hold Masonic intercourse with any lodge or individual Mason holding allegiance to the Grand Lodge of Peru.

All of which is respectfully submitted.

R. B. DONALDSON,
E. G. DAVIS,
MYRON M. PARKER,
Committee on Jurisprudence.

Adopted.

On motion of Past Grand Master Matthew Trimble the report was received, its recommendations concurred in, and the Grand Secretary directed to have copies thereof printed and distributed among the several Grand Lodges with which this Grand Lodge is in communication.

Past Grand Master Matthew Trimble, chairman of Special Committee on Proposed Removal of Grand Lodge Library, &c., submitted the following report which, on motion of Past Grand Master Harrison Dingman, was adopted.

WASHINGTON, D. C., *May* 11, 1898.
To the M. W. Grand Master, Wardens,
and Members of the Grand Lodge, F. A. A. M.

BRETHREN: When your committee made its report in December last on the proposed plan of leasing the entire second floor of the Masonic Temple for Grand Lodge purposes the Grand Lodge had a proposition from the Masonic Hall Association whereby the latter agreed to lease said premises at an annual rental of $1,600.

Since then, viz., on May 9, 1898, the Masonic Hall Association has reconsidered its proposition and withdrawn it, on the ground that a rental at the sum named would result in a loss to the Association, but at the same time the Association renews a proposition previously made, viz., one at an annual rental of $2,000, which includes the main hall and all the rooms connected with it with the use of chairs and settees in various rooms.

In our report of December 27, 1898, your committee submitted what was thought to be a liberal estimate of the yearly expenses of this Grand Lodge in event the $1,600 proposition was accepted. By said estimate it was shown that the expenses of the Grand Lodge would increase about $400 per year, which did not include the cost of putting the rooms in proper condition for Grand Lodge purposes, and now that the proposed rental has been fixed at $2,000 our increase in expenses would be about $800 per year.

Your committee have given the subject careful and earnest consideration and while we still firmly believe that it is highly desirable, almost necessary, for this Grand Lodge to have better and more commodious quarters for its officers and library, yet in view of the fact that our yearly expenses might be increased to the amount of nearly $800 by the proposed change and that it would cost this Grand Lodge from $600 to $1,000 to put the entire second floor in proper condition for rental and Grand Lodge purposes, your committee recommend to this Grand Lodge that the proposition of the Masonic Hall Association be not accepted.

In this connection we desire to call attention to what must be apparent to anyone using the Grand Lodge Library, and that is, that the cases for the reception of books need renovating and repairing, and to the end that this may be done, as well as other repairs about the library, your committee recommend the appropriation of $200, or so much thereof as may be necessary, the same to be expended under the direction of a special committee.

MATTHEW TRIMBLE,
WM. R. SINGLETON,
JAMES A. WETMORE,
THOMAS H. YOUNG,
LURTIN R. GINN,
Committee.

The Grand Secretary offered the following motion, which was lost:

That the committee be authorized to interview the Board of Directors of the Masonic Temple, and if they are willing to accept the rent of $1,800 that the committee is hereby authorized and directed to make such contract in the name of the Grand Lodge and proceed at once to make all necessary arrangements for removal; that the M. W. Grand Master be authorized to appoint a committee of three to take charge of said removal and make all proper arrangements for the rental of the main hall and anterooms for public purposes, to continue until the annual communication, and are hereby authorized to pay all necessary sums by warrants as provided in the Constitution.

The Assistant Grand Secretary moved an appropriation of $50 for rent to June 1st, proximo. Carried.

A communication was received from the M. W. Grand Master of Italy and referred to the Committee on Jurisprudence.

No further business appearing the Grand Lodge closed in ample form. Prayer by the Rev. and W. Grand Chaplain.

WM. R. SINGLETON,
Grand Secretary.

SPECIAL COMMUNICATION.

WASHINGTON. D. C., *May* 16, 1898.

A Special Communication of the Grand Lodge, F. A. A. M., was held at Masonic Temple at 8 o'clock a. m. for the purpose of attending the funeral of our late brother, Peter H. Hooe, Past Deputy Grand Master, whose death occurred at his home in Maryland on the 12th instant.

PRESENT.

Bro. SAMUEL C. PALMER   .   M. W. Grand Master.
Bro. HARRISON DINGMAN as R. W. Deputy Grand Master.
Bro. WM. G. HENDERSON . R. W. Senior Grand Warden.
Bro. HENRY S. MERRILL as R. W. Junior Grand Warden.
Bro. WM. R. SINGLETON   . R. W. Grand Secretary.
Bro. W. S. JENKS   . . as R. W. Grand Treasurer.
Bro. ROBT. A. DELLETT   as W. Grand Lecturer.
Bro. C. B. SMITH . . . . Rev. and W. Grand Chaplain.
Bro. JOHN N. BIRCKHEAD as W. Grand Marshal.
Bro. R. V. GODMAN . . as W. Senior Grand Deacon.
Bro. F. P. HAYS . . . as W. Junior Grand Deacon.
Bro. W. H. TEEPE   . . as W. Grand Sword Bearer.
Bro. J. B. NORTH . . . as W. Grand Pursuivant.
Bro. C. C. HELMICK . . as W. Senior Grand Steward.
Bro. M. D. HUME   . . as W. Junior Grand Steward.
Bro. JOHN N. BIRCKHEAD . Grand Tyler.

The Grand Lodge was opened in ample form.

The following appointments were then made, viz: Pallbearers for the Grand Lodge, H. Dingman and W. S. Jenks;

for Washington Commandery No. 1, Henry S. Merrill and F. Behrens; for St. John's Lodge, No. 11, R. A. Dellett and W. H. Teepe; for Centennial Lodge, No. 174, Maryland, C. C. Webster and W. H. Gibbons. Deputations from Washington Commandery, No. 1, and from St. John's Lodge, No. 11, of which bodies Bro. Hooe was a member, accompanied the Grand Lodge.

The Grand Lodge then proceeded to the Baltimore and Potomac Depot and by that railroad went to Croome Station, near which was the residence of Bro. Hooe, where carriages were in waiting, to convey the brethren to the house. The Grand Lodge then took charge of the remains and proceeded in carriages to the church of St. Thomas (Protestant Episcopal), where religious services were conducted by Rev. F. P. Wielles; after which the casket was borne to the grave near the church and the Masonic services were performed according to ancient usage. During the religious service, the sun reached an altitude whereby the rays through an upper window shone down upon the casket and produced a beautiful scene which was inspiriting to the audience. After the ceremonies the brethren were conveyed in carriages to Upper Marlboro' where dinner had been previously ordered and the guests enjoyed the same.

The Grand Lodge returned to the city and to the Temple and was closed in ample form.

WM. R. SINGLETON,
Grand Secretary.

SPECIAL COMMUNICATION.

WASHINGTON, D. C., *October* 18, 1898.

A Special Communication of the Grand Lodge, F. A. A. M., of the District of Columbia was held at the Northeast Temple, H street near Twelfth, northeast, at 3.30 o'clock p. m.

PRESENT.

Bro. SAMUEL C. PALMER   . M. W. Grand Master.
Bro. JOHN H. SMALL, Jr.   . R. W. Deputy Grand Master.
Bro. JAS. A. WETMORE . as R. W. Senior Grand Warden.
Bro. HARRY STANDIFORD . R. W. Junior Grand Warden.
Bro. WM. A. GATLEY   . . R. W. Asst. and Act'g G. Sec.
Bro. CLAUDIUS B. SMITH   . Rev. and W. Grand Chaplain.
Bro. GEO. H. WALKER . as W. Grand Marshal.
Bro. ANDREW K. LIND . as W. Senior Grand Deacon.
Bro. J. E. BURNS . . . as W. Junior Grand Deacon.
Bro. Z. T. JENKINS . . as W. Grand Sword Bearer.
Bro. GEO. W. ULINE   . as W. Senior Grand Steward.
Bro. JOSEPH JOUY   . . as W. Junior Grand Steward.
Bro. JOHN H. BIRCKHEAD . Grand Tiler.

Representatives and Past Masters of Lodges Nos. 5, 10, 11, 14, 15, 16, 21, 22, and 27.

The Grand Lodge was opened in ample form.

Labor was dispensed with in the third degree and a lodge in the first degree declared open.

The Grand Master stated that he had called the Grand Lodge together to assist him in laying the corner-stone of the Douglas Memorial M. E. Church, he having been invited to perform that service by the building committee.

The following appointments were then made: Bro. Jesse M. Harr, No. 27, bearer of the Great Light; Bro. Thomas A. Perry, W. M., No. 27, bearer of the Square; Bro. Charles A. Pike, No. 27, bearer of the Level; Bro. John A. Moyer, No. 27; bearer of the Plumb; Rev. Bro. S. Bilheimer, No. 5, bearer of the Goblet of Corn; Bro. Frank Thomas, P. M., No. 5, bearer of the Goblet of Wine; Bro. William Scherer, No. 5, bearer of the Goblet of Oil.

The procession was then formed, under the direction of the Grand Marshal, and proceeded to the site of the church, corner of Eleventh and H streets, northeast.

The religious services having previously been held in the Northeast Temple (owing to the inclemency of the weather), the M. W. Grand Master, with the assistance of the other Grand Officers, laid the corner-stone in ample form in accordance with the ancient usage of the craft.

The Grand Lodge then returned to the Northeast Temple. Labor was resumed in the third degree and the Grand Lodge was closed in ample form.

WM. A. GATLEY,
Asst. and Acting Grand Secretary.

ANNUAL COMMUNICATION.

WASHINGTON, D. C., *November 9*, 1898.

The Annual Communication of the Grand Lodge, F. A. A. M., of the District of Columbia was held at Masonic Temple at 6 o'clock p. m.

PRESENT:

Bro. SAMUEL C. PALMER . M. W. Grand Master.

Bro. JOHN H. SMALL, JR. . R. W. Deputy Grand Master.

Bro. WM. G. HENDERSON . R. W. Senior Grand Warden.

Bro. HARRY STANDIFORD . R. W. Junior Grand Warden.

Bro. WM. R. SINGLETON . R. W. Grand Secretary.

Bro. WM. A. GATLEY . . R. W. Asst. Grand Secretary.

Bro. C. B. SMITH . . . . Rev. and W. Grand Chaplain.

Bro. J. S. RAEBURN . . as W. Grand Marshal.

Bro. GEORGE H. WALKER . W. Senior Grand Deacon.

Bro. JAMES A. WETMORE . W. Junior Grand Deacon.

Bro. LURTIN R. GINN . . W. Grand Sword Bearer.

Bro. WALTER A. BROWN . W. Grand Pursuivant.

Bro. FRANCIS J. WOODMAN W. Senior Grand Steward.

Bro. A. B. COOLIDGE . . W. Junior Grand Steward.

Bro. JOHN N. BIRCKHEAD . Grand Tiler.

Past Grand Masters: R. B. Donaldson, Isaac L. Johnson, E. G. Davis, Myron M. Parker, Jose M. Yznaga, Harrison Dingman, James A. Sample, Thomas F. Gibbs, L. C. Williamson, Henry S. Merrill, David G. Dixon, George W. Baird.

Past Deputy Grand Master Joseph H. Jochum.

Past Junior Grand Wardens George W. Balloch, George E. Corson.

REPRESENTATIVES:

LODGES.	W. MASTERS.	S. WARDENS.	J. WARDENS.
Federal, No. 1	R. B. Nixon	H. M. McDade	H. B. Mason
Columbia, No. 3	Herbert Wright	J. C. Kelper	L. F. Speer
Naval, No. 4	H. P. Cook		
Potomac, No. 5	Jas. S. Raeburn		A. W. Hudson
Lebanon, No. 7	J. H. Tatspaugh		
New Jerusalem, No. 9	B. Parkhurst	Edw. Matthews	H. D. Feast
Hiram, No. 10	W. F. R. Phillips	John Breen, Prox.	John T. Meany
St. John's, No. 11	W. T. Jones	J. S. Beach, Prox.	
National, No. 12	Joseph E. Falk		Abner P. Wilde
Wash'n Centen'l, No. 14		Edson Phillips	
B. B. French, No. 15	H. MacNamee, P.		F. St. C. Thompson
Dawson, No. 16	F. G. Harbaugh	Ed. S. Holmes, Jr.	B. F. Odell
Harmony, No. 17		C. T. Caldwell	
Acacia, No. 18		S. T. Covert	
Lafayette, No. 19	Thos. P. Morgan	B. S. Graves	H. S. Selden
Hope, No. 20	C. C. Van Horn	N. S. Meyers	G. A. Cohill
Anacostia, No. 21	W. F. Gude	A. Gude, Proxy	
Geo. C. Whiting, No. 22	B. W. Murch		J. H. Taylor
Pentalpha, No. 23		Wm. J. Wallace	W. L. Price
Stansbury, No. 24	G. C. Pearson	Henry Yost, Jr.	
Arminius, No. 25		M. Glaeser, Proxy.	
Osiris, No. 26	F. A. Harrison	C. H. Buckler	W. H. DeShields
King David, No. 28	C. E. Baldwin		
Takoma, No. 29	H. J. Long		

Past Masters: No. 1, W. S. Jenks, J. S. Tomlinson, G. Y.
AtLee; No. 3, A. M. Muzzy, W. H. Decker, G. S. King, W.
S. Macgill; No. 4, G. W. Harrington, K. N. Harper; No. 5,
F. Thomas, W. S. Waddey; No. 7, T. Taylor, Thomas H.
Young, H. K. Simpson, W. W. Ludlow, W. F. Gatchell;
No. 9, A. W. Kelley, R. V. Godman; No. 10, Joseph Jouy,
M. R. Thorp; No. 11, James E. Hutchinson, A. McKenzie,
W. H. Douglas; No. 12, Joseph M. Eggleston, C. W. Otis;
No. 14, H. P. Marshall, E. C. Elmore, C. H. Smith, W. B.
Pettus, F. W. Harper, J. J. Hill, C. K. Berryman, R. Con-
nell, H. F. Riley; No. 15, H. M. Gillman, W. A. Meloy,
H. M. Schooley; No. 16, F. A. Sebring, R. Williss; No. 17,
W. H. Smith, W. C. Babcock; No. 18, G. W. Koonce, C. J.
O'Neill; No. 19, A. F. Fox, W. H. Olcott, W. Brown; No.
20, F. P. Hays, J. H. Cunningham, W. A. Craig, C. W.
Henshaw, J. S. Mills; No. 21, S. E. Shields, W. S. Dodge,
H. Kuhn; No. 22, Charles Becker; No. 23, W. P. H. Crews,
William J. Naylor, S. A. Hollingshead, J. C. Johnson, H. A.
Trembley; No. 24, G. W. Balloch, J. W. Ray, W. E. Nalley,

Thomas Calver, T. M. F. Dowling, Angus Lamond, F.
L. Summy; No. 25, J. Toense, Moritz Glaeser; No. 26, C. S.
Hyer, W. L. Boyden, W. L. Sears; No. 27, J. E. Burns;
No. 29, Theo. Friebus.

Grand Representatives: Mississippi, Victoria, R. B. Donald-
son; Illinois, L. C. Williamson; Connecticut, George E. Cor-
son; Indiana, James A. Sample; Idaho, E. G. Davis; Indian
Territory, I. L. Johnson; Michigan, Charles H. Smith; New
Hampshire, G. W. Balloch; New York, H. S. Merrill; New
Zealand, S. C. Palmer; North Dakota, William A. Gatley;
Nova Scotia, W. A. Craig; Ohio, Venezuela, Jose M. Yznaga;
South Australia, W. G. Henderson; South Dakota, D. G.
Dixon; Texas, T. F. Gibbs; Wisconsin, John H. Small, Jr.;
Montana, G. H. Walker; South Carolina, J. A. Wetmore;
Nevada, George W. Baird; Arizona, Cuba, Federal District
of Mexico, Hidalgo, Jacob de Molay, Jalisco, Lower Cali-
fornia, Missouri, Morelas, New South Wales, Vera Cruz,
Vincente Guerrero, William R. Singleton.

The Grand Lodge was opened in ample form. Prayer by
the Rev. and W. Grand Chaplain.

The minutes of the Semi-Annual Communication held May
11, 1898, and Special Communications held May 16 and October 18, 1898, were read and approved.

The M. W. Grand Master then read the following address:

GRAND MASTER'S ADDRESS.

BRETHREN OF THE GRAND LODGE: I congratulate you upon
the happy auspices under which we are permitted to assemble in
this the Eighty-seventh Annual Communication of the Grand
Lodge. Harmony and prosperity prevail throughout the lodges
of the jurisdiction, and our fraternal relations with sister Grand
Lodges, with the exception of the Grand Lodge of Peru, have
been undisturbed; and I anticipate with pleasure the probable re-
sumption of intercourse with that Grand Body, within whose
jurisdiction the "Great Light of Masonry" has been restored upon
their altars.

Before proceeding with the formal report of my actions during the year, I deem it meet and proper to pay our tribute of respect and sorrow to the memories of our brethren who have passed to the higher life.

OUR FRATERNAL DEAD.

The records of our constituent lodges will show the names of a number of deceased brethren during the present Masonic year, and among them will be found the name of Bro. Peter H. Hooe, Past Deputy Grand Master of this Grand Lodge and Past Master of St. John's Lodge, No. 11. Bro. Hooe died at his residence, near Croome, Md., May 12, and was buried May 16, 1898. R. W. Grand Secretary Wm. R. Singleton communicated with M. W. Grand Master Thos. J. Shryock of Maryland, who readily assented to the suggestion that the burial services should be conducted by this Grand Lodge, and in company with a number of the Grand Officers and a delegation from St. John's Lodge, No. 11, and Washington Commandery, No. 1, K. T., I repaired to the late residence of the deceased, and, assisted by a number of members of Centennial Lodge, No. 174, located at Cheltenham, Md., accompanied the body to the place of interment, where it was buried with Masonic services, as provided by our beautiful ritual, after the solemn service of the Episcopal Church had been concluded. I recommend that a page of our printed proceedings be set apart as a memorial to Past Deputy Grand Master Hooe, and a suitable number of pages be inscribed to the memory of other deceased members of our jurisdiction. "After life's fitful fever they sleep well."

> "Oh, perfect rest, divinely full and deep,
> Safe from the storms which earthward o'er us sweep—
> For so He giveth His beloved sleep."

A number of distinguished brethren of other jurisdictions have also passed away, and from the many we record the names of—

M. W. Bro. John Quincy Adams Fellows, Past Grand Master of Louisiana. Died November 28, 1897.

M. W. Bro. William B. Taliaferro, Past Grand Master of Virginia. Died February 27, 1898.

M. W. Bro. John Patterson Fitzgerald, Past Grand Master of Virginia. Died June 10, 1898.

M. W. Bro. William Francis Drinkbard, Past Grand Master of Virginia. Died July 9, 1898.

M. W. Bro. William H. Best, Past Grand Master of North Dakota. Died May 3, 1898.

M. W. Bro. James R. Boyce, Sr., Past Grand Master of Montana. Died April 2, 1898.

M. W. Bro. Daniel Striker, Past Grand Master of Michigan. Died April 11, 1898.

M. W. Bro. Henry C. Cook, Past Grand Master of Kansas. Died June 12, 1898.

M. W. Bro. Parker Job Pillans, Past Grand Master of Alabama. Died June 12, 1898.

M. W. Bro. James M. Harkey, Past Grand Master of Arkansas. Died September 28, 1897.

R. W. Bro. John W. Widderfield, Past Deputy Grand Master of Colorado. Died July 4, 1898.

R. W. Bro. William Abram Dove, M. D., Past Deputy Grand Master of Georgia. Died January 22, 1898.

R. W. Bro. Charles C. Stevenson, Grand Secretary of Grand Lodge of Idaho. Died February 28, 1898.

R. W. Bro. George C. Davis. Died October 21, 1897.

R. W. Bro. J. Henry Leonard, Past Deputy Grand Master of New Brunswick. Died April 21, 1896.

DISPENSATIONS.

I have granted the following dispensations during the year:

January 11th, to Federal Lodge, No. 1, to enable said lodge to receive application of Mr. N. M. Carpenter for the degrees of Masonry in accordance with a provision of its By-Laws.

January 11th, to Takoma Lodge, No. 29, to confer the Master Mason's degree upon Bro. George W. Parkins in advance of statutory period, as the brother was about to remove from the jurisdiction.

April 6th, to St. John's Lodge, No. 11, to confer the Master Mason's degree upon Bro. S. Albert Fishblate one week in advance of the regular time, the brother being in poor health and desirous of leaving the city.

May 7th, to Myron M. Parker Lodge, No. 27, to confer the Master Mason's degree on Bro. Orlando L. Pettebone in advance of statutory time, provided the brother was proficient in the work of the second degree.

May 7th, to La Fayette Lodge, No. 19, to receive the report of a committee and ballot upon petition of Mr. Etbelbert L. B. Brackenridge previous to statutory time, and, if elected, to confer the first degree on him May 19, 1898, resident members of the lodge to be notified of proposed action.

May 7th, to La Fayette Lodge, No. 19, to confer the Master Mason's degree upon Bro. Nat. Tyler, Jr., at a special meeting of the lodge to be held May 14, 1898, said brother having been initiated February 17 and passed May 5, 1898, and under orders to leave the city May 20, 1898, in connection with the U. S. Geological Survey.

May 24th, to La Fayette Lodge, No. 19, to confer the second and third degrees upon Bro. J. O. A. Kansche, an Entered Apprentice of the lodge, prior to June 4, 1898, at which time said brother would sail for Europe, to be gone possibly several years.

June 18th, to La Fayette Lodge, No. 19, as will appear in the subjoined application and answer:

"WASHINGTON, D. C., *June* 18, 1898.
"MR. SAMUEL C. PALMER,
  "*Grand Master of Masons of the District of Columbia.*

"DEAR SIR AND M. W. BROTHER: I have the honor to request dispensation to hold a special meeting of La Fayette Lodge on Wednesday, the 22d instant, to receive the report of a committee on the petition for the degrees of Mr. George C. Schafer, and, if elected, to confer the first, second, and third degrees upon him on that evening.

"The circumstances are as follows: Mr. Schafer is twenty-three years of age, now resides at 439 Sixth street, southwest, and has been a resident of the District of Columbia since his birth. He has been lately appointed an assistant paymaster in the U. S. Navy, and is on waiting orders, liable to be sent to his ship any day. This young man is favorably known for a number of years by Past Master John H. Olcott and Bro. Max Fischer, both of La Fayette Lodge, who highly commend him and are anxious that he should go to the front as a Mason.

"If you can see your way clear to grant this dispensation, it will be highly appreciated.
      "Fraternally yours,
            "THOMAS P. MORGAN,
                  "*Worshipful Master.*"

"WASHINGTON, D. C., *June* 18, 1898.
"MR. THOMAS P. MORGAN,
      "*W. M. La Fayette Lodge, No. 19, F. A. A. M.*

"DEAR SIR AND BROTHER: Your letter of this date is at hand, and, in accordance with your request, dispensation is hereby granted La Fayette Lodge, No. 19, F. A. A. M., to hold a special meeting on Wednesday, the 22d instant, to receive the report of a committee on the petition of Mr. George C. Schafer for the degrees of Masonry, and, if elected, to confer the first, second, and third degrees upon him on that evening. As Mr. Schafer has received an appointment in the U. S. Navy, and is liable to be sent to his ship any day, I recognize this as a very urgent case, and suggest that an extra effort be made to secure his proficiency in the work of the degrees before his departure, if conferred.

"You will notify your resident members of the proposed action of the lodge.
      "Fraternally yours,
            "SAMUEL C. PALMER,
                  "*Grand Master.*"

August 3d, to Osiris Lodge, No. 26, to confer the first and second degrees upon Mr. Ira J. Pennewill, if elected, at a regular meeting of the lodge of this date, the applicant being a traveling man, who is necessarily absent from the jurisdiction a great part of the time.

September 8th, to George C. Whiting Lodge, No. 22, to hold its regular communications of September 8 and September 22, 1898, in the annex to the Masonic Hall, Georgetown, D. C., in consequence of repairs being made to lodge room.

September 9th, to Columbia Lodge, No. 3, to confer the Fellow Craft's and Master Mason's degrees upon Bro. Bernard Herman in advance of the statutory period, as said brother would leave the city on the 20th instant to enter an institution of learning at Boston, Mass., for an extended course of study.

September 15th, to Hope Lodge, No. 20, authorizing said lodge to confer the third degree upon Bro. Dale Sheriff in advance of statutory time, as the brother, a sailor in the U. S. Navy, would be ordered away by the 20th instant, care being taken to insure his proficiency in the degrees.

September 19th, to Potomac Lodge, No. 5, to hold such meetings of the lodge as may be necessary in the banquet hall of Masonic Hall, Georgetown, D. C., while repairs were being made to its regular lodge room.

October 17th, to Washington Centennial Lodge, No. 14, to confer the Master Mason's degree upon Bro. Mark Hatch ten days prior to statutory time, provided Bro. Hatch was proficient in work of second degree.

DECISIONS.

The only decisions I have been called upon to make of sufficient importance to present to the Grand Lodge are the following:

March 9, 1898, I received a communication from William F. Meyers, Worshipful Master of Arminius Lodge, No. 25, of which the following is an extract:

"In our last meeting a candidate, whom the committee had favorably reported and recommended, received a black cube on the first and second ballot. Every brother present seemed astonished, and before I could announce the result some brethren expressed a suspicion that by carrying the old ballot-box around it could happen that a black cube could get into the box, and, on motion of Bro. Louis Goldsmith, I ordered and requested every brother to cast another ballot (the third); no objections. This ballot was clear, and accordingly I declared the candidate duly and legally elected. Since then a member of our lodge asserts that this ballot was illegal. Will you kindly send me your opinion, so I can satisfy the brother who is in doubt?"

To which I made the following reply:

"WASHINGTON, D. C., *March* 12, 1898.
"MR. WILLIAM F. MEYERS,
"*Worshipful Master Arminius Lodge, No.* 25, *F. A. A. M.*

"DEAR SIR AND W. BROTHER: Your letter of the 9th instant, in which you ask my decision as to the legality of your action in taking a third ballot upon the application of a candidate for the degrees of Masonry in your lodge, has been received.

"Section 9, Article XX, of Grand Lodge Constitution, provides that where one black ball (cube) appears in the first ballot it shall be immediately retaken, 'when, if a single black ball (cube) again appears, no further ballot can be taken for said applicant for the space of six months.'

"In contemplation of the law, a mistake may happen on the first ballot, but it is hardly probable to occur the second time, and it would be highly improper for each member of the lodge to make known how he voted, as that course would destroy the secrecy of the ballot, which should be carefully guarded.

"If, as suggested, it is possible for a cube to find its way into the ballot without being cast, owing to faulty construction of your ballot-box, a perfect box should be provided.

"In view of the law quoted, I am of opinion that the third ballot was illegal, and so decide. The candidate must be regarded as having been rejected.
"Fraternally yours,
"SAMUEL C. PALMER,
"*Grand Master.*"

"WASHINGTON, D. C., *January* 31, 1898.
"SAMUEL C. PALMER, Esq.,
"*M. W. Grand Master of the Grand Lodge,*
F. A. A. M., District of Columbia.

"DEAR SIR AND BROTHER: In view of the fact that the present meeting place of Osiris Lodge, No. 26, F. A. A. M., was the birthplace of this lodge and has been its place of meeting ever since, and in consideration of the present situation, I desire (as Worshipful Master of said lodge) your official opinion as to whether Osiris Lodge may continue to meet in its present quarters (1007 G street, northwest) indefinitely.
"Respectfully and fraternally,
"FRANK A. HARRISON,
"*Worshipful Master.*"

"WASHINGTON, D. C., *February* 2, 1898.
"MR. FRANK A. HARRISON,
"*Worshipful Master Osiris Lodge, No.* 26, *F. A. A. M.*

"DEAR SIR AND BROTHER: I have carefully considered your communication of January 31, 1898, in which you ask my 'official opinion as to whether Osiris Lodge may continue to meet in its present quarters (1007 G street, northwest) indefinitely,' and beg to say in reply that the sanction of the Grand Lodge must be obtained for such continued occupancy of a lodge room in which other than Masonic organizations meet.

"Truly and fraternally,

"SAMUEL C. PALMER,

"*Grand Master.*"

Several other questions have been presented for consideration, but a reference to the Grand Lodge Constitution rendered a formal decision of any of them unnecessary.

GRAND REPRESENTATIVES.

I have the pleasure to report that in accordance with our system, February 5, 1898, a commission was issued to Bro. William A. McBride, appointing him Grand Representative near the Grand Lodge of Indian Territory.

February 5, 1898, a commission was issued to Bro. Joseph A. Miller, appointing him Grand Representative near the Grand Lodge of Nevada.

April 30, 1898, a commission was issued to Bro. Charles W. Pomeroy, Deputy Grand Master, appointing him Grand Representative near the Grand Lodge of Montana.

June 2, 1898, a commission was issued to Bro. Robert S. Gaskill, appointing him Grand Representative near the Grand Lodge of New Jersey, at the request of the Grand Master of New Jersey, in place of Bro. James H. Durand, who represents another Grand Lodge, that jurisdiction having determined to have one brother to represent only one Grand Lodge.

The following brethren have received commissions as Grand Representatives near this Grand Lodge:

Bro. George W. Baird, Past Grand Master, from the Grand Master of Nevada; Bro. James A. Wetmore, W. Junior Grand Deacon, from the Grand Master of South Carolina; Bro. George H. Walker, W. Senior Grand Deacon, from the Grand Master of Montana.

MASONIC FAIR AND EXPOSITION.

At the last Installation Communication of the Grand Lodge I invited your attention to, and requested your earnest support of, the proposed National Masonic Fair and Exposition, to be held in April of the current year, and it now gives me pleasure to report its complete success. The attendance exceeded anticipation, and the profit resulting forms a substantial nucleus for the fund necessary to construct a new temple in this beautiful city. I received the following invitation to be present and assist at the opening exercises:

"MR. SAMUEL C. PALMER,
"*M. W. Grand Master of the Grand
Lodge of the District of Columbia.*

"DEAR SIR AND M. W. BROTHER: I have the honor, in behalf
of the Board of Control, to invite you and the officers of the Grand
Lodge to be present, in full regalia, on the evening of April 11,
1898, at 8 o'clock, and to formally open the National Masonic Fair
and Exposition, to be held at Convention Hall, in this city.

"The program outlined for the evening, which I trust will meet
with your approval, is as follows:

"Prayer by the Grand Chaplain of the Grand Lodge. Music.
Presentation of the Most Worshipful Grand Master by the President of the Board of Control to open the fair. Presentation of the
President of the United States by the Most Worshipful Grand
Master for the purpose of turning on the lights at the various
booths as a signal that the fair is open. Grand chorus of three
hundred voices.

"This order of exercises has been submitted to the President of
the United States, who has expressed his approval of the same,
and states that he will be present if public business will permit.

"An answer at your earliest convenience will be appreciated.
"Fraternally yours,
"J. H. SMALL, JR.,
"*President.*"

Which I accepted, and on the evening in question, accompanied
by the Grand Officers and a large number of our distinguished
Past Grand Masters and other notable brethren, had the honor of
opening the fair in the following short address:

ADDRESS OF THE GRAND MASTER.

LADIES, GENTLEMEN, AND BRETHREN OF THE MASONIC OR-
DER: We are assembled this evening for the purpose of assisting
in the opening ceremonies of an enterprise which has for its object the formation of a fund to assist in the erection of a temple in
this city to be dedicated to the uses of the fraternity of Free and
Accepted Masons—a temple which is expected to be commensurate
with the needs of the fraternity of this jurisdiction, capable of
accommodating the National Bodies of Knights Templar and the
General Grand Chapter of the United States; an ornament to the
Capital of our Nation, and an asylum for the wayfaring brothers of
all lands.

I will not attempt to recapitulate the details of the work which
has led to this consummation; suffice it to say that the brethren
intrusted with the various duties connected therewith have labored
in season and out of season to insure success, and the result of their
labors will presently be presented to your admiring gaze. In this
work they have been ably assisted by the ladies, the wives, daughters, mothers, sisters, and sweethearts of members of the craft who

have willingly given their best efforts in preparation for the event, and will lend the grace and beauty of their presence in the conduct of the business of the fair, and by their persuasive arts contribute in large measure to its financial results.

They have also been encouraged by the support and indorsement of the highest officials of the national as well as city governments, many of whom are with us in person to testify to their interest in this great and glorious undertaking. We therefore confidently hope that a nucleus will be formed by this Masonic fair which shall expand and grow until it shall result in the construction of a temple, the plans of which will be conceived in wisdom, strength be displayed in its construction, and the beauty of harmony prevail in its interior and exterior adornment, that it may prove for ages yet to come a joy to the sojourner in our midst as well as a shrine to attract our brethren of all tongues and climes.

It was expected that our illustrious brother, William McKinley, President of the United States, would be present with us on this occasion and assist in the ceremonies. The exigencies of public service, however, prevent his attendance; nevertheless, he is with us in spirit and assures our R. W. Deputy Grand Master of his good wishes for the success of our endeavors, and in order to emphasize that feeling has provided electrical connection between this hall and the executive office, and at the proper time will bring us to further light, when the Masonic Fair and Exposition will be duly open for the transaction of business.

Tuesday evening, April 12, 1898, was set apart as "Blue Lodge Night" by the Board of Control of the Masonic Fair, and, in accordance with their suggestion, I requested the Worshipful Masters of the several lodges to assemble their members at the Masonic Temple at 7.30 o'clock on the evening in question to act as an escort to the Grand Lodge Officers and to attend the fair, and it is especially gratifying to be able to state that the attendance was so great as to congest the available space in the fair room and prevent the carrying out of the full program of reception.

The further control of the temple project is now vested in a board of managers by act of Congress, and it is earnestly hoped that that body may ere long be enabled to mature a plan whereby the realization f the desires of the promoters of this great enterprise will be fully consummated, known as "The Masonic Temple of the District of Columbia," of which Past Grand Master R. B. Donaldson is President; Deputy Grand Master John H. Small, Jr., Vice-President; Past Grand Master E. H. Chamberlin, Secretary; and Bro. Samuel H. Walker, Treasurer.

INVITATIONS.

Under date of January 14, 1898, I received an invitation from M. W. Bro. George W. Fortmeyer, Grand Master of New Jersey, to attend the annual communication of the Grand Lodge of New Jersey, in the city of Trenton, on Wednesday, January 26th, and sincerely regret that imperative engagements prevented my acceptance thereof.

The exigencies of the times compelled my declination of the courteous invitation of M. W. Bro. William A. Sutherland, Grand Master of New York, to attend the opening session of the one hundred and seventeenth annual communication of the Grand Lodge of Free and Accepted Masons of that State, Tuesday afternoon, June 7, 1898, which was accompanied by an invitation from R. W. Bro. Joseph Morris Ward to meet the M. W. Grand Master in company with a brother whom I might select at dinner on the evening of the day named. I tender my thanks for the courtesy extended and deep regret for my enforced inability to accept the same.

I also have to acknowledge receipt of invitation from Bro. William J. Kelley, R. W. Grand Master of Pennsylvania, to accompany him to Harrisburg to lay the corner-stone of the new capitol building on the 10th day of August, but, owing to a previously arranged visit to Maine, covering the date mentioned, I was unable to participate in that historical ceremony.

I have also received a number of invitations from brethren of our jurisdiction to unite with them at their anniversary banquets and other social entertainments, several of which I had the pleasure of attending, and others the misfortune to be compelled to decline for various reasons, and I desire to testify to the fact that at every gathering of Masons where I have had the opportunity of being present, I have, as Grand Master, been accorded the seat of honor and shown the greatest courtesy and respect.

WASHINGTON CENTENNIAL OBSERVANCE.

I have received the appended letter from Deputy Grand Master K. Kemper, chairman of the Committee on the Washington Centennial Observance, appointed by the Grand Lodge of Virginia, which I acknowledged under date of August 8th, expressing my intention of appointing the committee to act in conjunction with the committee of the Grand Lodge of Virginia. I now ask your concurrence in that action, in order that the Grand Lodge of the District of Columbia may be suitably represented in the ceremonies commemorative of that illustrious brother, George Washington:

"*ALEXANDRIA, VA., August 4, 1898.*

"MOST WORSHIPFUL SIR AND BROTHER: At a meeting of the Committee on the Washington Centennial Observance, held at Mt. Vernon, July 30th, the following resolution was unanimously adopted:

"*Resolved,* That the Grand Master of the Grand Lodge of the District of Columbia be cordially invited to co-operate with this committee in the work assigned them by the Grand Lodge of Virginia; and to that end that he be requested to appoint a committee of five Master Masons to act in conjunction with this committee.

"Hoping that this may receive your early and favorable consideration, I remain,   Yours fraternally,

"To SAMUEL C. PALMER,   "K. KEMPER,
        "*Grand Master.*"   "*Chairman.*

MASONIC BOARD OF RELIEF.

At several of the grand visitations I have called attention to the good work being accomplished by the Masonic Board of Relief in protecting our lodges from imposition, and in this connection present the following explanatory letter from the efficient Secretary, Bro. Lurtin R. Ginn, and earnestly recommend the Grand Lodge to assume the payment of the actual traveling expenses to the biennial sessions of the General Association of the two delegates which this Grand Lodge is entitled to send. The amount required will be very small in comparison with the benefits accruing to our lodges through the efforts of this truly valuable organization:

"*WASHINGTON, D. C., October 24, 1898.*
"SAMUEL C. PALMER, Esq.,
        "*Grand Master of Masons of the District of Columbia.*

"M. W. SIR AND DEAR BROTHER: As Secretary of the Masonic Board of Relief it has been my custom to give the Grand Master each year a little account of the condition of the Board and what we have been doing. I have not sought to burden you, inasmuch as the report of our Auditing Committee is published each year in the Grand Lodge proceedings.

"I am happy to state that the affairs of the Board continue in a prosperous condition, perfect harmony prevails in the deliberations of the Board, as has been the case in all the years of its existence, and the officers and members alike are zealous and watchful in all the work that properly belongs to us. The fund placed in our custody is carefully guarded and applied to its legitimate and proper uses; the worthy applicant is aided to the extent that his real and reasonable necessities require; the unworthy applicant gets nothing, and is noted and published by our General Association, thus limiting or cutting off altogether his ignoble career of mendicancy and falsehood.

"We have had less than the usual number of applicants during the year, and it is gratifying to note that it has been found necessary to levy but one assessment of five cents per capita, thus demonstrating beyond all question the effectiveness for good of the Board's work.

"There is one matter about which I have spoken to you personally and about which I wish to make mention in this report. By virtue of our membership with the General Masonic Relief Association of the United States and Canada, our Grand Lodge, as well as our Board, is entitled to send two delegates to the biennial sessions of the General Association. Located as we are at the National Capital, it seems essential for our own good and for the good of the craft in general that this Grand Jurisdiction should always be fully represented.

"Heretofore the brethren who have been selected to represent our Grand Lodge have always borne all of their own expenses to and from the place of meeting of the General Association, and until a very few years ago this has also been the case with the brethren who represented the Board.

"It has seemed to me and to all familiar with our relief work, in consideration of the importance of it, that this burden should not be borne in its entirety by the brethren who may be selected as our delegates, and that it would seem only right and proper that the Grand Lodge bear the actual railroad expenses of its delegates. By limiting it to actual railroad expenses, the journey could never take on any of the characteristics of a mere junketing tour, and the whole expense to the Grand Lodge every two years would probably not average more than thirty-five or forty dollars; a very small sum, when the vast amount of good accomplished is taken into consideration.

"The matter is thus brought to your special attention, in the hope that, after a careful consideration of the subject, you may see your way clear to making some special recommendation to the Grand Lodge in your address at the November communication.

"Thanking you for your uniform courtesy, and wishing you all the blessing which peace and prosperity can bring to any of us, I have the honor to be,

"Sincerely and fraternally yours,
"LURTIN R. GINN,
"*Secretary.*"

THE WASHINGTON GAVEL.

One of the most highly-prized souvenirs in possession of the fraternity is the historic gavel owned by Potomac Lodge, No. 5, of this jurisdiction, known as the Washington gavel, which was used by our immortal brother in laying the corner-stone of the U. S. Capitol, and has since been used in many memorable ceremonies. On August 4th I received a communication from R. W. Bro. William J. Kelley, Grand Master of Pennsylvania, requesting my good offices in obtaining the loan of the gavel to be used in laying the corner-stone of the capitol building at Harrisburg, Pa. I telegraphed to Bro. James S. Raeburn, M. W. of Potomac Lodge, No. 5, who was in Atlantic City, N. J., at the time, and received his reply to the effect that he would attend to the request, and upon his return to the city he convened his lodge, and obtained permission for its use. Subsequently I received from Worshipful Master Raeburn the following report of his action:

"August 12, 1898.

"S. C. PALMER, Esq.,
       "M. W. G. M., F. A. A. M., D. C.
   "DEAR SIR AND BROTHER: As per your request under date of August 4th, Potomac Lodge, No. 5, F. A. A. M., held a special meeting and unanimously authorized the use of the historical Washington gavel on the occasion of the laying of the corner-stone of the State Capitol at Harrisburg, Pa., by the Grand Lodge of that State, said gavel to be in custody of the usual committee of three members of the lodge.
   "The committee, composed of James S. Raeburn, W. M., F. W. Daw, S. W., and F. Thomas, P. M. and Secretary, arrived at Philadelphia on the evening of August 9th and proceeded on the morning of August 10th, together with the Grand Lodge of Pennsylvania, to Harrisburg, where, by the use of the Washington gavel, the corner-stone of the State Capitol was laid with Masonic ceremonies by Bro. William J. Kelley, R. W. G. M., F. and A. M. of Pennsylvania.
   "The committee was shown every courtesy and attention it was possible for them to receive, and it is with a great deal of pleasure I, as chairman of the committee, offer you this official communication, that you may be assured of the fulfillment of your request.
               "Courteously and fraternally,
                       "JAMES S. RAEBURN,
           " Worshipful Master, Chairman Committee
                       Washington Gavel, Potomac Lodge, No. 5."

I have also to acknowledge the courtesy of Potomac Lodge, No. 5, in granting the use of the gavel for the purpose of laying the corner-stone of the Douglass Memorial Methodist Church, corner 11th and H streets, northeast, which, with the assistance of the Grand Lodge officers and a number of brethren, I performed on the afternoon of October 18, 1898, by request of the officials of the church.

ORDER OF EASTERN STAR.

This order is composed of Master Masons, their wives, daughters, sisters, mothers, and widows, and is in a most flourishing condition in this District, where its chapters are permitted to hold their meetings in lodge rooms dedicated to Masonic purposes. At the meeting of the General Grand Chapter in this city, September 27–30, 1898, the local Grand Chapter reported eight constituent chapters, with a membership of about 1,400. The work of the order is beautiful, and its teachings instructive and elevating, and I commend it to our brethren as a valuable auxiliary in the benevolent work of our lodges.

Under authority of the resolution of the Grand Lodge, adopted May 13, 1896, I have granted permission for Mizpah Chapter, No. 8, to hold its meetings in the room of Potomac Lodge, No. 5.

THE MASONIC MUTUAL RELIEF ASSOCIATION.

Notwithstanding the fact that in many of our sister jurisdictions Masonic insurance associations are regarded with disfavor, I cannot refrain from calling your attention to the Masonic Mutual Relief Association of the District of Columbia, and recommend it to your favorable consideration. It is essentially a local institution, and if the eligible members of the fraternity will unite themselves with it, under the present system of graded assessments, and limited benefits, they will obtain protection for their dependent loved ones at a minimum cost of insurance. I quote the following from the address of its worthy President, Bro. H. L. Biscoe, November, 18, 1898:

"Since its organization, thirty-two years ago, it has paid to beneficiaries a grand total of over three-quarters of a million dollars, having paid during the past year almost $24,000.

"The relief and consolation it has brought to the sad hearts of many widows and helpless orphans, and the benefit it has been to Masonry in this jurisdiction, is incalculable. When we remember that it has never yet disappointed a widow or an orphan, and that every claim against it has been paid in full, we should pray God it may ever continue on its beneficent mission, and that the brethren may more fully realize its benefits and importance, and accord to it all the support which it so justly deserves."

ST. JOHN'S MITE ASSOCIATION.

This association still continues to perform its beneficent work, and I ask for it the generous support of the lodges of the jurisdiction. Its charity, like mercy, falleth as the gentle dew from heaven, blessing them that give, as well as them that receive. Its usefulness promises to be greatly increased in the near future.

MASONIC BURIAL LOT.

February 21, 1898, upon application of Bro. Joseph Gawler, I granted permission for the burial of the remains of the widow of Bro. Goldsborough Bruff in the grave of her husband in the lot at Congressional Cemetery.

ANNUAL GRAND VISITATIONS.

The annual grand visitations to the several constituent lodges of the District of Columbia commenced on the evening of Tuesday,

October 4, and ended Monday evening, November 7, 1898, and the series proved fully as interesting as those of any preceding year. Exercises were of a diversified character, and consisted of able and instructive addresses, interspersed with vocal and instrumental music, and in two instances, after the formal proceedings of the lodges were concluded, members of the families of the brethren participated in the pleasures of the occasion.

The lodges, with the few exceptions, were found to have increased their membership, and the financial condition of all showed them to be in a very healthy condition.

The Grand Master received many substantial tokens of regard, which he will ever cherish as mementos of those delightful occasions.

AN EVENTFUL YEAR.

The present has been an eventful year, and we cannot but feel deeply interested in the result of its stirring events, in so far as they affect our ancient order and control the destinies of our beloved country.

As American citizens we rejoice in the signal victories vouchsafed our arms on land and sea; victories unsurpassed in the annals of the world, whose far-reaching consequences our wisest statesmen cannot foresee. As members of that world-wide fraternity of Free and Accepted Masons, whose cardinal principle is a belief in the "Fatherhood of God and the Brotherhood of Man," we give heartfelt thanks that "grim-visaged war hath smoothed his wrinkled front" and that the Angel of Peace spreads her wings of healing over our land.

In our newly-acquired possessions across the seas, I believe that our order will prove a potent factor in the work of civilization, and greatly promote the blessings of liberty, justice, and fraternity for all the people. May the good work go on and the time speedily come—

> "When the war-drum throbs no longer,
>   and the battle-flags are furled,
> In the Parliament of man,
>   the Federation of the World."

CONCLUSION.

Brethren, I have presented to you the record of my official actions, which I trust may meet your unqualified approval.

I now desire to thank my associate Grand Lodge officers for the efficient support they have given in discharge of the duties imposed by our laws and customs. Especially do I express my obligations to R. W. Grand Secretary Singleton, whose fund of Masonic knowledge has been cheerfully and willingly placed at my disposal at all times and seasons. May he be spared in health and strength to serve us for years to come.

And, finally, my brethren, as we approach the labors of this communication, I pray that we may have wisdom to conceive and strength to execute such measures as may redound to the best interests of the craft, and promote the harmony and good will we so highly appreciate.

SAMUEL C. PALMER,
Grand Master.

On motion of the R. W. Grand Secretary the address was referred to a committee of three, consisting of Past Grand Masters Thomas F. Gibbs, L. Cabell Williamson and David G. Dixon for distribution; report to be made the same evening.

The Committee on By-Laws, through the chairman, Past Master Martin R. Thorp, Hiram Lodge, No. 10, made the following report, which was received and adopted, viz.:

REPORT OF COMMITTEE ON BY-LAWS.

WASHINGTON, D. C., November 9, 1898.
To the Most Worshipful and Grand Master, Wardens,
and Brethren of the Grand Lodge, District of Columbia:

BRETHREN: Your Committee on By-Laws beg to report that they have received during the year communications from Harmony Lodge, No. 17, and Naval Lodge, No. 4, Lebanon Lodge, No. 7, recommending slight changes in their By-Laws. After ascertaining that the proposed changes was not in conflict with the Constitution of the Grand Lodge, your committee promptly approved them.

Fraternally submitted,
M. R. THORP,
A. GUDE,
Committee.

The R. W. Grand Secretary submitted a recent amendment to the By-Laws of St. John's Lodge, No. 11, and on his motion it was approved, as follows:

WASHINGTON, D. C., *November* 1, 1898.

WM. R. SINGLETON,
 Grand Secretary of the Grand Lodge of
  F. A. A. M. of the District of Columbia:

DEAR SIR AND BROTHER: The following amendment to the
By-Laws of St. John's Lodge, No. 11, regularly adopted at the
stated communication, held on Friday, October 28, 1898, is hereby
submitted for the approval of the Grand Lodge.

Amend Section 5 of Article VI, fifth line, by striking out 20 and
inserting 10, so that the clause shall read "and 10 per cent. of all
money received for degrees," etc.

Yours fraternally,

EDWIN A. NIESS,

239 10th street, northeast.   *Acting Secretary.*

The chairmen of the Committees on Grievances and Jurisprudence reported that nothing had been referred to their respective committees for consideration.

The chairman of the Committee on Correspondence stated
that his report was nearly completed and would be ready for
publication.

The R. W. Grand Secretary stated that the protracted illness of the R. W. Grand Lecturer had prevented the preparation of his report and moved that the report, when prepared,
be included in the minutes of this communication.   Carried.

REPORT OF GRAND LECTURER.

WASHINGTON, D. C., *December* 23, 1898.
M. W. Grand Master, Wardens, and Brethren of the
 Grand Lodge, F. A. A. M., of the District of Columbia:

As I was unable to attend the Annual Communication of the
Grand Lodge on the 9th of November, and failed to make a report
at that time, I deem it the proper thing to do at this late date, to
submit a report as to visits made to the different lodges.

VISITS TO LODGES.

Federal Lodge, No. 1.   January 11, May 24, August 9, September 13, 1898.

Columbia, No. 3.   December 17, 1897; March 18, July 1, 1898.

Naval, No. 4.   March 3, May 19, August 4, 1898.

Potomac, No. 5.   December 6, 1897; March 7, August 4, 1898.

Lebanon, No. 7.   March 4, June 17, August 19, 1898.

New Jerusalem, No. 9.   December 23, 1897; February 10, June 23, 1898.

Hiram, No. 10.   February 4, June 3, September 2, 1898.

St. John's, No. 11.   February 11 and 25, May 27, August 26, 1898.

National, No. 12.   December 7, 1897; April 5, July 19, 1898.

Washington Centennial, No. 14.   January 5, May 18, August 17, September 21, 1898.

Benjamin B. French, No. 15.   January 3, May 16, July 18, 1898.

Dawson, No. 16.   December 13, 1897; February 14, May 23, July 25, 1898.

Harmony, No. 17.   January 13, May 11, September 14, 1898.

Acacia, No. 18   November 23, 1897; February 8, May 24, September 13, 1898.

La Fayette, No. 19.   December 2, 1897; March 17, July 7, 1898.

Hope, No. 20.   January 28, March 11, June 10, August 26, 1898.

Anacostia, No. 21.   January 17, June 5, 1898.

George C. Whiting, No. 22.   January 27, May 26, July 11, August 1, 1898.

Pentalpha, No. 23.   January 3, May 2, June 27, October 3, 1898.

Stansbury, No. 24.   January 24, May 9, August 8, 1898.

Arminius, No. 25.   November 22, 1897; February 14, June 13, September 12, 1898.

Osiris, No. 26.   December 1, 1897; May 4, September 7, 1898.

Myron M. Parker, No. 27.   January 18, May 17, August 16, 1898.

King David, No. 28.   March 15, June 21, 1898.

Takoma, No. 29.   December 28, 1897; May 10, August 23, 1898.

Fraternally submitted,

JOSEPH HAMACHER,
W. G. Lecturer.

The Special Committee appointed at the Semi-annual Communication to make necessary repairs in Grand Lodge Library room reported that they failed to see any necessity for the expenditure of money for repairs, beyond the setting of one or two panes of glass in book-cases, which could be attended to by the Librarian. The M. W. Grand Master therefore rescinded the order to expend the $200 which had been appropriated for the renovation of the library room.

Bro. Frank A. Harrison, W. M. of Osiris Lodge, No. 26, stated the conditions under which said lodge discontinued its occupancy of a lodge room at 1007 G street, northwest, presented urgent reasons why it should be permitted to resume occupancy of said premises and expressed the hope that authority would be granted it to do so. On motion of the R. W. Grand Secretary the desired permission was given.

The R. W. Grand Secretary stated that he had several papers referring to Masonry in Peru, Mexico, and Cuba and moved that they be referred to the Committee on Jurisprudence with permission to report at the Installation Communication.

Past Grand Master James A. Sample, as Corporator of the Grand Lodge in the Masonic Temple Association of the District of Columbia, requested permission to present at the Installation Communication, certain matters pertaining thereto, involving, possibly, an appropriation, which request was granted.

The R. W. Grand Secretary presented to the Grand Lodge, Bro. James B. Sener, of Fredericksburg Lodge, No. 4, Fredericksburg, Va., a member of a committee appointed by the Grand Lodge of Virginia, to make the necessary arrangements for the celebration of the centennial anniversary of the death of our revered brother, George Washington, which is to take place at Mt. Vernon, December 14, 1899. Bro. Sener was delegated by said committee to solicit the co-operation of this Grand Lodge, also of Federal Lodge of this jurisdiction, which attended the funeral as a body. Later in the evening, Bro. Sener addressed the Grand Lodge, giving the details of the order of exercises, as far as perfected, and suggesting the part which this Grand Lodge could most advantageously take therein.

The R. W. Grand Secretary gave notice of the appointments of Bros. George H. Walker, P. M., Hiram Lodge, No. 10, James A. Wetmore, P. M., Benj. B. French Lodge, No. 15, and Past Grand Master George W. Baird, as Grand Representatives near this Grand Lodge of the Grand Lodges of Montana, South Carolina, and Nevada, respectively, and on his motion, they were received and acknowledged as such.

The Committee on Distribution of the Grand Master's address made the following report:

NOVEMBER 9, 1898.

To the M. W. Grand Master, Officers, and Members of the Grand Lodge of the District of Columbia, F. A. A. M.:

Your committee to whom was referred the address of the M. W. Grand Master for distribution report as follows: We recommend that this Grand Lodge confirm the appointment of Grand Representatives made by the M. W. Grand Master; and that the Grand Representatives, near this Grand Lodge, as reported by the M. W. Grand Master, be duly received and acknowledged as such.

That memorial pages in the proceedings of the Grand Lodge be set apart to perpetuate the memory of deceased brethren as recommended by the M. W. Grand Master.

The decision of the M. W. Grand Master in the case of taking a third ballot in Arminius Lodge where one black ball appeared in the two preceding ballots is, in the opinion of the committee, in conformity with the Grand Lodge Constitution, and therefore recommend its approval. That decision of the M. W. Grand Master respecting the indefinite occupation of lodge room by Osiris Lodge, No. 26, in which other than Masonic organizations meet be approved.

We recommend the approval of the action of the M. W. Grand Master in appointing a committee to assist in the observance of the Washington Centennial ceremonies.

That the recommendation of the M. W. Grand Master respecting the payment of actual traveling expenses of two delegates from this Grand Lodge to the biennial sessions of the General Masonic Relief Association of the United States and Canada be approved.

We further recommend the approval of the other acts and doings of the M. W. Grand Master as reported by him in his very able address.

Respectfully submitted,

THOMAS F. GIBBS, P. G. M.,
L. CABELL WILLIAMSON, P. G. M.,
D. G. DIXON, P. G. M.,
Committee.

On motion of Past Master Charles H. Smith, Washington Centennial Lodge, No. 14, the report was received and adopted.

All business having been disposed of the M. W. Grand Master announced that the time had arrived for the election of the Grand Officers for the ensuing Masonic year and directed that ballots be prepared for the office of M. W. Grand Master. On collecting and counting the ballots, Bro. John H. Small, Jr., was declared duly elected M. W. Grand Master.

The following Grand Officers were then regularly elected, viz.:

Bro. Wm. G. Henderson, R. W. Deputy Grand Master.

Bro. Harry Standiford, R. W. Senior Grand Warden.

Bro. Malcolm Seaton, R. W. Junior Grand Warden.

Bro. Wm. R. Singleton, unanimously re-elected R. W. Grand Secretary.

Bro. Chas. C. Duncanson, unanimously re-elected R. W. Grand Treasurer.

Bro. Arvine W. Johnston, W. Grand Lecturer (Bro. Jos. Hamacher having, by reason of ill health, declined to be a candidate).

Bro. Claudius B. Smith, unanimously re-elected Rev. and W. Grand Chaplain.

Bro. George H. Walker, unanimously elected W. Grand Marshal.

Bro. James A. Wetmore, unanimously elected W. Senior Grand Deacon.

Bro. Lurtin R. Ginn, unanimously elected W. Junior Grand Deacon.

Bro. Walter A. Brown, unanimously elected W. Grand Sword Bearer.

Bro. Francis J. Woodman, unanimously elected W. Grand Pursuivant.

Bro. A. B. Coolidge, unanimously elected W. Senior Grand Steward.

Bro. Henry K. Simpson, W. Junior Grand Steward.

Bro. John N. Birckhead, unanimously re-elected Grand Tiler.

Past Grand Master R. B. Donaldson, unanimously re-elected Corporator of the Masonic Hall Association.

APPROPRIATIONS.

Masonic Hall Association, rent for six months, $50.00; J. S. Tomlinson & Son, miscellaneous printing, stationery, and postage, $24.25; Frederick W. Behrens, carriage hire, $15.00; total, $89.25.

Past Master Charles H. Smith, Washington Centennial Lodge, No. 14, moved that a committee, to consist of three Past Grand Masters, be appointed to procure a suitable testimonial to be presented to the retiring Grand Master.

The motion prevailed, and Past Grand Masters R. B. Donaldson, E. G. Davis, and James A. Sample were designated as such committee.

Past Master Charles H. Smith moved an appropriation of $50 as extra compensation for Grand Tiler, Bro. John N. Birckhead, and it was so ordered.

. No further business appearing, the Grand Lodge was closed in ample form. Prayer by the Rev. and W. Grand Chaplain.

WM. R. SINGLETON,
Grand Secretary.

RETURNS OF THE CONSTITUENT LODGES

UNDER THE JURISDICTION OF THE

Grand Lodge of the District of Columbia

FOR THE YEAR 1898.

———

[The star (*) indicates life members, the dagger (†) hononary members.]

——— ———

FEDERAL LODGE, No. 1,

Meets on the Second and Fourth Tuesdays in each Month.

OFFICERS.

RICHARD B. NIXON, Worshipful Master.
HENRY M. McDADE, S. Warden. HARRY B. MASON, J. Warden.
GOODWIN Y. ATLEE, Secretary.   W. S. JENKS, Treasurer.

PAST MASTERS AND PAST GRAND OFFICERS.

Goff A. Hall, P. S. G. W.; R. B. Donaldson, P. G. M.; John Lockie, P. D. G. M.; J. D. Bartlett, Geo. D. Patten, jr., Jos. Hamacher, W. H. Miller, W. S. Jenks, J. J. Burrows, I. Fairbrother, W. H. Proctor, W. W. Lesh, J. S. Tomlinson, Geo. Z. Colison, G. Y. AtLee, W. R. Sheid, W. T. Reed, W. S. Knox, S. E. Tomlinson, J. J. Faber, H. M. Johnson, J. L. Nichols, W. A. Brown, Arthur Barnes, M. Dorian.

LIST OF MEMBERS.

Abrams, W. D.
Allen, Jacob S.
Ammann, Wm. P.
Anderson, Robt. L.
Arnold, A. J.
AtLee, G. Y.
Austin, James E.
Baker, James M.
Banks, Alex. R.
†Bar, Levi
Barker Howard H.
Barker, Howard W.
Barnes, Arthur
Bartlett, John D.
Bartlett, Jos. W.
Bauman, Chas. H.
Bayly, Charles B.
Beckman, Edwd. F.
*Behrend, A.
Bell, John W.
Belt, Francis A.
*Benjamin, Chas. F.
Benson, Thomas R.
Benton, A. J.
Berry, Allen P.
Binns, Douglas
Black, George D.
Boteler, John W.
Boyd, William A.
Brantley, C. J.
Brown, Andrew R.
*Brown, Joseph T.
Brown, Walter A.
Bryan, William
Buchler, John A.
Burk, William H.
Burrows, John J
Butterfield, F. H.
Campbell, Chas. B.
Carlin, Lewis A.

Carpenter, N. U.
Catts, Geo. S.
Chancey, John T.
Childs, William H.
Choate, Warren
Choate, Warren R.
Chung, Mun Yew
Clark, John W.
Cohen, G. M.
Cole, Isaac N. C.
Cole, Thomas H.
Colison, George Z.
Covington, Wm. H.
Cragg, William B.
*Crowley, J. P.
Crystal, James A.
Dalton, George A.
Davis, Eugene
Davis, Madison
Davis, Sidney H.
Davis, W. W.
*Dearing, George T.
Denson, James F.
Desio, Salvator
Dickens, James R. S.
Dinsmore, Ruel A.
*Donaldson, R. B.
Donovan, William J.
Dorian, Frank
Dorian, Marion
*Dummer, George E.
Early, William
Eberbach, G. H.
Edwards, James S.
Emory, William E.
Faber, J. J.
Fague, Joseph R.
Fairbrother, Isaac
Fischer, Herrman
Fowler, George Wm.

Fowler, Thomas W.
Fugitt, N. B.
Gale, Thomas M.
Gantz, William
Getchell, Edwin P.
*Gibson, George
Gibson, Thomas A.
Gleason, Thomas E.
Gleason, Thos. W.
Goldsmith, Max
Goodrick, Lewis M.
Grant, Percival B.
Greenfield, Wm. E.
Greer, Charles E.
Griffin, B. B.
Groot, Simon I.
Haislip, John W.
Hale, George C.
Hall, Albert G.
Hall, Goff A.
Hamacher, Joseph
Hamilton, Stephen F.
Hardy, William B.
Harries, William A.
Haswell, John H.
Hawley, H. Reed
Hazen, George W.
Heitmuller, Anton
Hibbs, James E.
Hitchens, W. F.
Hobbs, Rev. G. W.
Hodgman, Allen W.
Hodgson, Joseph F.
Holmes, Charles E.
Houchens, Joseph B.
Hough, Burr W.
Hough, Henry H.
Hughes, James
Irey, C. William
Jenks, W. S.

Johnson, Elwood A.
Johnson, Hosmer M.
Johnson, J. William
Johnson, Richard M.
Jolly. John H.
Karr, Jacob
Keller, Thos. W.
Keyes, C. W.
Knox. George V.
Knox, John O.
Knox, William S.
Lamb, Robert H.
Lesh, William W.
Lewis, James F.
Lewis, J. Hall
Lewis, John S.
Lewis, Samuel E.
Lewis, William I.
Libbey, Israel P.
*Lockie, John
Lord, Francis B., jr
†Lord, John B.
Lord, Millard F.
Lovejoy, J. W. H.
Macarty, Daniel J.
McCleary, Eben S.
McDade, Henry M.
McDade, Louis H.
McDermot, E. H.
McDermot, F. G.
Macfeely, William
McKeever, H. H.
Markward, Geo. C.
Martin, W. T.
Mason, Harry B.
Matile, James H.
Middleton, Rosier
Miller, Isaac A.
Miller, Jacob O.
Miller, John H.
Miller, William H.
Minnix, William H.

Moore, Silas H.
Morgan, Edward
*Morsell, S. T. G.
Muehleisen, William
Nephew, F. D.
Nichols, John L.
Nixon, R. B.
Norris, Brison
Nutze, Charles T.
Nye, Francis
O'Connor. Arthur H.
Ohm, Frederick C.
Oppenheimer, Max
*Patten, Geo. D., Jr.
Pendleton, E. Gray
Pfeiffer. George B.
Phillips, Richard W.
Pierce, Frank H.
Pierce, James H.
Platt, William
Playter, Henry J.
Powell, William B.
Pressey. Harry A.
Proctor, William H.
Pruess, Peter
Quinter, Joseph R.
Raub, Samuel C.
Rearden, George W.
Reed, William T.
Reeves, James J.
Reynolds, Austin H.
Richardson, W. H.
Riggles, J. Richard
Robbins, Willard S.
Rock, Andrew J.
Roper, Daniel C.
Russell, Alex. A.
*St. Clair, F. O.
Sanderson, A. J.
Schultz, Rev. J. R.
Schutter, Hubert
Schweinhaut, Francis

Scrivener, Peyton
Settle, Joseph A.
Shears, George W.
Sheid, William R.
Shelton, William R.
Shumate, E. J.
Simmons, John B.
Slater. Isaac C.
Slick, John E.
Smith, James D.
Smoot, Chas. M.
Spang, Edward H.
Speir, William E.
Springmann, Fredk.
Springmann, J. T., jr.
Springmann, Jos. M.
Sprinkle, J. V.
Steever, Edgar Z.
Stewart, Alonzo H.
Street, Harlowe L.
Talcott, Alfred B.
Taylor, Leroy M.
Thomas, Sylvester F.
Thompson, Chas. N.
Thompson, Wm. P.
Thorn, Charles G.
Tomlinson, John S.
Tomlinson, S. Edw.
*Topham, James S.
Tuckey, Wm. W.
*Turner, S. S.
Turner, W. Lee
Turton, George H.
Vaughn, Walter J.
Vermillion, J. Oliver
Wardwell, Eugene
Warner, Joseph R.
Webb, Martin V.
Wheeler, William B.
Willett, James P.
Williams, Parker
Williams, Wash. B.

Willis. Charles B.   Wilson, Howard E.   Wonn, W. W.
Willis. Edward M.   Wilson, J. L. C.   Woods, Elliott—253.
                        Wilson, Philip R.

DROPPED FOR N. P. D.

Gill, Edw. C.   Purman, W. J.   Winfree, W. W.
Layton, Wm. E.   Schafhirt, E. F.

COLUMBIA LODGE, No. 3,

Meets on the First and Third Fridays in each Month.

OFFICERS.

HERBERT WRIGHT, Worshipful Master.
J. CLAUDE KEIPER, S. Warden.   LUTHER F. SPEER, J. Warden.
W. S. MACGILL, Secretary.   GEO. S. KING, Treasurer.

PAST MASTERS AND PAST GRAND OFFICERS.

Josiah M. Vale, Arthur M. Muzzy, Andrew Cauldwell, Albert
K. Williams, Alex. F. McMillan, Wm. H. Wetzel, Thos. F. Gibbs,
P. G. M.; Jas. L. Falbey, Edmond Cotterill, Winfield S. Macgill,
Millard J. Moore, Wilmer W. Wetzel, George S. King, Wm. P.
Tullock, Wm. H. Decker, Bunyan Olive, Robt. G. Tinkler, Saml.
H. Moore, Jacob F. Raub.

LIST OF MEMBERS.

Anderson, Gustave   Christiani, Charles   *Edelin, W. R.
Austin, Robert J.   Christensen; Anthon   *Edson, John Joy
Babendrier,Arthur O.   Churchill, Frank L.   Eglin, John Henry
Baker, Wm. T.   Collins, Frank S.   English, John R.
Baker, Willie W.   Cotterill, Edmond   Esty, Warren B.
Baum, Henry   Dean, Russell   *Falbey, James L.
Boswell, Henry F.   Decker, Wm. H.   Farabee, Louis T.
Bowdler, Robert   *Deneane, Joseph W.   Farrer, Edw. T.
*Cauldwell, Andrew   Duschere, Edward   Fernandez, M. W.

*Fowler, Charles H.
Frazier, James A.
Frazier, Wm. H.
Frederich, A. A.
Frederich, L. L.
*Freeman, Wm. P.
Fugitt, Lemuel
Gibbs, Herbert A.
*Gibbs, Thomas F.
Gooch, Charles J.
*Goodno, Charles E.
Grenfell, Fred. W.
Haislip, James
Hammack, J. La F.
Hansen, Christian
Harbaugh, Yost D.
Hawes, W. H. H.
Herman, Bernard
Hitner, Joseph H.
Holer, Emil
Horrigan, James J.
House, Samuel P.
Hughes, Britton
Hummer, G. W. F.
Hummer, W. F.
Huntoon, Andrew J.
Irwin, Joseph L.
Isham, Charles H.
Jaeger, Henry
Jenkins, Henry
Jones, C. Page
*Joyce, John A.
Kautenberg, Matt. N.
Keiper, J. Claude
*King, George S.
Knill, Alfred E.
Koch, Harry B.
Kramer, James S.
Lewis, Silas D.

*Limerick, John A.
Little, Joseph W.
*Lothrop, John P.
Macgill, Winfield S.
Mackall, Upton B.
Marshall, William
McConnell, Theo. F.
*McMillan, Alex. F.
*McNeill, Hector
Moore, Millard J.
Moore, Samuel H.
*Muzzy, Arthur M.
Neale, George W.
Newell, Charles
Offterdinger, H. T.
Olive, Bunyan
Page, Henry
Patterson, L. H.
Pearson, Aven
Phillips, Everett L.
*Pike, B-z D.
Proudfit, Samuel V.
Raub, Jacob F.
Reed, Thomas W.
Reiplinger, John
Reynolds, W. H.
Rich, Louis
*Richardson, W. T.
Riley, Wm. Wallace
Robinson, Jesse D.
Robinson, John S.
Rogers, James R.
Ryan, Harvey E.
Ryon, Owen C.
Rutherford, Wm. A.
Sandstrom, Ernst V.
*Schnebel, Charles
Sellhausen, E. A.
*Shuey, Theo. F.

Sillers, Frederick
Silverman, Louis J.
Simmons, Wm. J.
Slee, Richard B.
Smith, Jay B.
*Smith, J. T.
Speer, Luther F.
Spooner, C. M. C.
Stern, Aaron
Stoddart, Armat
Stryker, Burdett
Sutton, John R.
Sutton, John R., jr.
Swan, Moses M.
*Tappan, Myron A.
Taylor, William K.
Thompson, Robert M.
Tinkler, Robert G.
Tullock, William P.
*Vale, Josiah M.
Wall, Julian
Wetzel, Charles J.
Wetzel, William H.
Wetzel, Wilmer W.
*Wheeler, Chas. S.
Wheeller, J. W.
*Whitaker, A. J.
White, John Q.
Wilson, Samuel
*Williams, Albert K.
Williams, W. H., jr
Winans, William
Wind, Henry A.
Works, Winfield F.
Wright, Herbert
Wright, Moses B. C.
Yoder, Charles T.
Zurhorst, George P.
—143.

DROPPED FOR N. P. D.
Bunyea, Emmet P.

NAVAL LODGE, No. 4,

Meets on the First and Third Thursdays in each Month.

OFFICERS.

HARRY P. COOK, Worshipful Master.
C. GLENN NICHOLS, S. Warden.   HENRY T. ADAMS, J. Warden.
I. H. McCATHRAN, Secretary.   ADAM GADDIS, Treasurer.

PAST MASTERS AND PAST GRAND OFFICERS.

Robert Clarke, P. D. G. M.; Charles Venable, Wm. E. Hutchinson, P. S. G. W.; E. B. Bury, George W. Harrington, Wm. H. Hoeke, Joseph H. Hartley, John Schultz, E. M. Boteler, Charles Shelse, C. A. Stockett, A. J. Symonds, Charles F. Warren, P. B. Otterback, Jas. Tindall, Geo. Thom, M. T. Dixon, K. N. Harper.

LIST OF MEMBERS.

Altemus, Frank S.
Anderson, Wm. T.
Altfather, Fred. M.
Adams, Henry T.
Avery Henry H.
†Bromwell, H. P. H.
Bromley, Alex. C.
Bright, Henry J.
Bury, Edward B.
Berkeley, David L.
Berkeley, Elmer S.
Boteler, Edward M.
Baker, John
Baker, Moses D.
Bradford, Chas. A.
Bradford, Thomas A.
Beaumont, Oliver T.
Brockman, Henry
Bennett, William
Brust, Albert G.
Browne, William E.
Beasley Willie H.
Buckey, C. M.
Bopp, William A.

Buckmaster, John L.
Bohannon, Geo. E.
Bunyea, Hubert H.
Bunn, John C.
Clarke, Robert
Chase, Isaac McKim
Cooper, William A.
Chapman, Rev.W. H.
Cooksey, Charles W.
Chambers, John L.
Childs, James W.
Childs, Albert
Childs, Frank H.
Ciscle, James
Cook, Harry P.
Cornell, George E.
Conner, John B.
Chadwick, Harry W.
Cornwell, Alton W.
Cassard, Rev.Wm.G.
Dellwig, Louis A.
Donch, Henry
Davis, John B.
Dalton, Robert

Donohue, Hugh
Dunn, Robert W.
Dunn, George W.
Dunn, Ernest A. A.
Dixon, Millard T.
Earnshaw, John T.
Earnshaw, Benj. B.
Ellis, Samuel S.
Ellis, Harry H.
Ellis, William H.
Falconer, Mortimer
Fox, J. William
Frank, Ferdinand
Gaddis, William
Gaddis, George H.
Gaddis, Adam
Gaddis, Lemuel
*Gulick, George F.
Goodman, Albert
Goodman, Rob't W.
Gambrill, Thos. D.
Hutchinson, W. E.
Hartley, Joseph H.
Hartley, Jos. C. F.

Hartley, Wm. R.
Harrington, G. W.
Hardester, Wm. B.
Hall, William R.
Harper, Kenton N.
Hawkins. Charles
Hagmann, Josef K.
Henderson, Robt. M.
Henderson, Wm. A.
Heimer, Augustus
Hogue, Geo. W.
Hodgson, Joseph E.
Hobbs, Salvador
Hoeke, Wm. H.
Jacobs, Thomas E.
Jones, Melville E.
Jones, Edwin D.
Jones, Lake W.
Jones, John F.
Kahlert, Herman
King, John J.
Lascallette, A. B.
Lascallette, J. W. H.
Latchford, L. A.
Lee, Theo. Samuel
Luce, Charles R.
Loane, John T. S.
McCathran, Isaac H.
McCathran, F. F.
McCathran, F. C.
McCauley, Henry C.
McClure, W. F.
†McKim, John W.
Marks, Henry E.
Mathis, William M.
Manuel, Silas A.
Mattingly, John F.

Mansfield, G. A., jr.
Miller, Anthony
Moulton, John B.
Mount, M. F.
Milstead, James W.
Moore, Lester D.
Morgan, Daniel M.
Nichols, C. Glenn
Otterback, Maurice
Otterback, P. B.
Ober, George C.
Olesen, Tory
Peake, William C.
Phillips, John X.
Palmer, William J.
Parsons, James L.
Pennell, Lewis S.
Petrola, Francis
Pierce, Harry H.
Pote, Harry W.
Quail, Harry A.
Reaney, Charles A.
Reynolds, Joseph S.
Richards, George G.
Ryon, Percy B.
Shelton, John H.
Sefton, Wm. M.
Schroeder, August
Scott, Napoleon B.
Scott, Isaac
Skidmoore, Geo. W.
Shelse, Charles
Sinclair, John S.
Stockett, Chas. A.
Stockett, George W.
Symonds, Arthur J.

Spurrier, Thos. H.
Scharr, George G.
Sousa, Antony A.
Spencer, Chas. L.
Sibley, Frank E.
Schaefer. Peter C.
Stevens, George F.
Schultz, John
Smith George E.
Smith, Thomas H.
Stahl, Arthur
Talbert, George W.
Talbert, Richard T.
Taylor, John S.
Taylor. Rhodia
Teachum, W. K.
Tindall, James
Thompson, Rev. W.J.
Thom, George
Vanderveer, H. S.
Veitenheimer, Foster
Venable, Charles H.
Venable, Joseph G.
Walton, David S.
Warren, Chas. F.
Wayson, Chas. A.
Ward, Charlie
Waite, Fred. C.
Wells, Joseph M.
Weber, L. F. W.
Williams, Chas. A.
Williams, Alex. H.
Winterhalter, Wm.
Wood, Court F.
Yost, Amos T.
Yost,William H.—181.

DROPPED FOR N. P. D.

Cooper, Jos. W.
Davis, Daniel D.

Moore, Bertrand C.
Peake, Millard F.

Scheller, Thos. K.
Truman, Geo. E.

POTOMAC LODGE, No. 5,

Meets on the First and Third Mondays in each Month.

OFFICERS.

JAMES S. RAEBURN, Worshipful Master.
FRED W. DAW, S. Warden.   ALPHEUS W. HUDSON, J. Warden.
FRANK THOMAS, Secretary.   WOLF NORDLINGER, Treasurer.

PAST MASTERS AND PAST GRAND OFFICERS.

J. Holdsworth Gordon, W. T. Wheatley, A. T. Brice, T. G.
Loockerman, Isaac Birch, J. B. Thomas, Frank Thomas, J. S.
Hays, Malcolm Seaton, G. J. Fritch, C. W. Cornwell, T. H.
Brinkman, W. S. Waddey, E. J. Hulse.

LIST OF MEMBERS.

Anderson, Edw. W.	Demar, C. H.	Leigh, M. C.
Adler, Maurice J.	Daw, Robert A.	McKnew, Benj.P.
Amery, Robert L.	Daw, F. W.	Miller, M. P.
Allen, George W.	Delzell, Samuel W.	Moll, Julius
Artz, Samuel	Dugan, George W.	Nelson, Rev. James
Akers, J. W.	Dwyer, E. E.	Nordlinger, Wolf
Blake, Eustace C.	Daughton, J. R., jr.	Nelson, Rev. H. E.
Brown, Edward H.	Fritch, Geo. J.	Orme, William B.
Brewer, Hiram H.	Fischer, Wm. C.	Offutt, Henry W.
Brice, Arthur T.	Fishel, Adolph M.	Oliver, Cornelius
Birch, George A.	Gordon, J. H.	Oliver, Jacob H.
Barrett, Hiram W.	Gross, Henry J.	Parker, John C.
Birch, Isaac	Hays, James S.	Peter, Armistead
Buchannan, J. M.	Hieston, Robert T.	Powell, Richard
Brace, William D.	Hulse, Edgar J.	Robinson, J. D.
Bennett, A. B.	Hudson, Alpheus W.	Rittenhouse, David
Brinkman, T. H.	Hunter, Montgomery	Robey, James T.
Billheimer, Rev. S.	Jones, Frank	Reintzell, C. H. F.
Core, John T.	King, Rev. Thos. A.	Raeburn, James S.
Cornwell, C. W.	Kurtz, John D.	Reynolds, George H.
Clokey, C. C.	King, George W.	Read, Rev. Edgar T.
Corbett, Edward	Linn, Wm. E.	Sweet, Parker H.
Cropley, Geo. W.	Loockerman, T. G.	Shinn, Riley A.
Doering, Jonas	Loveless, James W.	Southerland, Rev.S.B
Dowling, Thomas	Lyman, W. H. H.	Sommers, Henry

Sinsheimer, Louis M.
Seaton, Malcolm
Sherrier, John C.
Shipley, Saml. P.
Simpson, James
Sommerville, F. N.
Stroman, H. C.
Stone, Joseph E.
Scherer, William
Scherer, Charles

Stearn, Thos. M.
Swindells, Simeon
Thomas, John B.
Thomas, Robert B.
Thomas, Frank
Waters, Joseph G.
Waters, T. Dyson
Wheatley, Walter T.
Waters, S. M.
Waters, John M.

Wagner, Henry G.
Woodward, C. J.
Wilson, Harrison
Williams, C. P.
Waddey, W. S.
Wilkenson, Josiah
Waters, George S.
Waters, Morris W.
Yarnall, J. H.—104.

LEBANON LODGE, No. 7,

Meets on the First and Third Fridays in each Month.

OFFICERS.

JOHN H. TATSPAUGH, Worshipful Master.

JOHN E. WALSH, S. Warden.   R. B. BRUMMETT, J. Warden.

WALTER W. LUDLOW, Secretary.   THOMAS TAYLOR, Treasurer.

PAST MASTERS AND PAST GRAND OFFICERS.

Andrew Glass, P. S. G. W.; Chas. W. Hayes, Eldred G. Davis, P. G. M.; Charles C. Duncanson, R. W. G. T.; David G. Dixon, P. G. M.; Thomas Taylor, John Boyle, Thomas H. Young, W. G. Lecturer; William J. Acker, Henry K. Simpson, W. J. G. S.; Edwin I. Nottingham, Joseph Comer, Theodore G. DeMoll, Eugene J. Bernhard, William Watson, Lewes D. Wilson, Walter W. Ludlow, Summerfield G. Nottingham, William F. Gatchell, William F. Coggins.

LIST OF MEMBERS.

Acker, Albert E.
Acker, Charles A.
Acker, Franklin J.
Acker, Nicholas A.
Acker, Walter H.

Acker, William J.
Addison, James C.
Akers, John F.
Akers, Robert S.
Allender, Chas. H.

Andersen, George
Anderson, Robert
*Angermann, John
Babbitt, Zenos B.
Banes, Albert

Batchelor, John H.
Bates, Geo. W.
Baum, Joseph
Behrens, Louis
*Bell, Samuel
Bernhard, Eugene J.
Berry, Raymond L.
Bifield, John
Bonar, Robert
Bourne, Caleb P.
*Bowen, James G.
Boyle, John
Boyle, Robert M.
Brethauer, August
Brooks, Richard H.
*Brown, John (1)
Brown, John (2)
Brown, Lewis
Brummett, R. B.
Buck, Cassius M.
Burdine, James W.
Burger, Joseph C.
Burns, Frank H., jr.
Burns, Frank H., sr.
Butler, James A.
Byrne, C. E.
Cameron, Robert L.
Campbell, Homer
Carew, A. J.
Carlsen, Carl
Chism, Wm. W.
Church, Wm. A. H.
Cissel, Thomas W.
Cissell, Frank M.
Cissell, Wm. H. H.
Clagett, Dorsey
Clark, A. P., jr.
Clarke, Shelby
Claxton, Arthur B.
Coggins, William F.
Collins, Charles H.
Comer, Joseph

Compton, Ludwell
Copenhaver, Wm. A.
Cornwell, R. W.
Cowell, Albert M.
Craig, W. Alexander
Crook, A. C.
Cross, Francis E.
Cross, Samuel
Curry, Edward
Davis, Augustus L.
*Davis, Eldred G.
DeMoll, Theodore G.
Dickinson, E. P.
*Dixon, David G.
Dodge, Herbert A.
Doell, Charles W.
Drew, John W.
Duncanson, Chas. C.
Dunnington, A. F.
Duvall, William A.
Eckstein, Charles A.
Engels, Charles E.
English, Lucius O.
Evans, Henry
Evans, John
Fisher, William H.
Fitzhugh, D. K.
Flint, Albert F.
Fonda, Charles B.
Forker, Joseph B.
Fowler, W. C.
Freund, William J.
Fries, Theodore A.
Gardiner, Edward
Gatchell, William F.
Gerlach, John
Gerlach, John L.
Gibbs, Charles E.
Gibbs, John B.
*Glass, Andrew
Goodall, Alfred
Goodrich, J. H.

Goodspeed, Alex.
*Gordon, Malcolm B.
Grass, August
Gray, George R.
Green, David S.
Guffey, Geo. B. M.
Guild, James
Haines, Walter S.
Hall, Joseph A.
Hall, Samuel K.
*Halley, James
Halliburton, L.
*Hamlin, John P.
Harding, R. N.
Hardy, Samuel F.
Harvey, John A.
*Hayes, Charles W.
Hazen, David H.
Hazen, W. P. C.
Heffner, James E.
Heinline, Wm. M.
Helmsen, E. A.
Herrmann, Aug. G.
Hockemeyer, John
Holtman, William J.
Howard, C. W.
*Huguley, Chas. W.
Hutchinson, Frank S.
*Imirie, John
James, Richard D.
Jameson, Albion B.
Jardella, Felix
Jardine, William
Jeffers, Joseph F.
Johnson, Esau L.
Johnson, William C.
Johnson, William H.
Jones, J. Gordon
Jordan, William W.
Kattelmann, C., jr.
Kattelmann, C., sr.
Keesecker, E. E.

*Kerr, James K.
*Kettler, Louis
Lansburgh. James
Lawrence, James E.
Lawrence, Joseph H.
Lee. Robert E.
Leese, Curtis A.
Le Mour, Ernst H.
Litchfield, F. H.
Littleton, Wm. B.
Lockwood, E. J.
Lomax, James C.
Low, Robert
Lucas, Eugene C.
Luerssen, H. G.
Ludlow, Walter W.
Macafee, Burton
MacKenzie, John B.
Maddox, Ferd. T.
Mades, Charles
*Maguire, Thos. F.
Makosky, Eugene C.
Marks, William S.
Marmaduke, M. M.
Marshall. George E.
Marshall, W. T.
Martin, David W.
Martin. James
Martin, W. H. R.
Mattern. Harry J.
McCall, Wm. A.
McCondach, James
McCutcheon, Wm.
*McElroy, John
MacFarlane, Duncan
McGregor, John
McGregor, Wm. W.
McKerichar, Alex.
*McKericher, Alex.
McKimmie, George
McLaughlin, John
Mead, Christopher

Membert, Jacob J.
Meyer, Louis
Middleton. Wm. B.
Miller, Douglas G.
Miller, Peter R.
Mitchell, John
*Mitchell, John N.
Mockabee, Geo. W.
Moeller, John N.
Moffitt, M. M.
Mooers, Frank H.
Moore, William B.
Murphey, J. J.
Musgrave, Will E.
Myers, George A.
Nolle, William W.
Nottingham, E. I.
Nottingham, S. G.
Nottingham, W. W.
Orth, Henry
Otto, Henry L.
Padgett, William E.
Page, Chas. F.
Palmer. L. F.
*Penfield, L. M.
Penney, Ernst A.
Petersen, Peter
Pirie, William
Pixley, W. P.
Pollard, W. A.
Ports, Albert D.
Price, Charles S.
Purks, Forrest H.
Ralph, Henry, jr.
Redman, William T.
Reyburn, Robert
Reynolds, Walter B.
Riggles, Fred D.
Riggles, George W.
Riggles, Lewis
Riggles, Thomas
Robinson, Charles G.

Robinson, Wm. H.
Rohange, Robert
Ross, Henry
Roux, John M.
Ruebsam, Adolph C.
*Ruebsam. Valentine
Ruppert, E. C. E.
Rupprecht, H. E.
Russell, John
Russell, John F.
Rynex, R. Frank R.
Sacks, Eckert J.
Santelmann, Wm. H.
Saunders, William
*Sautter. Charles A.
*Scheel, John E.
Schneider. Charles F.
Schneider, Ferd. T.
Schneider, Harry M.
*Schriftgeisser, P. L.
Schultz, John G.
Scott, S. Oden
Scott, Thomas W.
Scott, Walter C.
Seibert, Edward G.
Shannon, James
Shepard, Charles
Simmerman, W. B.
Simpson, Charles J.
Simpson, Henry K.
Singleton, Thos. D.
Skellenger, Danl. W.
*Skerrett, Wm. H.
Skidmore, James L.
Smith, Arthur H.
*Smith, Charles B.
*Smith, John M.
Spignul, William H.
Spransy, George
Steele, John M.
Stephens, F. H.
Sterling, Franklin R.

Stewart, George S.
Stinzing, John P.
Stodder, Carl W. P.
Stodder, John S.
Storey, Henry
Sweeney, Hugh
Sweeney, Thos. W.
Talbert, James A.
Tatspaugh, Geo. W.
Tatspaugh, John H.
Taylor, Thomas
Taylor, William A.
Thompson. L. L.
Torney, John H.
Townsend, Frank C.
Trussell, Willie J.

Turner, Duane C.
Tyler, J. DeMotte
Van Buskirk, H. K.
Van Ness, Charles
Venable, Charles H.
Vogt, John F.
Voigt, Fred. P.
Voigt, Joseph C.
Walsh, John E.
Ward, William A.
Waters, Somerset R.
Watson, James A.
Watson, William
Wells, Huyler Z.
West, Edward S.
Westfall, John H.

Wetzel, Emil P.
White, R. E. L.
*Williams, Benj. F.
Williams, Edgar W.
Wilson, Lewes D.
Wilton, Charles
Windsbecker, Julius
Wood, George O.
Wylie, Henry J.
Yetton, William E.
Yingling, David C.
Yoeckel, John L.
Young, George D.
Young, Thomas H.
—313.

DROPPED FOR N. P. D.

Cowl, De Witt P.   Green, Grant

———

NEW JERUSALEM LODGE, No. 9,

Meets on the Second and Fourth Thursdays in each month.

OFFICERS.

BENJAMIN PARKHURST, Worshipful Master.
EDW. MATTHEWS, S. Warden.   HOWARD D. FEAST, J. Warden.
WM. E. DENNISON, Secretary.   ROBT. V. GODMAN, Treasurer.

PAST MASTERS AND PAST GRAND OFFICERS.

Aug. Lepreux, sr., Frank A. Jackson, Robert V. Godman, W.
S. Thompson, J. Tyler Powell, Joseph H. Jochum, P. D. G. M.;
George J. Mueller, Edward H. Chamberlin, P. G. M.; E. F. Law-
son, S. T. Schofield, Andrew W. Kelley, William G. Henderson,
R. W. S. G. W.; William E. Dennison, Martin O'Conner, Harrison
Dingman, P. G. M.; S. S. Burdett, Joseph W. Howell, George

W. Nagle, sr., James B. Henderson, W. T. Spencer, S. C. Thompson, James O. Roller, M. F. Eggerman, John Henderson, jr., Thomas A. Chandler, James S. Gray, W. W. Trego.

LIST OF MEMBERS.

Adams, John Lee
Adams, John R.
Allen, Charles
Allen, Samuel E.
Allison, A. M.
Aldrich, S. F.
Anderson, Notley
Archer, James B.
Arnold, William L.
Appich, J. J.
Atkinson, F. G.
Atkinson, Dr. W. H.
Augusterfer, J. A.
Baker, W. H.
Bardroff, J. E.
Banes, C. E.
Bachrach, E. A.
Bradburn, J. D.
Barthel, John A.
Blackburn, J. W., jr.
Baier, Geo. K.
Baruch, Albert
Baum, C. S.
Baurman, A. P.
Bayles, R. N.
Beall, W. A.
Breitbarth, George
Benzler, Herman
Berry, Charles E.
Bergheimer, H. C.
Breck, John
Birmingham, H. L.
Brill, Charles O.
Borland, C. C.
Bolster, Theodore
Bowers, W. W.
Boyle, Bernard

Brown, Frank W.
Brown, Gus. R.
Brockway, B. H.
Botsch, Charles W.
Bowman, C. L.
Burdett, S. S.
Burnett, W. A.
Burton, B. L.
Burgess, H. S.
Burgdorf, Ernest
Butt, Charles, jr.
Boyd, George W.
Button. John F.
Chamberlin, E. H.
Chamberlin, H. O.
Carter, W. G.
Callahan, Robert
Casilear, G. W.
Clarkson, Robert
Champlin, E. P.
Callisher, D. L.
Cramer, B. D.
Carlton, Guy
Crain, E. B.
Crane, S. L.
Carlisle, E. H.
Chapin, A. A.
Chandler, T. A.
Cheesman, George
Collins, J. H.
Cook, J. J.
Cole, Charles D.
Cole, Fred. H.
Cornwell, S. G.
Coxen, Charles
Coffman, D. J.
Coon, W. R.

Conley, W. L.
Conradis, Aug.
Coombs, C. C.
Coombs, C. W.
Crump, James E.
Daetz, Aug.
Daly, W. W.
Dakin, B. E.
Dauterich, H. L.
Dennison, J. E.
Dennison, Wm. E.
Denny, S. W.
Diehl, John A.
Dingman, H.
Downs, R. S.
Douglas, J. F.
Duffey, H. C.
Dunn, M. F.
Eaton, A. J.
Eiseman, J. B.
Eggerman, M. F.
Eliot, Rand L.
Entwistle, J. C.
Engel, N. T.
Esher, Emil
Esher, George C.
Estler, T. W.
Ellyson, R. M.
Edmonds, I. K.
Fagan, W. J.
Fearson, W. H.
Feast, H. D.
Fred, Charles H.
French, J. W.
Fields, Thomas M.
Fischer, Charles
Fowler, James G.

Galt, Ralph L.
Galloway, Thomas
Grady, J. M.
Gebhart, Urban
Green, Edward
Geoghegan, Samuel
Gheen, B. W.
Gleason, Albert
Griesbauer, J. A.
Griswold, F. E.
Gibson, David
Godman, R. V.
Goodman, N.
Gray, James S.
Gross, Isaac
Golway, W. W.
Gottsman, J. A.
Haas, E. E.
Halley, T. F.
Hammond, John
Hanvey, F. L.
Harley, W. M.
Harrison, A. M.
Harrison, J. T.
Harmon, J. O.
Harper, R. N.
Hanley, Peter
Hayward, John
Heimerdinger, H.
Henderson, G. W.
Henderson, John, sr.
Henderson, John, jr.
Henderson, J. B.
Henderson, R. W.
Henderson, T. C.
Henderson, William
Henderson, Wm. G.
Hennage, J. H.
Henry, William M.
Heyl, John K.
Hobday, Harold
Hoffman, George

Hoofnagle, W. B.
Holmes, U. T.
Herdman, J. D. E.
Herman, Isaac
Holdridge, H. E.
Howell, Jos. W.
Howison, R. B.
Hosch, Chas. L.
Hosford, F. H.
Hunt, William F.
Hughes, W. L.
Hutchins, G. E.
Hutchinson, J. T.
Hynes, Thomas
Isham, F. H.
Jacobs, Benjamin
Jacobsen, Charles
Jacobsen, H.
Jackson, F. A.
Jackson, J. P.
Jochum, J. H.
Jochum, J. H., jr.
Jochum, Wm. I.
Johansen, H. P. T.
Johnson, Charles
Johnson, J. O.
Johnston, W. A.
Jones, H. Clay,
Jorss, A. F.
Keating, W.
Keating, W. C.
Keely, Thomas
Kelley, A. W.
Kennedy, S. A.
Kennedy, William
Kent, M. W.
Kettler, C. H.
Keys, C. Fen.
Krey, Louis P.
Krey, Chas. H.
Killmon, C. A.
King, M. R.

Knight, F. H.
Kober, Charles
Kolb, Joseph A.
Kuerschner, H.
Lackey, W. S.
Landon, T. E.
Lansdale, E. G.
Latterner, Peter, jr.
Lawson, E. F.
Lee, Jesse B. K.
Lemon, Rev. J. L. M.
Lemkowitz, J.
Lepreux, A., sr.
Lepreux, A., jr.
Lind, E. G.
Linger, W. H.
Lipp, C. M.
Lippert, George
Little, William E.
Littlefield, H. B.
Lewis, F. M.
Loeb, Myer
Lodge, Lee D.
Long, C. H.
Lucas, J. W.
Mack, J. C.
Magill, C. J., jr.
Major, John W.
Mann, Jesse
Matthews, C. B.
Matthews, Edward
Mattingly, O. F.
McBlair, C. R.
McCauley, Joseph
McCulloch, G. M. D.
McGeorge, H. W.
McKay, G. H.
McKeon, John
McNeir, William
McKenney, C. F.
McKenzie, William
McReynolds, R.

Meyer, Charles E.
Miller, J. S.
Miller, W. E.
Mitchell, J. E.
Montague, A. P.
Morris, Roy T.
Morsell, Herndon
Mueller, George J.
Nagle, Geo. W., jr.
Nagle, Geo. W., sr.
Nauck, C. G.
Nauck, F. C.
Nieman, Henry
Norton, H. R.
O'Brien, M. W.
O'Conner, M.
Oliver, P. R.
Oetzel, William
Omohundro, G. N.
Parkhurst, Benjamin
Payette, George N.
Prime, W. T.
Price, Millard
Powell, J. Tyler
Prosise, J. L.
Plugge, H. O.
Purcell, H. G.
Railey, S. W.
Ragan, R. A.
Rapley, W. H.
Ratcliff, Howard
Raub, George T.
Reedy, Thomas
Reeves, J. C.
Reiter, C. H.
Reiter, Henry
Riezenstein, C. H.
Rieman, J. M.
Riddle, A. S.
Robbins, E. W.
Robbins, N. H.

Rock, Joseph C.
Roller, C. C.
Roller, J. O.
Rothrock, H. C.
Ruff, F. Albert
Rullman, I. A.
Sacks, George P.
Saur, Fenelon
Saur, Rudolph
Schafer, G. F.
Schafer, John
Schafer, J. C.
Shade, N. B.
Staples, O. G.
Stranley, G. C.
Searles, R. B.
Selecman, John
Sheiry, Franc. E.
Sheiry, J. S.
Shehan, George A.
Shekell, George A.
Schneider, J. A.
Schneider, J. F.
Schneider, W. I.
Scott, John B.
Simmons, J. H.
Sheehy, C. A.
Spencer, W. T.
Stein, Nat
Shipley, Pembroke
Springman, C. E.
Strickland, M.
Smith, C. E. (1)
Smith, C. E. (2)
Smith, Frank A.
Smith, George W.
Smith, William H.
Somborn, E. K.
Schofield, A. J. W.
Schofield, S. T.
Stokes, E. S.

Stoops, J. B.
Shumate, O.
Shute, D. K.
Shuster, E. A.
Sturbitts, William
Sylvester, Richard
Taylor, L. W.
Taylor, Thomas S.
Trego, W. W.
Thomas, F. H.
Thomas, G. W.
Townsend, William
Thompson, Frank M.
Thompson, S. C.
Thompson, W. E.
Thompson, W. S.
Tucker, George H.
Trunnell, S. W.
Vaughan, W. W.
Von Gluemer, R.
Vonderheide, H.
Vonderheide, W. J.
Voneiff, George
Von Walleghen, Jos.
Waddey, John A.
Waggerman, J. F.
Walker, O. N.
Walker, T. B.
Walters, C. C.
Waters, F. J.
Weaver, M. C.
Weber, Philip
Welty, A. L.
Wigginton, C. E.
Wheeler, Frank
White, F. L.
Williams, A. R.
Wills, Sidney
Wills, W. H.
Wilmarth, W. B.
Wright, W. H.

Wright, W. W.	Young, Philip	Youngs, R. B.
Wolf, A. L.	Young, William	Zea, E. W.--366.

DROPPED FOR N. P. D.

Carll, J. H.	Martin, R. H.	Webb, John N.
Clarke, Jas. M.	Tribby, C. G.	

HIRAM LODGE, No. 10,

Meets on the First and Third Fridays in each Month.

OFFICERS.

W. F. R. PHILLIPS, Worshipful Master.
—— ——, S. Warden.   JOHN T. MEANY, J. Warden.
JAS. W. WRENN, Secretary.   PHILLIP H. WARD, Treasurer.

PAST MASTERS AND PAST GRAND OFFICERS.

Louis D. Wine, P. D. G. M.; M. R. Thorp, J. B. Lambia, J. M. Fernandez, Robt. Armour, John D. Newman, Jas. W. Wrenn, Ira W. Hopkins, W. C. Bickford, Geo. H. Walker, F. I. Hunter, F. W. Ritter, jr., Jos. Jouy, C. L. Patten, W. L. Stuard, George W. Linkins, John Breen, A. S. Tabor, Geo. W. Uline.

LIST OF MEMBERS.

Armour, Robert	Brown, Edmund H.	Buck, Rev. J. A.
Ash, William M.	Birch, Henry	Barton, J.
Ashton, John C.	Biscoe, Henry L.	Bispham, Rev. C. W.
Ashby, Welby L.	Bex, Frederick	Bieleski, Rev. Alex.
Bassett, Geo. T.	Bickford, Warren C.	Biscoe, Henry E.
Blackburn, L. L.	Bradbury, R. F.	Carlson, C. A.
Berry, James	Brandenburg, F. H.	Cuthburt, James
Barbee, J. Russell	Brandenburg, Ed. C.	Chase, William
Byram, James H.	Berger, Oscar L.	Clements, John W.
Bremmerman, L. T.	Breen, John	Cranmer, David
Biedler, Andrew J.	Bell, Aaron H.	Campbell, Edwin
Borland, Alex. T.	Bird, Henry E.	Davis, C. W. T.

Davis, John A., jr.
Dixon, Henry M.
Donaldson, John T.
Donaldson, R. B.
Duckett, Walter G.
Draper, W. S. T.
Dunn, William
Danforth, R. Foster
Doton, Charles O.
Danforth, M. E.
Donnelly, Richard J.
DeReamer, George C.
Duncan, Rev. Geo. S.
Eisenman, Moses
Erney, Charles A.
Earl, Robert
Earnest, J. Paul
Eldridge, M. A.
Evans, Henry, jr.
Exley, Thomas M.
Eaton, P. H.
Ennis, Rev. H. W.
Edwards, Ed.
Fishell, Samuel J.
Fardon, A. P.
Fairfax, Arthur W.
Fernandez, J. M.
Fentress, Augustus
Fisher, Marvin P.
Fisher, Milton L.
Fletcher, Benj. F.
Frankenfield, H. C.
Frey, Levin S.
Fought, Joseph
Fearson, John B.
Fairfax, Charles W.
Freund, Harry P.
Flack, William P.
Gawler, Charles J.
Garner, Lucien
Garnett, Phillip
Gawler, Alfred H.

Gittings, Jed
Gray, Evan J.
Gray, Samuel
Gleason, James
Gayle, Robert E.
Harner, W. A.
Hoffman, Will A.
Harkness, Robert H.
Hege, S. B.
Hopkins, Ira W.
Hopkins, S. G.
Hunter, Fielder I.
Hodges, Yulee
Hinternach, C. R.
Hancock, A. W.
Helmuth, E.
Hunter, Frank T.
Harding, Rev. A.
Howes, William H.
Hilton, James M.
Hempstone, H. L.
Hamlin, John
Hall, Philip T.
Hunt, Rev. E. L.
Hunt, John T.
Henderson, Jos. C.
Johnson, J. Hiram
Jenner, H. W. T.
Johnson, Alvord G.
Johnson, Ashbury R.
Johnson, George A.
Johnson, Daniel
Jones, Ed. T.
Jouy, Joseph
Johnson, George W.
Johnson, Daniel, jr.
Johnson, Robert W.
Johnson, Enoch G.
Johnson, Wm. M.
Johnston, George C.
Krahenbuhl, August
Kolb, John

Koppell, Herman
Kraus, Charles A.
Kelley, John T., jr.
Koontz, Marcellus
Lowe, W. T.
Lambia, James B.
Linkins, George W.
Linkins, James N.
Lyons, Hugh
Lynch, John
Mann, Richard C.
Martin, Henry B.
Mechlin, F. S.
Milton, James H.
Myer, James C.
Maddox, W. R.
Morse, Bryan H.
MacNab, John F.
Magruder, R. L.
Magee, James F.
Maxwell, Martin V.
McGlue, George T.
McIllhenny, Jas. S.
McLaughlin, Jas. B.
Morris, Henry F.
Miller, Harry T.
Moffitt, Benjamin F.
Meany, John T.
Myers, Ed. E.
Madden, Daniel
Moore, Charles J.
Nichols, Charles B.
Newman, John D.
Newton, George
Norris, Eppa
Nelson, Charles W.
O'Connell, John
Parker, Jesse L.
Price, John A.
Patten, Charles L.
Perry, Charles H.
Perry, George N.

Peterson, Jacob E.
Pearson, Isaac
Potts, Frank C.
Poultney, W. W.
Phillips. W. F. R.
Power, John A.
Runyan, I. N.
Raub, Ezra W.
Raymond, Samuel J.
Reynolds, George R.
Riley. William T.
Ritter. Fred. W., jr.
Routt, Alphonso
Ramsey, Richard H.
Randall, John A.
Strasberger, Isaac H.
Smith, F. W.
Sanner, Jerome F.
Sauer, Charles H.
Salter. George W.
Schmid, Ernst
Shultze, John H.
Simpson, W. I.
Smith, Fred. H.
Sems, John H.

Sothoron. Elmer
Stearn, William G.
Stuard, William H.
Sutton, Robert M.
Sutor. Fred G.
Smith, H. B.
Schneider, Charles B.
Schneider, Fred A.
Sousa, John P.
Sardo. A. E.
Sears, John F.
Thomas, William A.
Taylor. Thomas J.
Thomas, Gideon A.
Thomas. Rev.W. S. O.
Tuck, Charles B.
Tallon, James F.
Taber, Alva S.
Taylor, A. B.
Thomas, John W.
Thorp, Martin R.
Tucker, H. Walker
Timmerman, W. H.
Texton, John A.
Uline, George W.

Vessey, Thomas L.
Vansant, Lewis
Wright, John W.
Williams, Henry E.
Wagner, John E.
Ward. Philip H.
Wescott. Edward S.
Weeden, James H.
Webber, Joseph E.
Wine, Louis D.
Wild, John F.
Witmer, Calvin
Wilson, Thos. M., jr.
Whiting, George W.
Wolfarth, E. S.
Wrenn, James W.
Whitiside, Benj. F.
White, A. G.
Walker, George H.
Wanstall, Frank B.
Wheeler, Benj. L.
Watterson, Robert J.
Zeigler, Jacob
Zimmer, M. J.—236.

SAINT JOHN'S LODGE, No. 11,

Meets on the Second and Fourth Fridays in each Month.

OFFICERS.

WILLIAM T. JONES, Worshipful Master.
REV. C. ALVIN SMITH, S. Warden.   CHAS. FERNALD, J. Warden.
ROBERT A. DELLETT, Secretary.   C. J. WATSON, Treasurer.

PAST MASTERS AND PAST GRAND OFFICERS.

Jesse W. Lee, jr., P. G. M.; Charles W. Hancock, P. G. S.;
George Wright, Charles J. Watson, Geo. A. Abbott, George P.

Bohrer, Louis Y. Mitchell, Wm. H. Douglas, Harry Standiford, Alex. McKenzie, Frank J. Foster, Edwin A. Heilig, Robert A. Dellett, Thomas Foster, Jas. E. Hutchinson, Vernon E. Hodges, Edwin A. Niess.

LIST OF MEMBERS.

Abbott, George A.
Adams, Thomas
Albertson, George H.
Altschu, Louis P.
Andrews, Robert
Angus, Job W.
Armstrong, Thos. H.
Austin, James B.
Bacon, Samuel H.
Balch, Samuel C.
Baldwin, Geo. E.
Barnhart, Samuel
Barton, William M.
Bass, William M.
Beach, John S.
Beck, Joseph F.
Belt, Anderson K.
Belt, William T.
Betts, Philander
Bishop, David J.
Bland, Charles W.
Bohrer, George P.
Boteler, James E.
Bowen, Charles
Boyce, John A.
Boyer, George W.
Bright, Albert W.
Brophy, Bernard
Brown, William B.
Browne, Philip
Brummitt, Arthur
Buckey, John D.
Buckler, Zach. S.
Bunch, Nazareth
Burbage, William D.
Burch, William L.

Burns, Thomas
Bussius, Allen
Byers, John S.
Callisher, Lewis
Cameron. Daniel D.
Campbell, Alberto
Campbell, James
Canfield, Andrew N.
Carr, George W.
Carter, Charles T.
Cavanaugh, Thomas
Chamberlin, F. T.
Chandler, Fred C.
Chapman, Edw. K.
Coen, Chas. M.
Cole, Elmer D.
Cole, Lamont E.
Cole, Samuel I.
Copenhaver, H. E.
Cottle, Albert
Crandall, Joseph E.
Crane, John H.
Craven, Henry N.
Crosby, William H.
Crush, James E.
Cummisky, Andw. J.
Daniel, Robert A.
Darneille, Hope H.
Dellett, Robert A.
Detweiler, Fred F.
Detweiler, Fred M.
Dobbs, Henry C.
Dodge, Arthur J.
Donaldson, A. L.
Donaldson, Martin L.
Doran, Albert L.

Douglas, William H.
Dubois, William
Dulin, Edward M.
Dyrenforth, Elias M.
Dyrenforth, Mitchell
Earnshaw,Richard J.
Eckels, Percy J.
Edgerly, Albert W.
Edmonston, Arch.
Elliott. Norman T.
Ellis, Dornin
Ellis, Henry
England, Wm. R.
Evans, Albert W.
Fernald, Charles
Fill, John C.
Fishblate, S. Albert
Fleming, Harry N.
Foster, Frank J.
Foster, Percy S.
Foster, Thomas
Fowler, Leonard F.
Froiseth, B. A. N.
Ganss, Isaac
Ganss, Samuel
Gardner, William H.
Gasch, Herman E.
Gawler, Joseph, jr.
Gawler, Joseph C.
Geyer, William F.
Gibson, William H.
Graham, John E.
Grevemeyer, Wm. H.
Guy, Benjamin W.
Hager, Peter
Hahn, Morris

Hahn, Selig F.
Hale, Charles F.
Hall, Charles C.
Hall, William C.
Hamlin, Harris C.
Hancock, Charles W.
Hannay, William M.
Hardester, Thos. J.
Harper, Joseph
Harper, Nicholas C.
Harris, Job
Harris, Reuben
Harrover, James D.
Harrower, John J.
Hart, Frank W.
Hart, Samuel
Heald, Edwin
Heilig, Edwin A.
Heller, Albert S.
Henry, Frank C.
Henry, Samuel W.
Hercher, Ferdinand
Hibbs, William B.
Hirsh, Morris S.
Hodges, Vernon E.
Hooe, Abram B.
Hooe, Robert A.
Hoover, Samuel F.
Hough, William I.
Houghton, John Q. A.
Howard, Joseph T.
Humphries, L. J.
Hunt, John D.
Hutchinson, Jas. E.
Hutchinson, W. T. (1)
Hutchinson, W. T. (2)
Jama, Alois E.
Jarvis, John F.
Jenkins, Frank M.
Jennings, L. de F.
Jones, Thomas H.
Jones, William T.

Joy, Herman S.
Karr, Henry C.
Kaufman, Henry
Kline, John M.
Kline, Seth Q.
Landergren, Thos. J.
Lanham, Charles L.
Laport, Frank F.
Larcombe, Howard
Larcombe, Rev. J. A.
Larcombe, Wm. M.
Lashhorn, Chas. H.
Lashhorn, Jesse V.
Lee, Jesse W., jr.
Lewis, David W.
Lightfoot, James H.
Lowe, Thomas
Maedel, Julius A.
Magruder, C. C., jr.
Markolf, Conrad G.
Marlow, Morris E.
Marlow, Walter H.
Massey, James H.
Merrick, Chaplin
Merrick, Eugene M.
Metzerott, Frank B.
Mitchell, Louis Y.
Mockbee, Henry E.
Molin, Nils
Moser, Joseph
McConnell, Abel
McCubbin, Charles J.
McIntyre, Thos. K.
McKenzie, Alex.
McKenzie, Alex. D.
McKnight, Wm. H.
Nailor, Allison, jr.
Nalle, Edmund C.
Nalle, Edmund P.
Niess, Edwin A.
North, Rev. Jos. B.
Otterback, Phillip

Owens, William E.
Parris, Joseph
Peach, Emanuel C.
Pentland, Andw. W.
Perrott, George
Pine, David E.
Plant, George H., jr.
Plumley, Addison
Polkinhorn, Jos. H.
Powers, Marcellus J.
Price, Washington R.
Price, Wm. H. H.
Prince, Abram D.
Pugh, James L., jr.
Reid, Esli D.
Richardson, M. N.
Ritchie, John P.
Robins, William L.
Rosenthal, Sidney E.
Ruff, Albert B.
Ryan, Richard W.
Ryneal, George, jr.
Sailer, Charles C.
Salvatore, E. A.
Samson, George C.
Sangston, Allan T.
Shedd, William A.
Shelton, George B.
Shoemaker, Chas. F.
Shreeve, Rev. Jesse
Shryock, Charles K.
Shuffle, Edwin
Simms, Richard D.
Slater, George W.
Slater, Jacob
Slater, Jacob S.
Slater, Luther W.
Slater, William F.
Sloan, Charles G.
Smith, Addison M.
Smith, Rev. C. Alvin
Smith, Jared G.

Smith, Jeff. D. F.
Smith, John N.
Snyder, Edwin H.
Sprigg, William M.
Standiford, Harry
Steele, Rev. John W.
Stephenson, Saml. L.
Stinemetz, Benj. H.
Stuart, Donald G.
Stutzman, Schell H.
Sunderland, Rev. B.
Swaine, John E.
Taylor, Harvey A.
Teepe, Wm. H.
Thomas, Amadeo L.
Tracy, Edwin D.
Trigge, Wm. A.

Turner, George
Tyree, Josiah S.
Unger, Calvin R.
Van Bibber, Wm. H.
Vinton, Leon R.
Wagner, William
Walker, John N.
Walker, Noble J.
Walter, John
Walter, William
Warren, William J.
Watkins, Victor E.
Watson, Charles J.
Watson, James
Watson, James M.
Watson, Johannes V.
Watson, Thomas H.

Watts, Walter
Weidman, John
Weller, Frank P.
Wells, Charles E.
White, Truman W.
Wilber, Jerome J.
Willasey, Edw.
Williams, Daniel
Winter, John T.
Wolfsteiner, Otto L.
Woltz, Charles A. D.
Woodbury, Henry E.
Wright, George
Wurdeman, John V.
Youngs, Elphonso
—283.

DROPPED FOR N. P. D.

Adams, James B.
Claus, John H.

Cline, Hugh M.
Cole, Henry D.

Lashhorn, Geo. A.
Vanderventer, S. C.

NATIONAL LODGE, No. 12,

Meets on the First and Third Tuesdays in each Month.

OFFICERS.

JOSEPH E. FALK, Worshipful Master.
F. W. BUDDECKE, S. Warden.   ABNER P. WILDE, J. Warden.
HARRY L. WALCOTT, Secretary.   G. TAYLOR WADE, Treasurer.

PAST MASTERS AND PAST GRAND OFFICERS.

I. L. Johnson, P. G. M.; R. C. Lewis, Edward Kern, P. S. Lesh,
T. J. Newton, Joseph M. Eggleston, J. J. Jones, H. L. Walcott,
Chas. F. Scott, Wm. E. Handy, Chas. W. Otis, John B. Hicklin.

LIST OF MEMBERS.

Adams, Edw. J.
Alburtis, John
Allen, Robert
Alvord, Thos. G., jr.
Armstrong, James R.
Arrington, Thos. M.
Ashley, Osborne
Barnett, John L.
Barry, Edmund
Bauer, George W.
Baum, Charles
Been, Henry
Beekman, Milton M.
Bieber, Samuel
Blout, Isaac L.
Blumenberg, M. R.
Bridger, J. D.
Brown, Charles W.
Buddecke, Fred W.
Burgee, Edw. E.
Bury, William F.
Cadick, Thos. W.
Chambers, Emmet B.
Cleland, William M.
Cole, Elisha H.
Crown, John O.
Cutler, Henry M.
Davis, James W.
Day, William H.
Donnell, George S.
Dunn, John
Dyer, Albert R.
Eggleston, Jos. M.
Eisenbeiss, Julius
Elliott, Alex., jr.
Enders, John
Engel, George W.
Ennis, William R.
Falk, Joseph E.
Fisher, George W.

Flamini, J. George
Flenniken, Wm. C.
Fout, Rev. Julius E.
Fulton, Horace G.
Ghiselli, Angelo
Gibson, John F.
Gill, John C.
Gill, Stephen F.
Giovannetti, Vincens
Goodier, John A.
Gummell, E. G.
Handy, William E.
Hansen, John
Harding, Clement T.
Harper, James L.
Hartman, C. A.
Hassler, Alpha M.
Hastings, William T.
Hawk, Samuel T.
Hawkes, Benj. F.
Helmuth, Valentine
Hicktin, John B.
Hobbs, Frank N.
Holl, Eugene A.
Huggins, James T.
Jarboe, Daniel W.
Johnson, Isaac L.
Jones, J. Jolly
Jordan, William H.
Jouvenal, Adolph H.
Jouvenal, Jacques
Kempner, Jake
Kern, Charles E.
Kern, Edward
Kern, George W.
Kern, J. Quincy
Kessler, Zadok W.
Kimmel, Carl
King, Albert H.
Kingsley, Albert F.

Kronheimer, Henry
Lerch, Frank S.
Lesh, Peter S.
Lewis, Richard C.
Lyles, Richard H.
McCormick, John F.
McLeland, Jerome F.
Martin, John L.
Measer, E. H. J.
Meyer, Simon N.
Nachman, David
Nass, John
Neitzey, William
Newman, Edward A.
Newton, T. John
Otis, Charles W.
Palmer, William J.
Parker, Harry B.
Pegues, Samuel W. E.
Porter, Harvey W.
Potbury, Edwin
Potter, Cyrus M.
Prosise, Logan
Rabbitt, John T.
Rae, George W.
Reiner, Frank
Rich, Max M.
Richmond, Jas. E.
Ridgeley, Augustus
Rothwell, Richard
Rouzer, George W.
Rouzer, Michael M.
Schinnerer, Wm.
Scott, Charles F.
Sherwood, M. A.
Silverberg, Bernard
Sinclair, William
Slater, John G.
Snyder, David J.
Stephan, Albert

Stickel, George D.
Stretton, Frank W.
Stück, Emil H.
Stutts, Rufus H.
Talbott, Robert W.
Taylor, Miles
Vaughan, Dan C.
Veerhoff, William H.

Vierbuchen, Peter
Wade, G. Taylor
Walcott, Charles W.
Walcott, Harry L.
Walker, George C.
Weber, William F. C.
Whitcraft, Walter
White, Josiah R.

Whiteside, Wm. D.
Whitney, Benj. B.
Wilde, Abner P.
Williams, Wm. C.
Wilson, Thomas M.
Wright, R. Franklin
Young, Sostman E.
—143.

DROPPED FOR N. P. D.

Basin, W. Finley

Essig, Charles
Macnichol, Chas., jr.

Smith, Bedford L.

WASHINGTON CENTENNIAL LODGE, No. 14,

Meets on the First and Third Wednesdays in each Month.

OFFICERS.

JOHN H. DAVIS, Worshipful Master.
EDSON PHILLIPS, S. Warden.   SAML. P. JOHNSON, J. Warden.
EMMETT C. ELMORE, Secretary.   WALTER S. BARKER, Treasurer.

PAST MASTERS AND PAST GRAND OFFICERS.

J. H. Hood, H. E. Riley, E. C. Elmore, C. H. Smith, H. P. Marshall, W. H. Baum, J. J. Hill, H. N. Keene, J. H. Small, jr., R. W. D. G. M.; E. C. C. Winter, W. B. Pettus, J. F. Stewart, J. H. McIntosh, R. Connell, H. F. Riley, F. W. Harper, C. K. Berryman.

LIST OF MEMBERS.

Anderson, C. C.
Atkisson, H. L. B.
Bailey, H. O.
Baker, John L.
Barber, George E.
Barber, J. R.

Barker, W. S.
Barr, John
Barrows, S. M.
Baum, Wm. H.
Bensinger, Samuel
Berg, John R.

Bergman, William
Berry, E. A.
Berryman, C. K.
†Bickford, W. C.
Bishop, A. A.
Bishop, V. R.

Block. Charles
Bogue. Dr. A. P.
Boughton. W. E.
Bouis, R. H. G.
Bouis. William R.
Brackett, George F.
Bradshaw, M.
Brantley. Thomas F.
Breast, James O.
Browne. John R.
Bruckheimer, Dr. M.
Bruckheimer, Saml.
Burdine, William T.
Burger, Leopold
Burgess, E. S.
Burney, H. P.
Burtt, E. J.
Burtt, George M.
Butterfield, George
Carson, William H.
Carter, H. P.
Carter, Thomas I.
Chambers, M. W.
Chapman, B. D.
Church, C. B.
Clapp, A. M.
Clark, W. S.
Cole, J. S.
Connell, Robert
Conway, George
Cooke, George H.
Copeland, A.
Crook, Dr. H.
Crowe, Rev. J. T.
Cummins, R. K.
Curran, Joseph H.
Curtis, J. L.
Dalgleish, J. E.
Daniel, E. H.
Davis, J. H.
DeLoach, Thomas
Dent, Louis A.

Dezendorf, F. C.
Dietz, Charles
Dillenback. Dr. W. J.
Doherty, E. W.
Donn, John C. T.
Donn. Thomas M. F.
Douglass. A. M.
Dowling, H. W.
Dulin, J. V., jr.
Durfee, R. B.
Eiseman. Gerson
Elliott. Robert F.
Elmore. Emmett C.
Field. Thomas
Finch, Erastus W.
Firor. F. M.
Fischer, Samuel
Fisher, A.
Fisher, John
Ford, E. R.
Ford, J. M.
Frank, Joseph M.
French, Evander
Garner, Thomas A.
Garrison, John S.
Getz, George H.
†Gibbs, Dr. T. F.
Godron, George
Goodman, S.
Graham, Thomas
Gray, C. W.
Gregory, J. W.
Greene, John A.
Gunnell, Dr. R. H.
Haliday, James B.
Hall, Ralph L.
Halleck, W. F.
Hanna, Read
Hansell, George B.
Harper, F. W.
Harshman, W. S.
Hartzell, W. E.

Hatch, Mark B.
Helmus, W. A.
Heffernan. Wm. A.
Herold, Charles
Hill, John J.
Hill, L. C.
Hinds, W. L.
Hiser, Daniel
Hodgkin, C. E.
Hoffa, Herz
Holder, Willis
Holmes, C. W.
Holtzclaw, W. B.
Hood, John H.
Hopkins, F. E.
Hopkins, John A.
Hopkins, Thad. A.
Hoskins, Dr. J. T.
Huddleson, H. P.
Hutton, H. T.
Jeuneman, H. E.
Johnson, S. P.
Jones, Edwin C.
Jones, Richard H.
†Jouy, Dr. Joseph
Keene, H. N.
King, Wm. R.
Kirby, E. E.
Knight, H. M.
Koch, William
Kraft, John
Laferty, I. D.
Langley, J. W.
Lawrence, C. H.
Leland, T. F.
Lemon, H. T. A.
Lemmon, Chas. F.
Long, A. M.
Long, John
Long, Dr. William
Longley, E. E.
Lusby, W. E.

Lytle, R. S.
Maedel, O.
Main, William H.
Malone, T. W.
Marshall, H. P.
McCorkle, George
McIntosh, J. H.
McKinley, J. Wm.
Meader, H. I.
Meador, Rev. C. C.
Merrill, C. M.
†Merrill, H. S.
Metzger, F. P.
Minnix, W. S.
Minster, A. L.
Mitchell, K. P.
Mock, Horace J.
Montgomery, C. F.
Moran, H. E.
Morgan, E. S.
Moreland, W. M.
Moores, E. S.
Morris, C. W.
Mosher, D. C.
Muir, Rev. J. J.
Mullineaux, H. H.
Oliver, G. W.
Olmstead, E. B.
Orndorff, L. G.
Otterback, W. H.
Oyster, James F.
Pardoe, C. S.
Parkinson, C.
Partridge, W. H.
Payne, R. H.
Peters, Eugene
Pettit, Smith
Pettus, W. B.
Phillips, Edson
Phillips, W. L.
Pless, William A.
Plumley, S. M.

Potts, Frank E.
Powell, J. W.
Rau, Herman A.
Rau, John C.
Raymond. Frank K.
Renz, Andrew
Richard, Edward
Ridley, C. W.
Riley, H. E.
Riley, H. F.
Roberts, Bowie
Rogerson, Fred
Rouse, F. L.
Roy, James
Rozycki, Stephen
Russell, I. C.
Sands, H. E.
Sanner, F. T.
Sargeant, T. B.
Sattes, P. R. R. M.
Scaggs, R. A.
Schmid, E. S.
Schram, M.
Schoepf, W. K.
Scott, Alex.
Seaman, Earnest
Sebree, W. E.
Sharp, James
Shaw, Alex. C.
Shepherd, William
Shipman, S. A.
Shunk, A. W.
Simms, C. E.
Simpson, C. W.
Skippon, H. H.
Small, C. A.
Small, J. H., jr.
Small, Joseph
Smallwood, W. C.
Smith, Chas. H.
Smith, James B.
Smith, John Speed

Smith, W. A.
Smith, William R.
Smith, W. Ryde
Speare, F. A.
Sprague, F. H.
Stearns, F. J.
Steinbrenner, A. C.
Stephenson, Thos. P.
Stewart, J. Frew
Stockton, A. W.
Stockton, I. C.
Stouffer, C. C.
Strait, Dr. N. A.
Streater, Wallace
Studds, Colin
Swingle, C. W.
Tanner, W. B.
Terry, Charles W.
Thompson, Dr. E. D.
Townsend, J. J.
Trusheim, J. H.
Trueworthy, B. T.
Trueworthy, O. W.
Vail, Benjamin
Vernon, C. W.
Walford, A.
Walker, A. G.
Walker, George E.
Walker, W. H.
Walters, J. E.
Ward, John B.
Ward, W. A.
Wells, A. B.
Wells, Josephus
Wendel, S. O.
Westerfield, J. W.
Wheeler, E. G.
Whitford, E. O.
Whitney, M. M.
Williams, Hugh H.
Williams, R.
Wills, J. W.

Wilson, C. S.	Woog, E. S.	Young, Dr. E. R.
Winter, Dr. E. C. C.	Wright, S. B.	Zeh, George F.—278.
Witten, James W.	Yerby, E. D.	

DROPPED FOR N. P. D.

Lilley, George	Turner, Edward	Worrell, C. W.
Messner, C. W.	Turner, William	

BENJAMIN B. FRENCH LODGE, No. 15,

Meets on the First and Third Mondays in each Month.

OFFICERS.

JOHN C. CHANEY, Worshipful Master.
ALEX. GRANT, S. Warden.   E. ST. CLAIR THOMPSON, J. Warden.
W. A. GATLEY, Secretary.   GABRIEL F. JOHNSTON, Treasurer.

PAST MASTERS AND PAST GRAND OFFICERS.

Warren H. Orcutt, P. J. G. W.; Val. N. Stiles, Ros. A. Fish, Frederick Johnston, George H. Lillebridge, John Tweedale, John R. Garrison, William A. Gatley, Samuel B. Evans, Myron M. Parker, P. G. M.; George Wallace, Samuel E. Slater, James A. Sample, P. G. M.; William H. Lemon, Charles R. Smith, Wm. Barnum, Gabriel F. Johnston, Nathan Hazen, Howard M. Gillman, Frank M. Kiggins, Frank F. Major, James A. Wetmore, Joseph A. Oliver, Henry M. Schooley, J. Hamilton Beatty, Durham W. Stevens, Francis P. Griffith, David D. Stone, John S. Tomlinson, John W. Moore, Convis Parker, William A. Meloy, Watson B. Mundell, Donald B. McLeod, Michael C. Connelly.

LIST OF MEMBERS.

Abbott, Ira C.	Allen, George W.	Atchison, Harris L.
Abraham, Alexander	Allen, John H.	Aukam, Frederick G.
Ailes, Milton E.	Arnold, Hunter	Bacon, L. Seward
Alderman, Z. Wilbur	Ashby, William F.	Bailey, William R.

Baker, Albert
Baker, Clarence
Baker, Edwin
Balch, George V.
Barbour, Fred E.
Barksdale, Wm. H.
Barksdale, Noel W.
Barnum, William
Bartlett, Edwin C.
Basset, Jesse M.
Bateman, Wm. W.
Baxter, John C.
Bayne, John W.
Beall, Howard
Beach, Seward S.
Beall, Richard J., jr.
Beatty, Chester H.
Beatty, J. Hamilton
Beatty, Louis K.
Beck, James H.
Becker, Conrad
Behrens, Fred W.
Bell, Alonzo
Belote, Albert S.
Bennett, George B.
Bennett, John S.
Beveridge, Daniel W.
Beveridge, D. W., jr.
Biehl, Wm. F.
Blake, Lovell L.
Blye, Benjamin F.
Boag, John O.
Boardman, Myron
Bolton, Robert F.
Bone, Wallace G.
Borches, Diedrich H.
Boswell, George H.
Bottomley, John
Bourn, Frank B.
Boveé, J. Wesley
Bowman, Samuel H.
Bowen, Charles H.

Boyer, Ulysses L.
Bradfield, Jeff. D.
Brandt, Adam
Bronson, Charles E.
Brodie, William T.
Brown, Dorsey
Brown, Rev. T. W.
Buie, Walter A.
Bumpus, Lorenzo D.
Bundick, John N.
Burnside, Robert W.
Burnstine, Bernard
Butler, Charles H.
Butler, William H.
Callaghan, Ferd. W.
Calvert, Charles H.
Calvert, Finley H.
Campbell, Mort. S.
Carré, Alfred D.
Carroll, John J.
Cattell, Henry P.
Caylor, Joseph J.
Chaney, John C.
Childs, Frank W.
Clark, Herman J.
Clear, Robert L.
Cleaveland, Chas. H.
Cobaugh, Harry A.
Cogswell, Theo. M.
Coleman, Chas. O'C.
Coleman, Silas B.
Connelly, Michael C.
Cook, John
Coon, David L.
Cornman, Ephraim
Cossart, William P.
Coumbe, Albert T.
Coumbe, Oscar H.
Cousar, Robert M.
Coville, Frederick V.
Cowell, Henry C.
Cranford, Joseph H.

Crawford, John J.
Creamer, William
Crook, William H.
Crosthwaite, F. B.
Crump, William T.
Cunningham, S. C.
Curtiss, Charles L.
Custis, Marvin A.
Davis, Henry C.
Day, James H.
Deans, Arthur C.
De Land, Theo. L.
DePuy, Edward K.
Dick, Harvey B.
Dickson, Samuel H.
Doe, William H.
Donally, Williams
Douglas, John F.
Downing, Robert L.
Drane, Albert G.
Duffield, Will Ward
Dyer, Frank L.
Eagan, Thomas
Easterling, Edwin H.
Eaton, Walter S.
Eberly, Samuel G.
Ellis, William K.
Emmons, George E.
Emmert, Frank R.
Ennis, Charles H.
Espey, Ferdinand
Evans, Harry R.
Evans, Samuel B.
Fales, Warren D.
Faller, Albert L.
Fellows, Harry A.
Fish, Roswell A.
Fitch, Sidney A.
Fleming, Robert I.
Flenner, George C.
Fletcher, William H.
Floyd, Albert C.

Follett, Fred W.
Foster, John J.
Fowler, Ernest W.
Frazier, Robert T.
Freeman, John F.
French, H. Orren
Garrison, John R.
Gatley, William A.
Geiseking, Fred C.
Gibbs, James T.
Giddings, Alfred W.
Gillette, Charles J.
Gillman, Howard M.
Gilmer, Thomas W.
Gladmon, Burgess K.
Glascock, Alfred E.
Glover, George N.
Glover, Horace D.
Gohr, Frank C.
Gold, Daniel L.
Goodrich, Louis P.
Gordon, Charles H.
Gosling, Henry L.
Grant, Alexander
Gray, Alexander P.
Gray, John W.
Greeley, Arthur P.
Green, John M.
Greene, John, jr.
Gridley, Lucius E.
Griffith, Francis P.
Groff, John M.
Groff, Samuel A.
Hadley, Amos
Haig, Fredk. J.
Hale, Robert J.
Hall, Henry W.
Hall, Powhatan
Halpenny, R. L. S.
Hamblitt, Orrin A.
Hamilton, William
Hammerly, Chas. J.

Hammond, John E.
Hanford, Hopkins J.
Hanna, William
Harmon, L. Willard
Harrald, Henry
Harris, John H.
Harsha, John W.
Havenner, George C.
Hazen, Nathan
Hazzard, John L.
Heiberger, Francis J.
Heiberger, F. J., jr.
Heimer, Joseph
Heller, Simon
Hendrick, David S.
Hendrick, John T.
Herbert, Leon H.
Herron, Charles S.
Heth, Henry
Heupel, John L.
Hills, Wallace H.
Hindmarsh, Walter B.
Hodgson, William M.
Hoiby, Henry
Holmes, John
Holmes, Lewis
Hood, Thomas B.
Hoover, Dickerson N.
Hoover, William D.
Hough, Joseph T.
Howard, Alonzo M.
Howard, Charles
Howison, Andrew J.
Howlett, John H.
Hoyt, George B.
Hullett, Archibald G.
Hunt, James A.
Hunter, James A.
Hussey, Dexter S.
Hutchinson, Wm. J.
Iardella, Charles T.
Jackson, Frank H.

Jannus, Frankland
Jasper, T. Edward
Jemison, Ewan H.
Johannes, Ira H.
Johannes, John G.
Johns, Walter R.
Johnson, William B.
Johnson, William W.
Johnston, Frederick
Johnston, Frank E.
Johnston, Gabriel F.
Johnston, Henry A.
Jones, Edward S.
Jordan, John J.
Judd, Oscar M.
Keithley, George
Kellogg, Albert H.
Kellogg, Wilbur F.
Kemp, James W.
Kennedy, John L.
Kerr, James
Kiggins, Frank M.
King, Charles W.
Kinsel, James C.
Klemroth, Edgar H.
Kneesi, Gustave A.
Knowles, William E.
Koones, Samuel S.
Lacey, Robert S.
LaFlesche, Frank
Lansburgh, Henry
Law, Frank A.
Lazenby, Benj. C.
Leech, John S.
Leech, Daniel P.
Lemon, William H.
Lewis, Charles E.
Lillebridge, Geo. H.
Lipscomb, Wm. P.
Loeffler, George S.
Logan, Alonzo T.
Lohmann, Jasper

Loving, Samuel B.
Luthy, John H.
Luttrell, John A.
Lyford, Benjamin F.
Lown, William G.
MacLeod, Donald B.
MacNamee, Herbert
McClure, Charles
McConnell, James C.
McDonald, Allen C.
McElroy, John
McIntyre, Edw. A.
McIntyre, John V.
McKee, Townley A.
McKnight, John W.
McNeil, Eaton K.
McNeil, Walter A.
McNelly, Arthur, jr.
McQueen, James G.
Mack, Frank E.
Major, Frank F.
Malcom, Granville
Manning, William J.
Marche, William B.
Marble, George R.
Mathewson, David N.
Maurer, George H.
Meloy, William A.
Merrill, Daniel F., jr.
Metcalf, Francis S.
Meyer, Leonard
Mickle, William H.
Miller, Claude E.
Miller, Thomas
Mitchell, John, jr.
Mitchell, Thomas H.
Moler, Robert L.
Moore, John R.
Moore, John W.
Moore, Thomas P.
Morgan, Henry
Morgan, William B.
Morrison, D. C.

Morton, George S.
Moses, Henry C.
Mulcare, James E.
Mullowny, Alex. R.
Mundell, Watson B.
Munson, Charles B.
Murray. Bentley P.
Myers, Charles G.
Myers, Melvin E.
Nauck, Oscar
Nevius. Joseph D.
Newton, Watson J.
Nichols, Harry H.
Niedfeldt, Herman J.
Norton, George F.
Norton, Solon L.
Norton, William H.
Nowlin, Homer E.
Nuber, Jacob L.
Oliver, Joseph A.
O'Neal, Lewis I.
Orcutt, Warren H.
Parish, James H.
Parker, Convis
Parker, David
Parker, Frederick W.
Parker, Harry P.
Parker, John E.
Parker, Myron M.
Parris, Albion K.
Parsons, John W.
Partello, Dwight M.
Patrick, Runnion M.
Payne, James G.
Peabody, William S.
Pearson, Samuel P.
Pease, F. Walter
Penicks, Thomas B.
Phillips, George W.
Pitney, Ora L.
Pittis, William
Plass, Nicholas J.
Pomeroy, N. Willis

Pomeroy, Willis B.
Potter, Joseph K.
Potter, William M.
Proctor, Arthur B.
Ragan, Andrew H.
Ramsay, William
Ray, James
Redman, Jacob S.
Reed, Wilson G.
Reid, John W.
Rice, Charles E.
Rich, Rev. Alex. M.
Richards, Byron
Richards, Robert M.
Ricketts, William M.
Riddick, Richard P.
Ringwalt, Charles G.
Roderick, Frank A.
Rogers, Archibald I.
Rogers, Thomas E.
Rollings, Geo. F. D.
Rountree, Hamet B.
Rudy, William D.
Ryder, Stephen M.
Saks, Isadore
Sample, James A.
Sanderlin, George W.
Sandoe, David L.
Scharf, Samuel R.
Schmedtie, August
Schooley, Henry M.
Scott, J. Foster
Searle, William D.
Senft, William
Shaw, Alexander P.
Shaw, William B., jr.
Shepard, Herbert L.
Sheppard, Thomas R.
Shelton, Charles W.
Shirley, Edward M.
Shoulters, George H.
Silver, William
Simons, Henry O.

Slater, Samuel E.
Slater, William J.
Smith, Charles B.
Smith, Charles R.
Smith, Frank B.
Smith, Frank E.
Smith, Frank P.
Smith, Richard W.
Smith, Robert E. L.
Smith, Thomas W.
Snyder, Charles L.
Sollers, James L.
Songster, Thomas
Spicer, Oliver O.
Spransy, Brower F.
Sprigman, James H.
Stakely, Rev. C. A.
Stallings, Benj. D.
Statham, Henry T.
Steuart, William M.
Stevens, Durham W.
Stewart, Charles T.
Stiles, Daniel F.
Stiles, Valentine N.
Stinemetz, Saml. W.
Stoddard, Charles J.
Stone, David D.
Strang, Harry L.
Stratton, James A.
Sturtevant, Chas. L.
Swayze, Charles P.
Swartzell, Geo. W. F.
Swem, Rev. Ed. Hez
Tallmadge, Theodore

Taff, T. A. Roszel
Thomas, George C.
Thompson, Chas. W.
Thompson, Ezra B.
Thompson, E. St. C.
Tilp, Frederick
Todd, William B.
Tomlinson, John S.
Trembly, Leslie R.
Trott, Charles V.
Troutman, Lynn H.
Tryon, Frederick M.
Tryon, Noah
Tweedale, John
Tydings, John H.
Tyers, William W.
Van Arsdale, Jos. S.
Vanderhoef, Lorenzo
Van Horn, John T.
Varela, Alexander C.
Verbrycke, Rev. J. R.
Walker, Alfred A.
Walker, Charles J.
Walker, Joseph E.
Walker, Littleton W.
Walker, T. Vivion
Walker, William T.
Wallace, George
Ware, Richard
Watson, Charles G.
Waugh, Albert P.
Webber, George W.
Weir, Jesse C.
Welch, George H.

West, George N.
Westfall, John W.
Wetmore, James A.
Wetzell, Charles M.
Wheeler, George L.
White, James K.
White, Oscar W.
White, Walter C.
Whitemore, J. F. W.
Whiting, Harry C.
Wight, Alpheus S.
Wilcox, Adolphus D.
Wild, Edward S.
Wilkin, Thomas A.
Wilkinson, Ernest
Willis, Charles S.
Willis, Spencer J.
Williams, Daniel J.
Williams, Edward A.
Williams, John E.
Williams, John M.
Williams, Leander P.
Wilson, Andrew
Wilson, John C.
Withers, William, jr.
Wood, William C.
Woodson, Warren A.
Wooster, Wilbur F.
Wright, Allen
Wright, Josiah
Wrightsman, Benj. J.
Young, Charles E.
Young, John M.
Yount, Albert G.—495

DROPPED FOR N. P. D.

Gibson, Campbell F.

Kellogg, Charles I.
Parke, Robert A.

Tibbetts, Frank J., jr.

DAWSON LODGE, No. 16,

Meets on the Second and Fourth Mondays in each Month.

OFFICERS.

EDGAR G. HARBAUGH, Worshipful Master.
EDWIN S. HOLMES, Jr., S. Warden.   B. F. ODELL, J. Warden.
RODOLPH WILLISS, Secretary.   S. H. WALKER, Treasurer.

PAST MASTERS AND PAST GRAND OFFICERS.

Jos. Gawler, Chas. Hadaway, Edwin S. Holmes, sr., Wm. A. DeCaindry, Jas. E. Bell, John N. Birckhead, Orville Drown, H. Harvey Hazard, Rodolph Williss, James H. Trimble, Henry C. Thompson, Benj. F. Larcombe, jr., Thos. T. Burke, Wilson H. Thompson, Samuel R. Bond, Jesse F. Grant, Francis A. Sebring, Claude F. King, Wm. M. Garrett.

LIST OF MEMBERS.

Abraham, Lewis
*Anderson, Wm. S.
Archer, Andrew
Atkinson, Colin
Avery, James D.
Backenheimer, Sol.
Baden, Wm. H.
*Bailey, Charles B.
Baldwin, Dr. Aaron
Ball, Dr. Charles A.
Barr, Lester A.
*Bartlett, Marcus M.
*Bell, James E.
Bell, William H.
Birckhead, George E.
Birckhead, John N.
Bittinger, Rev. B. F.
Bogan, Alex. L.
Bogan, Dr. Fred M.
*Bogan, Dr. Saml. W.
Boggs, Rev. Harry
*Bond, Samuel R.
Bond, Dr. Samuel S.

Bornkessell, Theo. C.
Botsch, Wm. C.
*Boyd, Robert
Brenizer, John L.
Brennan, Patrick J.
Brittain, William B.
Brown, James C.
Brown, Andrew J., jr.
Browning, Wm. H.
Buchanan, Roberdeau
*Bundick, Charles P.
Burdine, Elbert F.
Burgess, Charles A.
Burke, Thomas T.
*Burnett, David L.
Burroughs, James E.
Burnside, John S.
Butts, Frank A.
Byers, Wm. J.
Caldwell, Dr. Wm. A.
Campbell, Edward B.
*Campbell, Robert G.
Cawson, Charles C.

Cawson, Frederick S.
*Chapman, James J.
Church, Charles W.
Clark, Charlton M.
Clark, Frank A.
Clark, John B., sr.
Clarke, Caleb C.
Clarke, Lucian A.
Clotworthy, James
Coburn, Frederick S.
Cochrane, James
Condra, Aaron M.
Cook, John C.
Costinett, Henry J.
Costinett, John J.
Coward, Robert H.
*Crampton, Job E.
Cranford, John W.
Croney, William A.
Crosby, Albert U.
Cullison, Eli T.
Cummins, Harry A.
Davenport, Wm. S.

Davis, Eugene A.
Davis, Frank P.
Davis, George P.
*DeCaindry, Wm. A.
Deffer, Philip A.
DePue, William B.
Dieudonne, Frank J.
Disney, William A.
Dobbert, John J.
Donn, Henry T.
Drew, William O.
*Drown, Orville
Dudley, William W.
Eaton, Alexander W.
Eldridge, Rev. E. O.
*Emory, John M.
Fitch, Arthur C.
Foster, Charles E.
*Fowler, James M.
Frost, Dr. Ellis F.
Frysinger, Henry
Garrett, William M.
Gawler, Joseph
Gilbert, William W.
Golden, George
Gordon, William W.
Gould, Ed. DuB.
Gould, Wm. H. H.
Grant, James H.
Grant, Jesse F.
*Gray, Edwin N.
Gregory, Samuel B.
*Hadaway, Charles
Hall, Theo. F.
Haller, Nicholas T.
Hammett, Dr. C. M.
Harbaugh, Edgar G.
Harr, Peter
Harris, William
Harrison, John M.
Harrison, Walton
Hazard, H. Harvey

Hepburn, Peter, jr.
Herrmann, Chas. F.
*Holmes, E. S., sr.
Holmes, Edwin S., jr.
Holmes, Hiram
Huguely, Oscar M.
Hurley, J. Edgar
Hutton, Harry D.
*Isdell, Nelson J.
*Jackson, Andrew
Jenkins, Allison C.
Kalusowski, H. E.
Karpeles, Leopold
Kearney, Michael H.
Kenon, Frank C.
King, Claude F.
Kingsbury, Thos. P.
Knapp, Milton M.
Koones, Charles M.
*Lafferty, Edward B.
Lannan, Wm. Frank
*Larcombe, B. F., sr.
Larcombe, B. F., jr.
Leffler, Milton L.
Leitch, James M.
Little, J. Marshall
Lutton, James H.
Macfarlane, William
Matthews, Wm. B.
*McClermont, Robert
McLaughlin, John
Merrill, Simeon H.
Merritt, Addis D.
Miller, Chas. F.
*Miller, Charles P.
Miller, Frederick J.
Miller, Wilson P.
Mitchell, John H.
Mitchell, Wm. Roy
Morgan, George W.
Morris, Abraham
Muirhead, William

Newman, Harry A.
Newman, Horatio D.
Newman, Walter E.
Nilson, Leonard J.
Odell, Dr. Benj. F.
Parkinson, Dr. C.
Parsons, Dr. Randall
Peabody, William F.
*Pearson, George W.
Pearson, Paul
Perkins, Edward D.
Petty, James T.
Phillips, William L.
Price, J. Clarence
Priest, Tellus
Proudley, George R.
Ramby, Samuel H.
Reed, Alvin L.
Reinhard, William
Reintzel, George W.
Rhodes, David H.
Riley, Thomas R.
*Royce, Fred W.
Saks, Samuel
Scalia, Simoni
Sears, William H.
Sebring, Francis A.
Sheriff, George R.
Siggers, Edward G.
Siggers, George W.
Simons, Charles G.
Simonson, Otto G.
Sims, Grant F.
Smith, Charles B.
Smith, Frank B.
Smith, J. Harrison
Snook, Lucius W.
Sonne, Charles
Starr, Rev. Jesse C.
*Stephenson, A. H.
Stephenson, John F.
Stephenson, Jos. G.

Stewart, William F.
Stidham, Albert D.
*Stoddard, Leonard
Strasburger, Jacob
Suddarth, Dr. Jas. L.
Swigart, Jesse E.
Thompson, Ernest G.
Thompson, Dr. H. C.
Thompson, Dr. M. F.
*Thompson, Wm. A.

Thompson,Wilson H.
*Trimble, James H.
Tucker, Thomas S.
Vieth, Henry A.
Vines, James A.
Wailes, William M.
Walker, Martin C.
Walker, Samuel H.
Walter, Robison S.
Webster, William A.

Wiekland, Christian
Williss, Rodolph
Wood, Frank Ivey
Wright, Irving M.
Wright, Preston B.
Yeatman, Robert H.
*Yeatman, William S.
Young, Carrington A.
Young, John R.—224.

DROPPED FOR N. P. D.

Cox, Frank H.
Davis, Walter O.

Melson, Theodore K.
Smith, Harry

Stock, C. August

HARMONY LODGE, No. 17,

Meets on the Second and Fourth Wednesdays in each Month.

OFFICERS.

SHERMAN J. BROWN, Worshipful Master.
CHAS. T. CALDWELL, S. Warden. HENRY E. TRIPP, J. Warden.
W. HAMILTON SMITH, Secretary. ORANGE S. FIRMIN, Treasurer.

PAST MASTERS AND PAST GRAND OFFICERS.

Samuel Baxter, R. W. Hardy, George E. Corson, P. J. G. W.;
N. C. Martin, O. S. Firmin, L. M. Saunders, E. J. Barden, J. F.
Blackmar, F. K. Swett, W. Hamilton Smith, L. R. Ginn, F. M.
Criswell, F. S. Williams, A. W. Johnston, C. L. Heilbrun, B. A.
Allen, W. C. Babcock, W. H. Slater, G. W. Hascall, W. T. Johnson, John Wilson.

LIST OF MEMBERS.

Abel, Jacob W.
Abel, Joseph
Achenbach, Fredk.

Allen, Bennett A.
Ambrose, Nathaniel
Andrews, Ross P.

Appleman, Frank S.
Atherton, Benj. F.
Atwater, George S.

Babcock, George W.
Babcock, Wallace C.
Bailey, Oliver T.
Baker, Frank B.
Barden, Edwin J.
Barnard, Louis E.
Barnes, Frank M.
Barnes, Henry S.
Barnhouse, Sidney J.
Barnitz, Robert McP.
Bawsel, Edward
Baxter, Samuel
Bean, Theodore T.
Bell, Joseph S.
Benjamin, Samuel C.
Beverstock, Edwin J.
Bieber, Henry J.
Birch, William T.
Bispham, Samuel T.
Black, Joseph S.
Black, Richard R.
Blackmar, John F.
Blair, John H.
Blethyn, Benjamin
Bloomer, Arthur F.
Blumer, Charles H.
Boss, John R.
Boyd, Virgil M.
Bragonier, James
Britt, James M.
Brown, Sherman J.
Brown, Thomas A.
Brown, William J.
Buckley, Richard B.
Burdick, Edson A.
Burke, George O.
Busch, Charles R.
Calderwood, Robert
Caldwell, Charles T.
Carman, Louis D.
Caywood, Charles B.
Ceas, Robert E.

Chambers, Wm. W.
Cheney, James W.
Churchill, John M.
Claflin, Price C.
Clawson, J. M.
Clear, James H.
Cochran, Henry D.
Compton, George
Conliff, John C.
Conrey, Albert C.
Conser, Frank M.
Corey, George B.
Corson, George E.
Covell, Luther W.
Cowles, Frederick L.
Creighton, Thos. B.
Criswell, Francis M.
Criswell, William T.
Crowell, Henry S.
Culverwell, Wm. B.
Dame, John W.
Daniels, Ara M.
Darby, Rufus H.
Davis, Walter B.
Denny, Louis E.
Dillon, Michael A.
Domer, Charles S.
Domer, William A.
Downs, John A.
†Douglas, William H.
Drury, William C.
Dunkhorst, Harry F.
Dyer, James W.
Edmonds, Newton
Edmonston, Chas. R.
†Eedle, Frederick J.
Eliason, John H.
Eliason, William A.
Ellis, J. Curtis
Evans, George O.
Evans, George W. B.
Evans, William A.

Farnesworth, Calvin
Farran, J. Walter
Ferris, Walter S.
Firmin, Orange S.
Floyd, Charles M.
Frazier, Henry L.
Freer, James A.
Fulkerson, Roe
Gentner, William G.
Gettinger, William
Gibbs, George L.
Gilmore, Frank B.
Ginn, Lurtin R.
Gleason, Arthur B.
Gleason, Walter G.
Graff, Carl J. F.
Gray, Isaac S.
Gray, Walter L.
Griffin, William Y.
Grinder, George W.
Gross, Charles E.
Haas, Frank
Haas, George, jr.
Hahn, William
Hall, Hilman A.
Hardester, John T.
Hardy, Robert W.
Harper, Blake
Harper, James E.
Harrell, Harrison S.
Harris, John K.
Harris, Joseph S.
Harvey, Heber McK.
Hascall, George W.
Hayes, John W.
Heilbrun, Andrew J.
Heilbrun, Charles L.
Heilbrun, Louis
Heilig, George W.
Helmus, William
Henry, Charles T.
Hilman, Nelson J.

Hills, Louis C.
Hodge, Edwin R.
Hohoff, Frederick H.
Holman, Benj. W.
Holtz, Henry T.
Hoover, Adam M.
Hopkins, L. H.
Houchen, John L.
Hoyle, Harry T. L.
Hughes, Charles T.
Humphrey, Jas. W.
Hurlebaus, Fred A.
Hurlebaus, Geo. W.
Huson, Wilber
Ingalls, Owen L.
Jacobi, Joseph
Jacobs, Charles P.
Jacobs, William P.
Jaisohn, Philip
Jarvis, J. McK. R.
Jennings, Walter B.
Jett, Edwin M.
Johnson, Wm. T.
Johnson, Val. M.
Johnston, Arvine W.
Jones, Robert C.
Kaufman, Levi J.
Keefer, Abraham B.
Keen, George T.
Keim, Charles F.
Kerr, Sterling. jr.
Kincaid, Douglas H.
King, John I.
King, William M.
Klopfer, Walter H.
Knowles, Robert
Krigbaum, Orlando
Kuehling, John H.
Lamb, J. Melvin
La Tourette, John W.
Leadley, George W.
Leonard. N. W. W.

Levers, Theodore F.
Lewis, Thomas G.
Lewis, William J.
Lindheimer, Samuel
Littlewood, James B.
Love, Harry W.
†Malmberg, Fred S.
Mann, Henry La F.
Martin, Nathan C.
Matchett, Thomas L.
Mattern, Adolph
Mattern, John E.
Matthews, Chas.
May, George R.
May, James B.
McComas, Percy G.
McDonald, John A.
McGinniss, Wm. S.
McKee, Thos. H.
McMillan, Ira C.
MacNulty, Wm. A.
McShea, Wm. A. E.
Medairy, Charles M.
Meetze, Dempsey P.
Mills, Samuel C.
Milne, Alex.
Mitchell, John A.
Morgan, Joseph D.
Mott, Albert
Moulton, Hosea B.
Myers, Albert P.
Neiter, John G.
Nelson, James
Nessmith, James M.
Nicholson, James E.
Norbeck, William G.
Noyes, Clarence
Noyes, George E.
Noyes, Isaac P.
Ogram, Thomas E.
Page, William R.
Parker, William E.

Parks, James H.
Parlin, Edward H.
Parselles, George E.
Patten, Alphonso
Patterson, John W.
Paul, Charles E.
Peery, Edwin H.
Perlie, Horace E.
Peters, David W.
Pfeiffer, David G.
Piper, Horace L.
Porter, Dernelle S.
Posey, Luther W.
Potts, Joseph Y.
Price, William B.
Prince, George
Prout, John B.
Pyemont, George E.
Ragsdale, Martin S.
Ramey, Daniel
Ramey, Elmer E.
Ramey, Harry B.
Ramey, Ulysses G.
Rand, Irving W.
Rawlings, Francis T.
Recher, Stanley N.
Redman, Mortimer
Redmiles, Alfred
Rheem, Clarence B.
Richmond, Paul
Riley, Thomas G.
Rose, Joseph R.
Rosenberg, M. D.
Rossiter, Ignatius N.
Saffell, Henry C.
†Salvesen, Peter T.
Sanger, Raphael
Saunders, Lorin M.
Scantlebury, William
Schafer, George A.
Schlosser, John G.
Schooley, James H.

Scott, Winfield
Shank, Charles D.
Shattuck, Amory H.
Sherwood, Chas. W.
Simmers, Charles L.
Simmons, George
Sixbury, Sidney A.
Slater, William H.
Smith, James A.
Smith, Robert A.
Smith, Richard B.
Smith, Walter F.
Smith, W. Hamilton
Smyser, William H.
Snyder, Harold C.
Sowers, Zachariah T.
Spangler, Albert D.
Speich, Emanuel
Spencer, George F.
Stalley, Henry N. S.
Steele, Morgan L.
Stern, Louis

Stevenson, Faber
Stone, Joshua
Streng, Charles H.
Stumph, Edward B.
Swett, Frederick K.
Taylor, George E.
Ten Eyck, Jerome B.
Tripp, Henry E.
Tweedale, Alonzo
Underwood, C. H.
Waddell, Hugh
Wagner, George
Wallingsford, C. M.
Ward, Wm. F.
Washburn, Wm. S.
Weber, Chas. E.
Webster, John T.
Webster, Wm. L.
Weller, Josiah P.
Wells, Martin
Whipple, Madison
Whitcomb, Jas. A.
White, James E.

White, Wm. S.
Wilkes, Thomas M.
Wilson, John
Wilson, Laurence
Williams, Edwd. H.
Williams, Frank S.
Williams, Robert C.
Williams, Stephen R.
Willige, John L.
Wise, Charles B.
Wixsom, Menzo
Wolf, David
Wolf, Martin
Wolhaupter, D. P.
Wood, Charles C.
Wood, John H.
Woods, Peter
Wright, Eugene L.
Wright, John C.
Yeates, Charles M.
York, Edward S.
York, James M.—328.

DROPPED FOR N. P. D.

Austin, James H.   McCormick, Chas. C.   Richards, John H.

ACACIA LODGE, No. 18,

Meets on the Second and Fourth Tuesdays in each Month.

OFFICERS.

CLARENCE B. LANGAN, Worshipful Master.
S. T. COVERT, S. Warden.   HYLAS T. WHEELER, J. Warden.
CHAS. J. O'NEILL, Secretary.   GEORGE W. KOONCE, Treasurer.

PAST MASTERS AND PAST GRAND OFFICERS.

C. W. Franzoni, W. P. Young, B. F. Fuller, P. D. G. M.; R. H. Thayer, W. M. Poindexter, Thos. Robinson, A. H. Holt, C. H. Elliott, G. W. Koonce, J. E. Hosford, J. A. Runyan, T. W. S. Phelps, H. W. P. Hunt, H. Sutherland, C. J. O'Neill, R. P. Williams, E. B. Hesse.

LIST OF MEMBERS.

Adams, A. C.
Amaties, Louis
Arnold, J. A.
Arwine, J. T.
Ashby, I. G.
Ashby, V. W.
Badinelli, J. L.
Barker, R. W.
Bates, C. H.
Bates, Stephen
Beatty, C. L.
Berryman, Silas
Bolgiano, F. W.
Boteler, H. S.
Bowers, Rev. J. C.
Boyd, William
Brannan, Emora
Broas, J. M.
Brown, H. G.
Burroughs, H. H.
Carden, F. W.
Cleaver, D. W.
Clements, W. A.
Covert, S. T.
Crane, E. A.
Davis, J. S.
†Davis, E. G.
†Douglas, W. H.
DuBois, R. C.
Ebaugh, T. O.
Edmonston, Gabriel
Ellinger, J. A.
Elliott, C. H.

Elliott, Rev. J. H.
Ellsworth, G. D.
English, Henry
Eppley, J. K.
Fischer, Emil
Franzoni, C. W.
Fraser, Daniel
Fuelling, J. L.
Fuller, B. F.
Garriott, E. B.
Gorman, A. P.
Gregory, H. I.
Grimes, S. T.
Gurley, W. B.
Hailer, G. W.
Hall, Rev. P. B.
Harban, W. S.
Harwood, D. J.
Hesse, E. B.
Hendley, J. W.
Hibbs, G. D. C.
Holt, A. H.
Hosford, J. E.
Hudson, T. J.
Hunt, H. J.
Hunt, H. W. P.
Hunter, John
Hurdle, C. W.
Jarvis, Thomas
Jenkins, J. H. B.
Johnson, H. G.
Johnston, G. J.
Knabe, Albert

Kolb, Edward
Koonce, G. W.
Kraemer, Charles
Langan, C. B.
Leipold, R. H. T.
Lippold, Wm.
Little, J. J.
Lucas, J. H.
Marr, Calhoun
Marshall, J. R.
Martin, E. N.
Martin, W. J.
Michael, J. W.
Miller, John
Minnich, J. H.
Morgan, Eugene
Morrison, Alex.
Motts, George
McAuley, R. C.
McCartee, Charles
McFarlan, Daniel
Nevitt, J. R.
O'Neill, C. J.
Orrison, A. L.
Owings, T. H.
Parson, Rev. W. E.
Perry, U. G.
Perry, R. Ross
Petersen, Emil
Phelps, T. W. S.
Poindexter, W. M.
Power, Rev. F. D.
Prentiss, D. W.

Reynolds, C. L.
Rives, Franklin
Robbins, H. A.
Robinson, Thomas
Roots, J. P.
Runyan, J. A.
Rebuschatis, W. W.
Sardo, A. E., jr.
Saumenig,Rev.H.F.
Sawtell, S. A.
Schmidt, Louis
Shope, E. I.
Smith, H. E.
Sommerville, J. W.
Sommerville, T., jr.
Sowers, J. C.

Speare, W. R.
Springer, C. A.
Steed, J. Nat
Srier, F. A.
Strasburger, A. H.
Strasburger, H.
Sutherland, Edw.
Sutherland, Heath
Sutherland, J. A.
Thayer, R. H.
Tiffany, E. A.
Tolman, A. J.
Todd, T. H. G.
Trout, Rev. J. W.
Tudor, Rev. W. V.

Ullery, Lee
Verdi, T. S.
Wall, William
Walsh, Ralph
Waters, D. S.
Watkins, Rev.W. F.
Weaver, M. J.
Weber, G. W.
Wheeler, H. T.
Wheeler, H. W.
White, G. H. B.
Willett, R. H.
Williams, Rev. R. P.
Xander, Chr.
Young, W. P.—145.

DROPPED FOR N. P. D.

Leach, G. W.   Middleton, W. E.   Ravenburg, R.

LA FAYETTE LODGE, No. 19,

Meets on the First and Third Thursdays in each Month.

OFFICERS.

THOMAS P. MORGAN, Worshipful Master.
BENJ. S. GRAVES, S. Warden.   HENRY S. SELDEN, J. Warden.
W. H. OLCOTT, Secretary,   A. F. FOX, Treasurer.

PAST MASTERS AND PAST GRAND OFFICERS.

Noble D. Larner, P. G. S. and P. G. M.; Henry A. Whallon, Edw. B. MacGrotty, Frank M. Marshall, Joseph S. McCoy, P. G. M.; Burton R. Ross, Albert F. Fox, William G. Powers, W. Harry Olcott, John H. Olcott, Samuel M. Yeatman, H. H. Martin, Wm. S. Parks, John W. Ross, Henry S. Merrill, P. G. M.; M. B. Strickler, John M. McKinney, C. Neilson, James H. Wardle, James F. Scaggs, Leonard C. Wood, Thomas W. Cridler, J. W. Townsend, A. B. Coolidge, F. W. Johnson, William Broun, P. J. Coston, John B. Daish, Orlo Epps.

LIST OF MEMBERS.

Abner, Christian
Acker, George N.
Acker, William B.
Alburger, W. H.
Alexander, C. W.
Alexander, D. A.
Alexander, J. N.
Allan, William P.
Alleman, H. C.
Allen, G. Edgar
Allen, Jeremiah C.
Alverson, J. L.
Amos, James T.
Anderson, Joseph W.
Anderson, Victor
Appel, Charles A.
Armstrong, W. S.
Atkins, Lewis S.
Auerbach, Joseph
Auerbach, Louis
Baar, Lewis
Babbitt, Kurnal R.
Backus, William M.
Bailey, James A.
Bailey, Joseph B.
Bailey, Richard H.
Bailey, Samuel U.
Baker, Davis
Baker, Henry M.
Ball, William Z.
Bare, R. B.
Barker, Arthur E.
Barker, F. C.
Barnes, George W.
Barron, Albert W.
Barrows, Harry A.

Bartlett, George A.
Bartram, E. S.
Bateman, W. G.
Beattie, Wray
Beck, Henry K.
Becker, James J.
Belt, David G.
Bennett, Conrad F.
Bennett, W. A.
Bernhard, Charles E.
Bernhard, Henry I.
Beyer, Louis
Bingham, Charles
Birth, H. N.
Blakelock, John W.
Blanton, Charles L.
Bliss, Alfred G.
Boernstein, Aug. S.
Bohrer, Alex. B.
Bokman, Wm. W.
Booraem, Edgar I.
Boudinot, George S.
Bowen, J. Chester
Bowen, Miles D.
Brandt, William E.
Branson, Philip H.
Brewood, Henry
Brookings, E. J.
Brooks, Floyd V.
Brooks, Walter J.
Broun, William
Brown, Charles W.
Brown, Frank B.
Brown, R. M.
Browne, William H.
Bruni, Charles

Brush, Harmon M.
Bryan, Ed. C.
Bryan, Paul S.
Bryarly, John E.
Budd, George T.
Bunnemeyer, B.
Burke, Thomas W.
Burns, Edward N.
Butscher, E. P.
Calvo, William W.
Cameron, John
Campbell, Frank L.
Campbell, Willard S.
Carroll, Timothy A.
Carter, Charles C.
Carter, Francis
Chandlee, Wm. E.
Childs, Charles
Childs, Howard P.
Christiancy, G. A. C.
Churchill, W. P.
Clark, J. Wingate
Coburn, Henry C.
Cochran, Joseph
Cochran, William E.
Coffron, Willard H.
Cohen, Myer
Cohen, Robert
Coldren, Fred G.
Cole, Charles C.
Collins, Homer K.
Cook, Robert
Cook, W. J.
Coolidge, A. B.
Coryell, George H.
Coston, Porter J.

Cottrell, Ed. B.
Craig, William
Crallé, Jefferson B.
Cridler, Thomas W.
Croggon, John R.
Cromwell, Z. W.
Cronk, A. M.
Cross, Brooks
Crux, George
Cunningham, Jas.
Curry, Daniel
Curry, Elmer E.
Daish, John B.
Dane, Harry H.
Darling, George A.
Darlington, J. J.
Davis, Guy L.
Decker, Earl J.
DeMontreville, W.
Dent, Alfred B.
Depue, Leidy S.
Dinsmore, A. F.
Dodge, Victor L.
Dole, Stephen A.
Doores, William C.
Downs, Samuel I.
Drake, Horace F. J.
Dripps, John H.
Duvall, James E.
Eager, J. H. L.
Easterday, H. C.
Easton, Edward D.
Eberle, Frederick A.
Eberly, August F.
Edes, James H.
Edgar, Owen T.
Einstein, Samuel
Ellis, Thomas
Emrich, Fred W.
Epps, Orlo
Espey, A. Louis
Espey, H. Clay

Evans, George W.
Fair, Charles
Fairfax, Ethelbert
Fairfax, Thomas
Fallas, Leroy H.
Farrington, Wm. H.
Ferguson, Howard
Fischer, George D.
Fischer, Max
Fisher, Howard C.
Flick, George M.
Floyd, David O.
Floyd, Henry
Fluckey, I. N.
Fookes, V. M.
Force, David W.
Forrest, Edwin
Forsyth, Robert H.
Foster, Jacob C.
Foster, William W.
Fox, Albert F.
Frahm, Henry
Franc, Henry
Franc, Henry, jr.
Franc, Sidney
Franklin, Benj.
French, John R.
Frickey, Irving
Fugitt, Robert E.
Funk, William
Gaither, John C.
Galliher, Charles E.
Galliher, William T.
Gessford, George W.
Gessford, Oliver C.
Gessford, William C.
Gibbs, James A.
Given, Harvey
Goenner, A.
Goodall, George W.
Gordon, Peyton
Gorham, Albert E.

Gough, M. LeRoy
Gough, Stephen E.
Gracy, George W.
Grafton, A. W.
Grafton, E. W.
Graves, Benjamin S.
Gray, James
Gregory, Alex. H.
Griggs, William L.
Guthridge, Walter H.
Hack, Elam M.
Hadfield, Robert H.
Haislett, Samuel J.
Hall, Harry O.
Halley, J. K.
Hammett, C. M., jr.
Hanger, G. W. W.
Hardcastle, Wm. M.
Hartung, Charles E.
Hartung, William L.
Havenner, P. B.
Hay, George W.
Headley, John P.
Helmick, C. C.
Helmus, John
Henderson, Thos. N.
Hensey, Melville D.
Hensey, Thomas G.
Hepburn, James H.
Herman, Abraham
Hermann, J. Philip
Herrell, Frank A.
Herrell, Henry A.
Heyl, Charles H.
Hickling, D. Percy
Hill, Allen E.
Hillman, Joel
Hine, Harry O.
Hipkins, W. A.
Hodges, Harry W.
Hodges, John G.
Hoffa, Frank

Holmes, David E.
Horner, Christopher
Howard, Thomas N.
Howe, Charles E.
Howison, Edwin
Howison, Samuel
Howser, Frank T.
Hubbard, George A.
Hughes, Percy M.
Hunt, Granville M.
Hunt, William M.
Hunter, Joseph H.
Hunter, Rosser L.
Huntzinger, Geo. L.
Irvine, Alfred C.
Jameson, Robert M.
Johnson, F. Warren
Johnson, Griffith L.
Johnson, Sherman A.
Jones, John E.
Judd, R. B.
Judd, T. A. T.
Kauschke, J. O. A.
Kayhoe, M. E.
Kean, William B.
Kearney, William F.
Keigwin, C. A.
Keller, Thomas T.
Kelley, J. Fred
Kets Kemethy, M.
Kimball, William H.
King, Harry
King, S. J.
Kingsman, Richard
Knapp, Daniel E.
Koch, Edward W.
Kondrup, H. E. R.
Korts, Charles H.
Lake, Asheton E.
Lang, Edwin G.
Larner, Noble D.
Larner, Robert N.

Lawrence, B. B. H.
Leidy, Augustus P.
Leonard Charles G.
Lewis, Charles M.
Lewis, Thomas D.
Lewis, William C.
Lewis, William E.
Lichliter, Jacob H.
Lightfoot, John J.
Lincoln, S. Dana
Lipscomb, A. A.
Lipscomb, C. E.
Lipscomb, Jno. McL.
Lockwood, Geo. M.
Long, Vernon W.
Lothrop, Alvin M.
Louthan, J. D.
Loving, Robinson
Luckett, Thomas T.
Lynch, Elmore T.
Lynch, Thomas H. ,
MacGrotty, Edwin B.
MacNamara, F. G.
McCallum, P. M.
McCartney, M. W.
McClelland, Joseph
McConchie, Jas. W.
McCoy, Joseph S.
McDowell, A. B.
McDuell, John M.
McElwee, George G.
McFarland, Wm. D.
McKay, Nathaniel
McKeever, James C.
McKinney, John M.
McKnew, Wm. H.
McMackin, Robt. H.
McMaster, David
McQuay, Ben. C.
Macey, C. K.
Mann, Elias
Manning, J. F.

Manson, Joseph O.
Marks, Albert S.
Marshall, C. E.
Marshall, Frank M.
Marshall, J. L.
Martin, Hiram H.
Masterson, Wm. L.
Mathews, William B
Maxcy, Frederick E.
Maynadier, G. B.
Mazzei, Frank A.
Meding, John J.
Merillat, John H.
Merrill, Henry S.
Merrill, Oliver R.
Mewshaw, Joshua S.
Meyers, Joseph W.
Milans, Joseph D.
Minor, Benjamin S.
Minster, Max M.
Montgomery, V. F.
Moore, Charles H.
Moore, Mark W.
Morgan, Thomas P.
Mortimer, Wm. W.
Mosher, Alex.
Muldrow, Robert
Mullican, Irwin
Munroe, Hersey
Murphy, William
Naimaster, Fred
Neal, D. R., jr.
Nebb, John F. C.
Neilson, Calvin
Nelson, Conant C.
Nelson, Halvor
Newman, F. A.
Nordhoff, William
Norris, William H.
Nye, Marvin H.
Olcott, John H.
Olcott, W. Harry

Olive, Winfield S.
Oliver, Robert
Olmstead, John F.
Olmsted, Victor H.
O'Neill, John F.
Ottinger, J. Eugene
Owen, Owen
Palmer, J. William
Parks, Frederick R.
Parks, William S.
Parmenter, H. H.
Pearson, Harry C.
Pennebaker, Chas. D.
Perley, James P.
Perry, Howard
Peters, Benj. F.
Petingale, Samuel K.
Pettengill, E. T.
Pickett, R. L.
Pike, Benjamin S.
Pillsbury, E. H.
Piper, E. W.
Pitchlynn, Lee
Pitzer, Frank
Pocock, Thomas S.
Postley, Charles E.
Powdermaker, H.
Powers, William G.
Pratt, Geo. W.
Prindle, George S.
Pritchard, S. M.
Proctor, John C.
Prosperi, Charles B.
Prosperi, William H.
Pruden, O. L.
Pullman, Ed. J.
Pumphrey, Ed. P.
Queen, Benjamin F.
Quisenberry, A. C.
Raabe, Henry
Ramage, Samuel C.
Rapp, Frank E.

Read, Albert M.
Reapsomer, Wm. R.
Reed, George F.
Reed, William A.
Remer, William A.
Rich, George W.
Rich, Walter I.
Rich, Warren W.
Richmond, D. L.
Robbins, T. A.
Roberts, Henry C.
Roberts, Horace H.
Roberts, J. O'Connor
Robertson, T. M.
Robison, Samuel H.
Robison, William B.
Rose, George U.
Ross, Burton R.
Ross, John W.
Rothrock, H. J.
Rothschild, Coleman
Ruffin, Sterling
Russell, Fred P.
Rutherford, James A.
Sadler, John T.
Sanders, Thomas B.
Santorelli, A.
Saum, D. F.
Saunders, William E.
Scaggs, James F.
Schafer, Emil G.
Schmidt, Fred A.
Schultze, A. L.
Schulz, Henry
Scott, Arthur L.
Scott, Wm. L.
Searles, James H.
Selden, Henry S.
Senior, Thomas R.
Sexton, G. W.
Shaffer, William E.
Sharp, Frank C.

Sharretts, G. E. W.
Sheibley, Sinclair B.
Sherman, Howard E.
Shuster, E. Harry
Siddons, Fred L.
Sletz, William E.
Simms, John W.
Simpson, G. Warfield
Simpson, Robert L.
Singer, Fred
Slaybaugh, Geo. H.
Smith, Arthur B.
Smith, Emmons S.
Smith, Fred S.
Smith, George W.
Smith, J. George
Smith, Lincoln B.
Smith, Peter H.
Smith, William H.
Smithson, George W.
Snapp, John H.
Snoddy, Titus B.
Snodgrass, Stanley
Sorrell, G. R.
Sorrell, Richard H.
Spalding, J. Berret
Spence, Adolph N.
Spottswood, Wm. G.
Springer, Horace P.
Stafford, Fred H.
Stenley, Orlando O.
Stearns, E. F.
Stellé, Joseph G.
Stewart, James A.
Stokes, John W.
Strachan, Samuel S.
Stratton, John T.
Strickler, M. B.
Stutler, Warner
Summers, Chas. W.
Suter, John T.
Sutor, Louis P.

Tappan, Samuel F.
Thomason, Saml. E.
Thompson, H. S.
Thompson, Lewis Z.
Toepper, G. E.
Toepper, John G.
Tompkins, Ed. L.
Towles, Henry O.
Townsend, Chas. H.
Townsend, J. Wilson
Trail, E. M.
Travis, John A.
Tune, Thomas E.
Tune, William I.
Turpin, Perry B.
Tyler, James W.
Tyler, Nat., jr.
Ubhoff, C. J.
Vedder, Rodney S.
Vowles, N. Elwyn
Walker, W. Frank
Wall, Howard C.
Waller, Edmund E.
Wallerstein, Nathan
Walter, Henry S.

Wardle, James H.
Waters, E. N.
Weaver, Clarence
Webb, James W.
Weber, Louis K.
Webster, Clarence U.
Webster, John E.
Weeks, Alonzo
Welch, Benj. T., jr.
Wertz, Edward S.
West, Sidney
West, William D.
Whallon, Henry A.
White, John
Whitman, B. L.
Wilkerson, W. L.
Wilkins, Frank P.
Williams, Edward
Williams, U. J.
Williams, W. E.
Williams, W. Mosby
Williamson, J. B., jr.
Willson, H. B.
Wilson, J. Edwin

Wilson, Z. G.
Withall, Judson J.
Wolf, Simon
Wood, George H.
Wood, Henry P.
Wood, Leonard C.
Wood, Rev. R. S. W.
Woodward, Chas. G.
Woodward, S. Walter
Wooster, Walter M.
Wright, George
Wright, John R.
Wright, Walter E.
Wright, W. Harry
Yates, Richard H.
Yeatman, George W.
Yeatman, Samuel M.
Yerkes, Wm. H., jr.
York, Clarence M.
Yost, John C.
Young, Alex. H.
Young, Charles H.
Young, Nick E.
Young, W. L. D.—559.

DROPPED FOR N. P. D.

Baker, Karl H.
Christie, Alex. S.

Douglass, W. O.
Harris, W. J.

Lane, John H
Quinby, Fred J.

HOPE LODGE, No. 20,

Meets on the Second and Fourth Fridays in each Month.

OFFICERS.

CHARLES C. VAN HORN, Worshipful Master.
NATHAN S. MEYER. S. Warden. GEO. A. COHILL, J. Warden.
WM. A. CRAIG, Secretary. CHAS. H. DICKSON, Treasurer.

PAST MASTERS AND PAST GRAND OFFICERS.

Saml. Houston, I. B. Ruff, R. Goodhart, C. O. Brown, P. S. G. W.; John Beck, sr., W. A. Craig, T. W. Sanner, F. N. Carver, George W. Baird, P. G. M.; F. G. Dieterich, J. S. Mills, W. P. Challice, Clarence Lewis, Wm. Briggs, J. H. Cunningham, C. I. Snook, W. A. Cohill, C. W. Henshaw, Paul Neuhaus, Frank P. Hays, Philip P. Rouse, Fred M. Stromberger.

LIST OF MEMBERS.

Adams, William H.
Anderson, Wm. L.
Arnold, Richard A.
Balbendrier, Fred L.
Baer, August
Baird, George W.
Baker, Alfred L.
*Baker, William S.
Ballou, John C.
Barber, Amzi L.
Barnhart, Grant S.
Beck, John, jr.
Beck, John, sr.
Bender, Charles M.
Beresford, Randolph
Beron, John
Bettes, Eugene
Betz, Ernest
Bevans, James W.
Bode, Oscar
Boesch, Henry
Boyer, Heinrich H.
Briggs, James S.
Briggs, William
Brown, Andrew J.
Brown, Charles O.
Buechler, Richard, A.
Burrows, Joseph T.
Burrows, Samuel C.
Callahan, Thomas
Cameron, John W.
Capell, Charles A.

Carnes, John H.
Carver, Frank N.
Chadwick, DeWitt C.
Challice, William P.
Cohill, Bion H.
Cohill, George A.
Cohill, Henry R.
Cohill, William A.
Collie, Robert
Collins, John F.
Conrad, Jeremiah H.
Cook, J. Robert
Courtis, Frank
Coxen, M. Fillmore
Craig, William A.
Creary, William E.
Crise, John F.
Cunningham, Jas. F.
Cunningham, J. H.
Denty, William L.
Dickson, Charles H.
Dieterich, Fred G.
Donaldson, Thos. A.
Doniphan, Edwin C.
Driggs, Wm. H.
Dunham, Samuel C.
Eberbach, Edward
Eberwine, John
Edmunds, Saml. W.
Emmner, Julius
Esch, Albert F.
Esch, Michael

Evans, Richard M.
Fleming, Dudley W.
Fleming, George E.
Ford, John
Forster, Herman
Friedlander, Philip
Giles, James L.
Gilmore, Charles F.
Godfrey, Jos. H., jr.
Goodhart, Richard
Goodman, Isaac H.
Gordon, James A.
Gorsuch, Albert A.
Grimm, August L.
Hahn, Charles M.
Hahn, Frank
Hahn, John
Hall, Charles E.
Hall, Frederick A.
Hansen, Johan
Hauck, Francis A.
Hausmann, Theodore
Hays, Frank P.
Heid, Jacob
Henshaw, Chas. W.
Hering, Thomas F.
Hickok, William T.
Hinternesch, J. D.
Hooper, Charles R.
Houston, Sam.
Hover, Lorenzo C.
Howard, Geo. E.

Hyler, Oscar D.
Jones, Harry S., jr.
Kaufman, David J.
Kaufman, Milford L.
Kerr, Leeds C.
Kinney, Addison D.
Korn, Charles L.
Lang, Charles B.
Leissler, Wm. D.
Lewis, Clarence
Linthicum, Benj. F.
Little, Peter P.
Loewenstein, Ferd.
Long, Charles
Lovering, Phillips A.
McBride, John R.
McCleery, John F.
McLeod, Robert
MacFarland, J. Wm.
Maddox, Maurice
Mallard, Charles F.
Martin, Wm. N.
Mayer, Theodore J.
Meacham,-Charles C.
Meeds, Benjamin N.
Meyer, Nathan S
Miller, Jasper C.
Miller, William R.
Mills, John S.
Milne, David
Moore, John Benson
Nelson, Edgar A., jr.

Neuhaus, Paul
Nicholson, Wm. C.
O'Donoghue, M. F.
Parker, Thomas J.
Perkins, Samuel F.
Petteys, Charles V.
Peyser, Philip
Phillips, Nicholas W.
Prendergast, J. Thos.
Raymond, Frank K.
Reed, John T.
Reily, George E.
Riedel, Gus. H.
Roche, Patrick H.
Rodney, Robert B.
Rouse, Philip P.
Rowe, Albert S.
*Ruff, Isaac B.
Sanner, Thomas W.
Saunders, Alfred W.
Schaum. F. Louis
Schoyer, Louis
Sheriff, Dale
Sherwood, Henry G.
Siegel, Samuel
Skeen, Stephen D.
Skinner, George D.
Snook, Charles I.
Spielman, Rev. A. E.
Stearns, Solomon S.
Stevens, Ed. A. L.
Stone, George W., jr.

Strattan, Ruloff R.
Stribling, C. K.
Strobel, George E.
Stromberger, F. M.
Suit, Henry T.
Taylor, Alfred H.
Taylor, Stark B.
Thomas, Jas. C., jr.
Thompson, John L.
Thompson, Marion C
Thompson, Wm. E.
Tongue, William T.
Trazzare, J. Frank
Van Horn. Charles C.
Vermillion, Edw. F.
Vogelsberger, August
Wachter, J. William
Wagner, Henry
Walford. Edgar C.
Walker, James
Warder, John B.
Watson, Robert A.
Werber, Gustavus
Whitney, Henry H.
Wilver, Edward J.
Wood, Charles E.
Wood, Francis
Wright, Addison
Wrisley, E. Mason
Youngblood, Robt. K.
—190.

DROPPED FOR N. P. D.

Cooper, Charles A.   Godfrey, Lewis H.

ANACOSTIA LODGE, No. 21,

Meets on the First and Third Mondays in each month.

OFFICERS.

WILLIAM GUDE, Worshipful Master.
JULIUS W. TOLSON, S. Warden.   WM. N. FREEMAN, J. Warden.
JOHN H. KING, Secretary.   CLAUDIUS B. SMITH, Treasurer.

PAST MASTERS AND PAST GRAND OFFICERS.

†N. D. Larner, P. G. M.; †J. Lockie, John H. Mills, W. H. Collins, C. B. Smith, H. Kuhn, S. E. Shields, J. E. Halley, A. B. Garden, A. Gude, W. S. Dodge, J. E. Minnix.

LIST OF MEMBERS.

Anderson, Christian
Bartscher, Chris. M.
Benz, Alex.
Beyer, Andrew J.
Biggs, William H.
Brent, James T.
Brooks, Charles L.
Burn, Samuel H.
Burns, John
Campbell, Wm. D.
Carter, James S.
Collins, William H.
Cook, Rev. Chas. O.
Crawford, James A.
Crosier, Horace
Davenport, Rev. W. G.
Davidson, Alexander
Dodge, Charles R.
Dodge, Wilbur S.
Dony, James H.
Dougherty, Daniel
Emmons, Charles M.
Eno, Frank T.
Eno, Henry W.
Ernest, Wm. H.
Feddon, James F.

Fisher, Willis W.
Flood, William
Fowler, John T.
Frazier, Samuel M.
Freeman, Wm. N.
Fugitt, Eugene W.
Garden, Alex. B.
Garden, John C.
Garden, Peter C.
Green, Andrew M.
Grimes, Alfred T.
Griswold, Henry A.
Gude, Adolphus
Gude, William F.
Halley, James E.
Harbaugh, Charles J.
Harnish, Nath. R.
Harrison, John S.
Hayes, William E.
Heath, Charles L.
Herrell, John E.
Hinwood, Joseph H.
James, Charles J.
Jones, Thomas O.
Kahlert, August
Kahlert, John H.

Kaufman, Abram
Kemp, William H.
King, John H.
King, Vinton G.
Kramer, Fredk. H.
Kuhn, Henry
Latimer, William J.
†Larner, Noble D.
Leonard, James C.
†Lockie, John
Loffler, Charles
McNamara, John P.
Mathers, Ezra A.
Mayberry, Elmer C.
Miller, Joseph
Mills, John H.
Minkler, Henry E.
Minnix, James E.
Moreland, Jeff. R.
Nalley, Thomas R.
O'Brien, Samuel E.
O'Donnell, John H.
Okey, Cornelius W.
Patterson, Robert T.
Pope, Frederick C.
Pumphrey, Otto S.

Pyles, Richard A.
Randall, George F.
Redd. Jefferson B.
Remick, Herman B.
Richardson. Alfred L.
Robinson. Edw. W.
Samuels, Amabile
Schellhorn. Christian
Schneider, Martin H.
Scott, Clarence E.

Scott, Jasper
Scott. John F.
Scott. William H.
Shields, Samuel E.
†Sherman. Thomas E.
Slye, Frank
Smith, Claudius B.
Steadman, George C.
Stevens, Charles A.
Stoker. Edward
Stow, Henry S.

Tavender, Henry
Taylor. Benjamin N.
Tindall. Daniel
Tolson, Julius W.
Torrey, Charles T.
Walson. Charles F.
Walz, Burnette V.
Walz. Herman J.
Watson, Thomas J.
Wiess, C. H.—109.

GEORGE C. WHITING LODGE, No. 22,

Meets on the Second and Fourth Thursdays in each month.

OFFICERS.

B. W. MURCH, Worshipful Master.

H. S. BARRICK, S. Warden.　　　　J. H. TAYLOR, J. Warden.
CHARLES BECKER, Secretary.　　　W. T. WEAVER, Treasurer.

PAST MASTERS AND PAST GRAND OFFICERS.

S. N. Thorne; S. C. Palmer, M. W. G. M.; F. W. Storch, Edwin Turkenton, W. H. Griffin, Charles Becker, H. C. Craig, J. C. Athey, I. L. Johnson, P. G. M.; E. Weston, W. B. Easton, F. I. N. J. Tennyson, C. G. Graham, J. F. R. Appleby, J. T.[Greaves, R. W. Darby, W. T. Weaver.

LIST OF MEMBERS.

Appleby, Jas. F. R.
Athey, John C.
Baer, Alphonse M.
Balser. Arthur C.
Barrick, Harry S.
Becker, Charles

Becker, Charles A.
Becker, Harry
Bell, William E.
Berry, John E.
Berryman, John S.
Blacklidge, C. F.

Birdsall, Charles W.
Bradley. Chas. H.
Bradley, Joseph H.
Bornheim, Wm. M.
Brown, Augustus
Brown, Ernest W.

Brown, Joshua A.
Burton, Harry T.
Butler, Robert
Chappel, N. Webster
Conlin, William J.
Copperthite, Henry
Craig, Henry C.
Cunningham, Wm. A.
Darby, Rezin W.
Daw, Edward J.
Daw, Samuel L.
Decker, George W.
DeLashmutt, L. O.
Divine, John
Dutrow, J. T.
Easton, William B.
Einstein, Benjamin
Eli, Daniel E.
Elliott, Wm. H.
Engel, Benjamin F.
Estler, George W.
Everett, Lewis R.
Flynn, David
Fowler, Enoch S.
Freeman, George
Friebus, Gustav
Gain, William M.
Geiger, Geo. Junius
Gilbert, H. P.
Giles, Thomas J.
Goodman, Emil
Gordon, J. B.
Graham, C. G.
Greaves, James T.
Greenbaum, M.
Griffin, William H.
Harper, Benjamin F.
Harrison, William H.
Haviland, Thomas G.
Herdman, Benj. F.
Herschman, Jacob

Hess, Charles A.
Hess, George A.
Hess, William P.
Higgins, Lucius C.
Hoester, August
Holmes, Joseph
Hughes, Henry R.
Jackson, Albert B.
†Johnson, I. L.
Kaufman, Marx
Kidwell, Samuel
King, Theodore J.
Kleinschmidt, C. H. A.
Lang, William H.
Larman, John Q.
Law, James
Lewis, Robert K.
Lichty, Martin B.
Lichty, Martin W.
Littlefield, L. A.
Lockhead, Charles
Lohman, H. R.
Lowe, George W.
Luckett, William F.
Mattingly, Chas. W.
Maus, Oliver P.
May, Peter J.
McCobb, Ernest
Middleton, Robert L.
Miller, J. Barton
Minnis, R. M.
Money, William W.
Monroe, Wm. D.
Murch, Benjamin W.
Myers, Charles C.
Myers, E. H. L.
Nordlinger, Bernard
Orcutt, Albert
Palmer, Samuel C.
Parkhurst, John H.
Payne, Wm. N.

Peacock, Albert
Perry, Theodore F.
Prather, Albert C.
Proctor, Alex. H.
Reynolds, David L.
Riley, Eli
Riley, John
Riley, Thomas F.
Robey, Frank F.
Saers, Caleb L.
Schafer, Frederick
Schwennecker, Wm.
Shafer, William M.
Shaffer, William C.
Shanks, James R.
Shaw, John Thomas
Shekell, Abram B.
Shinn, Vincombe
Shoemaker, Isaac E.
Sinsheimer, Benj.
Smith, Chas. G., jr.
Smith, Hilliary M.
Sommerville, C. W.
Statz, H. M.
Steinbraker, Chas. H.
Storch, Frederick W.
Storm, J. A.
Strauss, Henry
Stroman, Henry C.
Stulz, Jacob
Swindells, John A.
Talbott, Edward H.
Taylor, Howard
Taylor, James H.
Tennyson, F. I. N. J.
Thorne, S. Norris
Thrift, Benjamin
Tincher, Timothy S.
Travers, Richard B.
Turkenton, Edward
Ullman, Samuel S.

Vinson, Webster
VonDachenhausen, G.
Walker, Edward
Wallace, James P.

Walther, Herman
Weaver, Walter T.
Wendel, John H.
Weston, Edmund

Weyss, John E.
Wilson, Downs L.
Works, A. Peyton
Young, J. T.—152.

PENTALPHA LODGE, No. 23,

Meets on the First and Third Mondays in each month.

OFFICERS.

GEORGE A. TAUBERSCMIDT, Worshipful Master.
WM. J. WALLACE, S. Warden.   WM. L. PRICE, J. Warden.
WM. P. H. CREWS, Secretary.   WM. K. MENDENHALL, Treas.

PAST MASTERS AND PAST GRAND OFFICERS.

Allan Rutherford, Wm. H. Appleton, J. M. Yznaga, P. G. M.;
W. K. Mendenhall, Edwin B. Hay, Arthur A. Birney, Matthew
Trimble, P. G. M.; John P. Torbert, Wm. P. H. Crews, Calvin
E. Town, Jerome B. Burke, John K. Robinson, Wm. R. Bushby,
Wm. J. Naylor, Harry W. Smith, S. A. Hollingshead, Joseph C.
Johnson, H. A. Trembley, Wm. R. Singleton, R. W. G. S.;
George P. Davis, Theo. B. Hibbs, †R. B. Donaldson, P. G. M.;
†H. P. H. Bromwell, P. G. M.

LIST OF MEMBERS.

Amiss, T. B.
Appleton, Wm. H.
Austin, James B.
Abbott, William E.
Abrams, George B.
Appold, W. B.
Amos, Henry C.
Amiss, William H.
Atkins, Joseph L.
Browne, Benj. W.

Barton, William H.
Bentley, A. J.
Beale, Buchanan
Bushby, William R.
Birney, Arthur A.
Burke, Jerome B.
Blodgett, William H.
Berlin, Henry S.
Brethauer, George J.
Barrett, James F.

Boss, Robert L.
Bennett, Adolphus
Brower, M. M.
Barton, W. M.
Beech, Eugene L.
Baumgarten, Leopold
†Bromwell, H. P. H.
Casey, Charles C.
Conner, L. A.
Crews, W. P. H.

Church, Robert A.
Craig, John G.
Coughlin, Dennis
Chesney, Charles S.
Coblenzer, George
Carusi, Nathaniel
Cooper, John W.
Crofts, Alfred E.
Colburn, W. E.
Clarkson, James A.
Carruthers, Lloyd E.
Dunwoody, W. P.
Durfee, Benjamin
DuBois, James T.
Dulin, Charles G.
Dyer, William A.
Davidson, Francis S.
Davis, Henry W.
Davis, John H.
Davidson, William J.
Darby, George W.
Dowrick, James A.
Davis, George P.
†Donaldson, R. B.
Eldridge, W. W.
Evans, D. J.
Elliott, Benjamin M.
Eberly, Daniel C.
Flint, Weston
Farden, James D.
Frey, Abram
Farden, Joseph S.
Ford, Edward C.
Frost, John W.
Griffin, E. W. W.
Graves, Rev. J. A.
Godwin, Harry P.
Grosner, Isidor
Green, William B.
Gifford, Leander W.
Galloway, Thos. F.

Grahe, J. H. C.
Gunderson, H. M.
Goodwin, O. W.
Higgins, H. A.
Hobbs, Isaac W.
Hood, William H.
Hood, James F.
Haworth, R. W.
Hay, William J.
Hay, Edwin B.
Halstead, Thomas
Henkel, August
Haldeman, W. C.
Heisley, George W.
Harlan, Benjamin A.
Hollingshead, S. A.
Henley, Travis F.
Hanks, Uriah S.
Hibbs, Theodore B.
Henry, William C.
Hess, Thomas L.
Hinton, John H.
Johnson, A. E.
Johnson, Joseph C.
Kipp, Eden
King, George E.
King, John F.
Kimmel, William A.
Kaiser, John H. (1)
King, Charles
Kraft, Henry E.
Keister, William H.
Kaiser, John H. (2)
Leese, Martin W.
Lotz, Jeremiah C.
Lowrie, Rev. R. W.
Lombard, A. J.
Lauder, John W.
Love, John P.
McKelden, Wm. B.
McKeldin, W. Harry

McKeldin, R. A. W.
Monroe, William H.
Morgan, Frank P.
Mendenhall, Wm. K.
Myers, Lewis
Michael, Richard
Malnati, Anton
Miller, George M.
Messenger, Frank C.
Montgomery, C. P.
Meston, Robert D.
Messervy, William
Murray, William J.
Mixer, Charles H.
Motz, Werner C.
Muller, Michael R.
Miller, Oscar
Musser, William
Meredith, Frank C.
Newman, Fred S.
Norris, James L.
Norton, H. D.
Naylor, William J.
Norton, Stephen W.
Ourand, Franck L.
Odell, William S.
Oppenheimer, Aug.
Prentiss, Charles A.
Parvin, Wash. L.
Pike, Yvon
Pennie, John C.
Price, William L.
Plitt, Charles F.
Patterson, Milton
Parker, W. H.
Plitt, George
Phillips, Robert D.
Plitt, Alexander H.
Parry, Richard L.
Parry, Albert S.
Parry, Francis B.

Robinson, John K.
Rutherford, Allan
Rupp, William H.
Reiter, Philip
Randolph, Fred J.
Richardson, Joseph
Robinson, Thos. A.
Rosen, David H.
Ries, Charles H.
Rhode, R. R.
Rice, Charles S.
Ridenour, W. S.
Singleton, Wm. R.
Stoek, J. F.
Stokes, George W. R.
Stephenson, James
Shaw, Josiah
Swan, Wm. D.
Stevens, Edward
Sontag, Rev. C. F.
Seegelken, Emil
Scholl, Robert W.
Spratley, Thomas W.
Smith, Harry W.
Scott, Harry C.
Sidwell, Thomas W.

Stewart, John C.
Stephens, L. Charles
Smith, John E.
Swormstedt, L. B.
Sidman, George D.
Sheetz, Elias M.
Sheckells, John E.
Snyder, J. William
Swainson, J. W.
Smith, John R.
Symonds, William
Stranahan, Geo. N.
Steidel, Charles L.
Shaw, Thomas K.
Stevenson, Rev. H. T.
Stoddard, Chas. J.
Sunderland, E. M.
Turpin, W. T.
Tisdel, W. P.
Torbert, John P.
Town, Calvin E.
Trimble, Matthew
Tauberschmidt, G. A.
Tupper, James A.
Teicher, John G.
Trembley, H. A.

Tauberschmidt, J. A.
Trembley. M. McC.
Underwood, H. G.
Upham, William C.
Utz, Harry A.
Von Bayer, Hector
Van Dorstan, A. W.
Vaughn, William A.
Voss. Charles H.
Van Arsdale, W. W.
Whitney, W. H.
Woodward, James
Whitaker, G. A.
Waugh. John H.
Whipkey, Allen
Wallace, W. J.
Weser, Charles H.
Wicklin, Charles S.
Wright, Marshall G.
Weed, Chester A.
Yznaga, José M.
Zimmerman, J. W.
Zange, Charles G.
Zellers, G. H. H.
—229.

DROPPED FOR N. P. D.

Clark, E. W.   Gardner, J. Anthony   Herbert, George R.

STANSBURY LODGE, No. 24,

Meets on the Second and Fourth Mondays in each month.

OFFICERS.

GEORGE G. PEARSON, Worshipful Master.
HENRY YOST, Jr., S. Warden.   CLYDE C. LAMOND, J. Warden.
WASH. E. NALLEY, Secretary.   GEO. W. BALLOCH, Treasurer.

PAST MASTERS AND PAST GRAND OFFICERS.

G. W. Balloch, P. J. G. W.; B. W. Summy, B. F. Martin, A.
G. Osborn, W. E. Nalley, H. Yost, sr., F. G. Alexander, P. G. M.;
T. M. F. Dowling, J. W. Ray, H. S. Lichau, †J. Hamacher, †W.
A. Gatley, T. Calver, F. L. Summy, A. R. McChesney, A. La-
mond, J. M. Mayne, Charles Brandt.

LIST OF MEMBERS.

Alexander, Fred G.
Alexander. John F.
Anderson, David B.
*Balloch, George W.
Bergmann, Wm. C.
Braddock, D. Scott
Brandt, Charles
*Brummell, Aug. O.
Butt. Charles
Calver, Thomas
Chappell, John W.
Charles, L. Nat.
Cissel, Thomas F.
Cogswell, Lem. H.
Colton, Andrew
Conradis, Henry
*Dowling,Thos. M. F.
Filbert, John E.
Freund, Louis
Freund, Frederick
Flack, Edwin B.
†Gatley, William A.
Gawler, Ferd.
Gibson, Frank E.
Glaum, John
Grant, Thomas
Haislip, Thomas M.
†Hamacher, Joseph
Hartig, Louis
Heine, Henry W.
Helbig, Fredk. W.

Horner, Firman R.
Javins, John F.
Johnson. Allen S.
Jones, William
Joy, Thomas H.
Kahlert, Fred W.
*Keene, Joseph R.
Keene, Will. A.
*Kennard, Rev. C. L.
King, Benj. C.
King, Charles R.
Klenk, George
Koss. Edward H.
Kramer. John C.
Kremb, Conrad
*Lamond, Angus
Lamond, Clyde C.
Landwehr, Louis
Leishear, William J.
Leishear, Samuel A.
Lichau, Henry S.
Lippold, George J.
Marcey, Lewis
*Martin, Benj. F.
Mathy, Joseph
Mayne, John M.
*Mattingly, Saml. L.
McCaully, Benj. F.
McChesney, Alg. R.
*Meyers, John G.
Miller, John

*Nalley, Wash. E.
*Osborn, Alfred G.
*Osborn, Marion
Passau, M. Ferd.
Pearce, Charles C.
Pearson, George G.
Pool, Benjamin G.
Purner, Ferd. G.
Rammling, Chris.
*Ray. John W.
Riley, Andrew J.
Scott, Richard T.
Shreve, Charles M.
Shreve, Wm. O., jr.
Springer, Francis A.
*Steele, Thomas M.
*Summy, Benj. W.
Summy, Frank L.
Swart, William W.
*Thomas, George W.
*Thomas, James A.
Thompson,Wm. H. C
Tucker, William J.
Walker, Redford W.
Walker, Allen
Westfall, Harry M.
White, Charles S.
Wicks, Marion
Yost, Henry, sr.
Yost, Henry, jr.—92.

ARMINIUS LODGE, No. 25,

Meets on the Second and Fourth Mondays in each month.

OFFICERS.

WM. F. MEYERS, Worshipful Master.

WM. BERGER, S. Warden.   CHAS. GERSDORFF, J. Warden.
H. H. GERDES, Secretary.   HENRY T. RIES, Treasurer.

PAST MASTERS AND PAST GRAND OFFICERS.

H. H. Gerdes, John Toense, J. C. Hesse, J. H. Meiners, L. Goldschmidt, M. Glaeser, Henry Brandes.

LIST OF MEMBERS.

Adler, Leon
Adt, Alexis
Alschwee, Henry
Altrup, Frederick
Baesgen, Joseph
Bartholomae, Wm.
Baumgarten, Herm.
Borcharding, Otto
Berens, F. C.
Berger, William
Bihler, Paul
Bischoff, Charles
Brakhagen, William
Brandes, Henry
Brodt, William
Burklin, Achille
Court, E. E.
Dahle, E. C.
Dempf, Joseph A.
Diemer, Jacob
Dietz, William
Dismer, Charles H.
Droop, E. F.
Egloff, Julius
Ehrlich, Siegm.
Eisenbeiss, H. J.
Escherich, Francis

Faber, Louis
Fischer, Henry
Ganzhorn, George P.
Gerdes, H. H.
Gerhold, Henry
Gerner, Charles E.
Gersdorff, Charles
Gerstenberg, Ernst
Glaeser, Moritz
Goldschmidt, Louis
Goldschmidt, Sol. E.
Giesler, Daniel
Hager, Christian
Hartenstein, Alvin
Herzog, Fr.
Hesse, J. C.
Heurich, Karl
Hinkel, J. P.
Hocheisen, Ferd.
Hollander, Justus
Horn, Karl
Illmer, Louis
Jakob, D. C.
José, Jacob
Katzenstein, Charles
Kehrle, Albert
Klinge, Henry

Koch, Werner
Kraemer, Henry
Latterner, Peter
Loeffler, Andrew
Loeffler, Charles
Loehl, Adolf
Maier, George J. P.
Meiners, J. H.
Meyers, W. F.
Michaelis, Abr.
Miller, George, sr.
Miller, George, jr.
Miller, Henry
Mueller, Charles
Naecker, Louis
Neumann, Henry
Ochs, Jacob
Olin, Andrew J.
Ockershausen, Wm.
Petersen, Carl
Reuter, F. W.
Rice, Wolf
Rieck, E. A.
Ries, H. T.
Rothschild, Harry
Ruppert, Ernst
Ruppert, Mathew

Schafer, Charles
Schaffert, J. L.
Schmidt, Aug.
Schnebel, William
Schneider, Chas.
Schuldt, Henry
Schulz, J. P.
Schwab, Conrad
Schwartz, Phil.
Schwarz, Aug.

Siegwart, William
Sonneberg, Joseph
Spiess, F. W.
Spitzer, David
Stahl, Ed.
Steinem, Em.
Steinem, Isaac
Stopsack, Henry
Teuber, Franz
Toense, John

Wagner, Emile
Waldmann, John
Walz, J. B.
Waterholder, F. W.
Wehner, Otto
Western, Clem.
Wiegand, Martin
Wilkening, Aug.
Worch, Hugo
Xander, Karl.—111.

OSIRIS LODGE, No. 26,

Meets on the First and Third Wednesdays in each month.

OFFICERS.

FRANK A. HARRISON, Worshipful Master.

C. H. BUCKLER, S. Warden.   WM. H. DE SHIELDS, J. Warden.
HERBERT P. GERALD, Secy.   WM. H. BARSTOW, Treasurer.

PAST MASTERS AND PAST GRAND OFFICERS.

L. C. Williamson, P. G. M.; †James A. Sample, P. G. M.; Wm. Oscar Roome, Wm. L. Sears, Fred E. Tasker, Wm. H. Barstow, Charles A. Riddle, Joseph Schiffman, Joseph C. Taylor, Charles S. Hyer, Wm. L. Boyden.

LIST OF MEMBERS.

Aaron, Robert
Adler, Victor E.
Andrews, Wm. W.
Barnett, Morris
Barstow, Edward C.
Barstow, William H.
Bartscher, J. G. W.
Baumgarten, Arthur
Baur, Joseph A.

Beach, Charles H.
Beattie, William W.
Behrend, Salm
Benner, George L.
Betker, John K.
Bigley, Frank C.
Bowles, William C.
Boyden, William L.
Brainard, Mark D.

Brainard, M. D., jr.
Brashears, Shipley
Briggs, Frederick
Buckelew, Joshua R.
Buckler, C. Howard
*Burns, William G.
Butler, Lafayette J.
Chisholm, Charles F.
Cohen, Jacob G.

Cohen. Max
Conley, Howard C.
Creecy, William B.
Danenhower, W. W.
De Shields. Wm. H.
Diehl. Charles L.
Dilliner, Joseph E.
Drew, George W.
Eisenmann, Jacob
Elliott, Charles B.
Esslinger, John A. F.
Fague, Solomon J.
Fischer. Samuel
FitzGerald, Wm. T.
Foos, William D.
Franklin, George E.
Fryer, John H.
Gapen, Clinton
Garner, William
Gerald, Herbert P.
Glaser, Samuel J.
Godwin, Thomas J.
Goldstein, Wm. N.
Gordon, Charles H.
Gorgas, Chas. S.
Griebel, Leonard
Haines, Mahlon N.
Harding, Theo. A.
Harlow, Reuben M.
Harrison, Frank A.
Harrison, George W.
Haynes, William R.
Hazelton, George C.
Heidingsfelder, Edwd.
Heimer, James F.
Henke, Charles E.
Herman, Albert
Herman, Meyer
Herman, Samuel
Herman, Samuel, jr.
Herzog, Joseph
Herzog, Sol

Hickcox, John S.
Hirsh, Salomon
Hoffa, Henry
Hope, William H.
Humphrey, Oscar W.
Hunter, Joseph H.
Hyer, Charles S.
Jackson, David
Jacobs, Sydney R.
Jobe, Isaac T.
Johnson, Howard F.
Jones, Edward E.
Jones, Henry C.
Kalbfus, Samuel T.
Kaufman, Joseph C.
Kaufman, Sigmund
Kellogg, Edward B.
Kimball, Charles C.
Kimpton, William C.
Lambert, Richard
Lampton, James J.
Latrobe, Benj. H.
Lee, Joel R.
Leitzell, Stuart M.
Lewis, William V.
Lippincott; Thomas
Lippman, Max
Losano, Francisco C
Macey, James T.
Maring, Delos T.
Marsh, A. Jay
Marx, Isaac
McCathran, W. A.
McNabb, Henry E.
*Meeds, James B. D.
Merrill, George W.
Miles, Frank H.
Monroe, Charles R.
Montgomery, Wm.
*Morgan, James D.
Murdoch, Lester H.
Musick, Wm. H. H.

Myers, Allen P.
Myers, Jacob
Nelson, Robert E., jr.
Norton, Frank P.
Oberheim, John
Oppenheimer, Saml.
Parker, Charles H.
Peirce. William E.
Pennewill, Ira
Peter, Arthur
Peterson, August
Pittman, Junius J.
Pool, Stephen D.
Ramsdell, Charles F.
Redhead, Geo. A.
Reed, Oliver H.
Rice, De La Pointe
Riddle, Charles A.
Roeder, John A.
Rogers, Charles S.
Roome, Albert W.
Roome, William O.
Rouzer, Lewis D.
Saegmuller, Geo. N.
Salomon, Benjamin
†Sample, James A.
Scheuerman, Geo. W.
Schiffman, Joseph
Sears, William L.
Sigourney, W. S.
Silcott, Thornton
Sondheimer, Julius
Steiner, Samuel
Strauss, David
Sugenheimer, Sol.
Tasker, Fred E.
Taylor, Benj. E.
Taylor. Charles H.
Taylor, John A.
Taylor, Joseph C.
Taylor, Leroy M., jr.
Thatcher, Frank H.

Thayer, Nelson C.
Tindall, William
Trudgian, Josiah B.
Tuley, Seth W.
Turner, Charles O.
Unsworth, Thos. H.

Van Vleck, James W.
Watson, Frank W.
Webb, Edwin D.
Webber, Ward D.
White, Henry
Williams, Alex. R.
Williamson, L. C.

Wilson, Walter A
Woods, Howard T.
Woods, Thomas E.
Yeoman, Wm. H.
Young, Samuel V.

—171.

DROPPED FOR N. P. D.

Grissom, Eugene, jr.   Jacobs, Henry H.   Patterson, Geo. S.

————

MYRON M. PARKER LODGE, No. 27,

Meets on the First and Third Tuesdays in each month.

OFFICERS.

Thomas A. Perry, Worshipful Master.
Joseph M. McCoy, S. Warden.   John A. Moyer, J. Warden.
Andrew K. Lind, Secretary.   J. Eldridge Burns, Treasurer.

PAST MASTERS AND PAST GRAND OFFICERS.

J. Eldridge Burns, A. K. Lind, J. C. Kauffman, A. S. Helton, F. E. Camp, Z. T. Jenkins, M. Schuster, H. F. Olmsted, B. P. Entrikin.

LIST OF MEMBERS.

Aregood, John W.
Babbitt, Robert A.
Belt, William L.
Bendheim, Moses
Biggs, Warren W.
Bitting, Jared D.
Bowdler, William T.
Bowen, Albert W.
Bowen, Ralph W.
Boyer, Woodward W.

Browning, Wm. S.
Bundick, Thomas J.
Burns, J. Eldridge
Burton, George C.
Camp, Francis E.
Camp, John J.
Carr, Arthur
Carr, Robert I.
Carson, Albert L.
Carver, Wilburn R.

Chappel, Albert W.
Christian, Robert W.
Clarke, James B.
Clark, Thomas J.
Cooke, Rev. Leslie
Cowsill, Arthur
Craig, Alvin L.
Cridler, David M.
Crisp, Thomas B.
Crowell, Charles E.

Crutchett, F. Edw.
Davis, Alfred A.
Davis, John F.
Davis, Frederick L.
De Silva, Dwight M.
Dewey, A. M.
Dickerson, P. B.
Dietrich, Chas. E.
Duffy, Michael
Emmons, George H.
Entrikin, B. P.
Entrikin, Samuel F.
Figg, Augustus W.
Forbes, Elmer A.
Fuller, John F.
Galiher, Samuel S.
Gilbert, Abel
Glenn, William G.
Goumpf, David S.
Greenman, E. L.
Handly, Edward J.
Hanen, Jeremiah L.
Hansell, George Y.
Hardesty, Reuben C.
Harr, Jesse M.
Henderson, Edgar
Heiser, David
Helton, Addison S.
Hess, Morris J.
Higinbotham, Chas.
Hunter, George

Jenkins, Zachary T.
Johnson, Victor H.
Johnson, Winfield B.
Kauffman, Joseph C.
Kolb, Edward L.
Leech, D. Olin
Ligon, John D.
Lind, Andrew K.
Lucas, James H.
Lybrook, Clifton H.
McCoy, Joseph M.
McCoy, William F.
Mackay, William F.
Maxwell, Lyman J.
Merrill, Norris H.
Morgan, Charles G.
Morgan, Joseph M.
Moyer, John A.
Myers, Charles E.
Nevitt, Robert I.
Olmsted, Hirah F.
Peake, John H.
Pennell, Edward
Pennington, Caleb
Perry, Thomas A.
Pettebone, O. L.
Pettigrew, Thomas J.
Pew, Alfred
Phillips, Ira G.
Pickens, M. C.
Pike, Charles A.

Powers, Ivan O.
Priddy, James V.
Quigley, Richard L.
Randall, Charles H.
Reid, Albert
Roberts, David J.
Rottmer, Harry E.
Rudy, Joseph P.
Schwab, George C.
Schuster, Michael
Silverberg, Lewis
Smith, P. W.
Snyder, Benjamin F.
Story, J. Johnson
Strieby, George F. W.
Stryker, Francis B.
Talbert, Charles R.
Tompkins, Edw. H.
Thompson, D. Darby
Truitt, John H.
Turner, Zachariah
Voneiff, George C.
Walter, L. D.
Wetmore, Wm. O.
Wheat, Eli M.
Wilkins, Frank
Wilkins, Wm. E.
Wilson, Stephen H.
Winchester, John M.
Woodruff, George G.
Young, Scott K.—123.

KING DAVID LODGE, No. 28,

Meets on the First and Third Tuesdays in each month.

OFFICERS.

CHARLES E. BALDWIN, Worshipful Master.
A. L. JACKSON, S. Warden. W. P. ARMSTRONG, J. Warden.
EBENEZER SOUTHALL, Secretary. JOHN B. LORD, Treasurer.

PAST MASTERS AND PAST GRAND OFFICERS.

Thomas G. Carmick, Wm. H. Stalee, J. Lewis Sherwood, H. McP. Woodward.

LIST OF MEMBERS.

Anderson, Wm. E.
Armstrong, Wm. P.
Baldwin, Charles E.
Burkes, George H.
Camp, Guy W. A.
Carmick, Thomas G.
Cass, Philip H.
Daniels, William S.
Davis, Daniel G.
Durfey, James G.
Ellis, Ebenezer
Etz, C. H.
Hackett, William T.

Hatcher, Eli
Holmes, Millard J.
Hull, Theodore Y.
Hurd, Judson B.
Jackson, Albert L.
Kinnan, Arthur F.
Lord, John B.
Lord, John B., jr.
Morgan, Ed. S.
Mull, M. D.
Penrod, Hiram J.
Phillips, Joseph
Quinn, William

Roth, Philip W.
Sherwood, J. Lewis
Sherwood, J. R., jr.
Small, John H.
Southall, Ebenezer
Stalee, William H.
Todd, Robert I.
Waudby, William S.
West, Robert R.
Whiteside, James L.
Woodward, H. McP.
†Young, Thomas H.
—38.

TAKOMA LODGE, No. 29,

Meets on the Second and Fourth Tuesdays in each month.

OFFICERS.

HORACE J. LONG, Worshipful Master.
H. M. CAMP, S. Warden.   O. D. SUMMY, J. Warden.
JAMES K. DEPUE, Secretary.   CHARLES M. HEATON, Treasurer.

PAST MASTERS AND PAST GRAND OFFICERS.

Theo. Friebus, James Morison, W. G. Platt, Theo. F. Willis, F. J. Woodman, †T. M. F. Dowling, †W. H. Douglas, †M. Trimble.

LIST OF MEMBERS.

Andrews, W. T.
Bailey, George H.
Bennett, H. M.

Brashear, C. H.
Burroughs, Joseph
Burrows, A. B.

Camp, H. M.
Cowl, B. G.
Curtis, Henry A.

Depue, James K.
Devine, James
Deitz, Charles J.
†Douglas, W. H.
†Dowling, T. M. F.
Dudley, L. F.
Eddy, Otis J.
Ferris, W. K.
Friebus, Theodore
Friebus. Theodore, jr.
Fugate, W. W.
Gillam, Frank
Gould, Ashley M.
Griffith, Rev. H. A.
Heaton, C. M.

Hitz, F. R
Jimerson, I
King, George W.
Kinnear, J. B.
Lawrence, A. L.
Long, H. J.
Longley, F. W.
Lung, F. J.
Mehn, William
Morison, James
Nowell James A.
Parkins, Alfred
Parkins, George W.
Parsons, Alfred V.
Perry, E. J.

Platt, W. G.
Pope, William H.
Roach, Frank C.
Shedd, S. S.
Shirley, John J.
Speer, Charles
Summy, O. D.
†Trimble, Matthew
Warren, George A.
Warren, H. E.
Wells, George H.
Willis, T. F.
Wilson, Rev. L. B.
Wine, M. J.
Woodman, F. J.—54.

DROPPED FOR N. P. D.

Alvey, William

Carroll, E. S.
Chapin, Gurden

Evans, H. C.

The following were Dimitted during the year 1898.

COLUMBIA LODGE, No. 3.

Henry M. Dixon...February 6, 1898
Wm. D. Haliday..October 7, 1898

NAVAL LODGE, No. 4.

Fredk. C. Waite...March 20, 1898

POTOMAC LODGE, No. 5.

Albert W. Paine..April 4, 1898

LEBANON LODGE, No. 7.

Robert E. Cozzens..June 3, 1898
Bellum Miller... December 17, 1897
J. W. Moore..December 3, 1897
Wallace C. Stratton...February 1, 1898

NEW JERUSALEM LODGE, No. 9.

A. H. Fiegenbaum...March 10, 1898
Joel Mann..October 13, 1898
Frank Taylor...October 13, 1898

HIRAM LODGE, No. 10.

Frank Fraser...February 4, 1898
F. K. Van Auken..February 18, 1898

ST. JOHN'S LODGE, No. 11.

Ril T. Baker...October 14, 1898
Fillmore Beall...October 22, 1897
Clarence D. Bowman...November 12, 1897
Samuel A. Collins..January 14, 1898
Martin Mangold...February 11, 1898
Henry R. Porter..August 26, 1898
James L. Wilmeth...March 25, 1898

NATIONAL LODGE, No. 12.

John J. Bier...December 21, 1897
Charles H. Nye...December 7, 1897

Washington Centennial Lodge, No. 14.

Dr. C. R. Johnson..May 4, 1898
J. C. McKie ....March 2, 1898

Benjamin B. French Lodge, No. 15.

George W. Albright...January 3, 1898
Wm. H. Emery.............. ....May 16, 1898
Millard J. Holmes........... .... December 6, 1897
Wm. O. Smith..January 3, 1898
Ernest L. Shepard...... ....March 21, 1998
Thos. A. Witherspoon...September 4, 1898

Dawson Lodge, No. 16.

Frank H. Quast...May 23, 1898

Harmony Lodge, No. 17.

Thomas G. Allan........... ....September 14, 1898
Oakes A. Caldwell..............:...........................November 11, 1897
William E. Stewart...September 14, 1898

Acacia Lodge, No. 18.

J. A. Harvey..November 9, 1897
Rev. C. L. Pate...August 23, 1898
J. J. Shirley..April 12, 1898
G. G. Wood............. ....March 22, 1898

La Fayette Lodge, No. 19.

W. H. Allen ....September 15, 1898
R. T. Bibb......... ....June 16, 1898
R. K. Cralle...... ....May 19, 1898
P. M. Hough..December 16, 1897
V. A. Moore...February 3, 1898
L. W. Naylor..December 16, 1897
George F. Robinson...June 16, 1898
C. A. O. Rosell..June 2, 1898
N. A. C. Smith ....June 2, 1898
R. E. Wiley...October 6, 1898

Hope Lodge, No. 20.

Guy C. Oder...October 14, 1898
P. Curtis Smith ....:May 27, 1898
Vernon C. Tasker...August 26, 1898

Anacostia Lodge, No. 21.

John T. Evely ....October 17, 1898

GEORGE C. WHITING LODGE, No. 22.

Obre R. Bourne...June 9, 1898

PENTALPHA LODGE, No. 23.

John Anderson...September 19, 1898
Alfred Pew..December 20, 1897

OSIRIS LODGE, No. 26.

Aaron Baldwin...March 16, 1898
Charles Hardin.. March 16, 1898
Alfred M. Lambeth...March 2, 1898
Josiah B. Perry...August 17, 1898
Robert W. Stevens..November 17, 1897
Leroy M. Taylor, sr..March 16, 1898
George Voneiff..January 19, 1898
Bartow L. Walker...September 21, 1898

MYRON M. PARKER LODGE, No. 27.

Alexander S. Barger...September 6, 1898
Samuel G. Cobb...March 1, 1898

TAKOMA LODGE, No. 29.

Julian C. Dowell..January 11, 1898
Charles S. Elliott...April 26, 1898

In Memory

Eighty-three Members

OF

Twenty-two Lodges of the District of Columbia

WHO HAVE DIED DURING THE MASONIC YEAR ENDING NOVEMBER 10, 1898.

FEDERAL LODGE, No. 1.

Richard H. Boswell, P. M...................................March 7, 1898
John A. Drawbaugh...May 27, 1898
Joseph F. Lucas..August 10, 1898
Thomas B. Marche.....................................September 22, 1898
Charles E. Van Arsdale..............................February 17, 1898

COLUMBIA LODGE, No. 3.

William F. Alden...October 29, 1898
William Bassett...March 12, 1898
William H. Myers..March 5, 1898

NAVAL LODGE, No. 4.

Frank W. Cross...August 2, 1898
John A. Foos, P. M.....................................February 21, 1898
William A. Scott...February 4, 1898
Thomas Somerville.....................................October 16, 1898

POTOMAC LODGE, No. 5.

John J. Beall, P. M., P. S. G. W..............February 17, 1898
Peter Dill...December 18, 1897
J. Edmund Thompson................................October 22, 1898

LEBANON LODGE, No. 7.

Clarence B. S. Adams..May 23, 1898
John Cochran...November 26, 1897
Charles Earl..July 13, 1898
William J. Gross.....................................February 2, 1898
John Jameson...................................November 14, 1897
Howard Q. Keyworth.................................January 22, 1898
John Robertson..July 25, 1898
Joseph Zadock Williams..........................May 27, 1898

NEW JERUSALEM LODGE, No. 9.

Samuel Bien...August 25, 1898
George Cochran...April 24, 1898

HIRAM LODGE, No. 10.

Alex. Campbell...May 7, 1898
J. C. Davison...March 2, 1898
Richard T. Fussell...................................June 4, 1898
John R. McMillan......................................May 25, 1898
Thomas H. Powell.................................January 26, 1898
John A. Rheem......................................May 18, 1898
Joseph E. Rawlings, P. M., P. J. G. W.............July 22, 1898

ST. JOHN'S LODGE, No. 11.

Edward M. Drew...................................... June 17, 1898
Peter H. Hooe, P. M., P. D. G. M.....................May 13, 1898
Jacob V. Lashhorn..March 18, 1898
Fred A. Snyder.......................................October 30, 1898
Albert H. Walcott...July 9, 1898
Knight C. Woodley.......................................May 7, 1898

NATIONAL LODGE, No. 12.

Frank T. M. Baird.......................................January 8, 1898
John H. Firor..March 30, 1898
Charles Freirich.......................................December 31, 1897
Stephen F. Gill, sr., P. M.............................March 10, 1898

WASHINGTON CENTENNIAL LODGE, No. 14.

Morris L. Ackerman......................................January 9, 1898
Charles E. Beller...July 3, 1898

BENJAMIN B. FRENCH LODGE, No. 15.

DAWSON LODGE, No. 16.

Joseph M. Labold..July 3, 1898
Benjamin Swallow.............................September 29, 1898
George Tatspaugh................................October 20, 1898

HARMONY LODGE, No. 17.

Edward Floyd Berryhill.....................................May 14, 1898
James Newman Sudduth................................August 11, 1898
Isaac S. Tichenor, P. M................................August 15, 1898

ACACIA LODGE, No. 18.

R. F. Baker..March 23, 1898
H. B. Elliott ....October 1, 1898
T. A. Howard..November 25, 1897
W. G. Moore.. July 12, 1898
P. E. Wilson...January 9, 1898

LA FAYETTE LODGE, No. 19.

J. Walter Blandford...................................March 12, 1898
John R. Francis...October 30, 1898
Jacob G. Jones..August 15, 1898
David C. Lobb...May 20, 1898
Frank B. Miller, P. M................................January 16, 1898
Thomas Mitchell, P. M.................................July 29, 1898
S. A. Muhlemann......................................February 14, 1898
C. E. Nordstrom...January 11, 1898
Alfred V. Robinson......................................August 2, 1898
W. D. Wyvill..April 8, 1898

HOPE LODGE, No. 20.

Walter S. McNairy..................................September 3, 1898
William Mertz, P. M....................................November 18, 1897
Lewis W. Shoemaker.................................March 2, 1898

ANACOSTIA LODGE, No. 21.

William H. Balser.......................................August 25, 1898

GEORGE C. WHITING LODGE, No. 22.

F. P. Davis, P. M..February 11, 1898

PENTALPHA LODGE, No. 23.

James H. Bonebrake.....................................April 7, 1898
J. Thomas Clements...................................January 25, 1898
William T. Johnson.....................................January 14, 1898

ARMINIUS LODGE, No. 25.

Herm. Burkhart..April 4, 1898
Frederick Dahler.............. ....September 7, 1898
Christian Schneider.... ....April 21, 1898
George Kerner.................................... ....December 22, 1997

MYRON M. PARKER LODGE, No. 27.

Homer Fellows, P. M..... ....March 25, 1898
James McCandlish....... ....October 30, 1898

TAKOMA LODGE, No. 29.

Solon Fisher........ ....October 27, 1898

TO THE MEMORY

OF

Bro. PETER H. HOOE,

PAST DEPUTY GRAND MASTER.

———

WORSHIPFUL MASTER OF ST. JOHN'S LODGE, NO. 11, FOR
THE YEARS 1852, 1853, AND 1854.

———

Died May 13, 1898.

TO THE MEMORY

OF

Bro. JOHN J. BEALL,

PAST SENIOR GRAND WARDEN.

———

Worshipful Master of Potomac Lodge, No. 5, for the years 1864 and 1865.

———

Died February 17, 1898.

TO THE MEMORY

OF

Bro. JOHN A. FOOS,

PAST MASTER.

———

WORSHIPFUL MASTER OF NAVAL LODGE, NO. 4, FOR
THE YEAR 1866.

———

Died February 21, 1898.

———————

TO THE MEMORY

OF

Bro. JOSEPH E. RAWLINGS,

PAST JUNIOR GRAND WARDEN.

———

WORSHIPFUL MASTER OF HIRAM LODGE, NO. 10, FOR
THE YEAR 1863.

———

Died July 22, 1898.

TO THE MEMORY

OF

Bro. STEPHEN F. GILL,

PAST MASTER.

———

WORSHIPFUL MASTER OF NATIONAL LODGE, No. 12, FOR
THE YEAR 1872.

———

Died March 10, 1898.

———————

TO THE MEMORY

OF

Bro. ISAAC S. TICHENOR,

PAST MASTER.

———

WORSHIPFUL MASTER OF HARMONY LODGE, No. 17, FOR
THE YEAR 1873.

———

Died August 15, 1898.

TO THE MEMORY

OF

Bro. FRANK A. MILLER,

PAST MASTER.

———

WORSHIPFUL MASTER OF LA FAYETTE LODGE, NO. 19,
FOR THE YEAR 1881.

———

Died January 16, 1898.

TO THE MEMORY

OF

Bro. THOMAS MITCHELL,

PAST MASTER.

———

MEMBER OF LA FAYETTE LODGE, NO. 19, BY AFFILIATION.

———

Died July 29, 1898.

TO THE MEMORY

OF

Bro. F. P. DAVIS,

PAST MASTER.

———

Worshipful Master of George C. Whiting Lodge
No. 22, for the year 1893.

———

Died February 11, 1898.

———————————

TO THE MEMORY

OF

Bro. HOMER FELLOWS,

PAST MASTER.

———

Worshipful Master of Myron M. Parker Lodge, No.
27, for the year 1896.

———

Died March 25, 1898.

INSTALLATION COMMUNICATION.

WASHINGTON, D. C., *December* 27, 1898.

The Installation Communication of the Grand Lodge, F. A. A. M., of the District of Columbia, was held at Masonic Temple at 6 o'clock, p. m.

PRESENT:

Bro. SAMUEL C. PALMER . M. W. Grand Master.
Bro. JOHN H. SMALL, Jr. . R. W. Deputy Grand Master.
Bro. WM. G. HENDERSON . R. W. Senior Grand Warden.
Bro. HARRY STANDIFORD . R. W. Junior Grand Warden.
Bro. WM. R. SINGLETON . R. W. Grand Secretary.
Bro. WILLIAM A. GATLEY . R. W. Ass't. Grand Secretary.
Bro. CHAS. C. DUNCANSON . R. W. Grand Treasurer.
Bro. CLAUDIUS B. SMITH . Rev. and W. Grand Chaplain.
Bro. MALCOLM SEATON . . W. Grand Marshal.
Bro. GEORGE H. WALKER . W. Senior Grand Deacon.
Bro. JAMES A. WETMORE . W. Junior Grand Deacon.
Bro. LURTIN R. GINN . . W. Grand Sword Bearer.
Bro. WALTER A. BROWN . W. Grand Pursuivant.
Bro. FRANCIS J. WOODMAN W. Senior Grand Steward.
Bro. HENRY K. SIMPSON . W. Junior Grand Steward.
Bro. JOHN N. BIRCKHEAD . Grand Tiler.

Past Grand Masters: Robert B. Donaldson, Myron M. Parker, Edw. H. Chamberlin, Harrison Dingman, James A. Sample, Thomas F. Gibbs, Henry S. Merrill, David G. Dixon.

Past Deputy Grand Master: G. A. Hall.

Visitors: K. Kemper, R. W. Junior Grand Deacon of the Grand Lodge of Virginia; W. H. Somerville.

REPRESENTATIVES:

LODGES.	W. MASTERS.	S. WARDENS.	J. WARDENS.
Federal, No. 1	H. M. McDade	H. B. Mason	Francis Nye
Columbia, No. 3	J. C. Kelper		H. A. Gibbs
Naval, No. 4	George C. Ober		
Hiram, No. 10	J. T. Meany	*J. Breen, Proxy.*	
National, No. 12		Abner P. Wilde	
Wash'n Centen'l, No. 14	E. Phillips	S. P. Johnson	E. H. Daniel
B. B. French, No. 15	*H. MacNamee, P.*	F. St.C. Thompson	J. F. Gibbs
Dawson, No. 16	E. S. Holmes, Jr.	*C. F. King, Proxy.*	
Harmony, No. 17	C. T. Caldwell.		
Acacia, No. 18	Seward T. Covert.		
Lafayette, No. 19	B. S. Graves	*H. Perry, Proxy*	
Hope, No. 20	N. S. Meyer	G. A. Cohill	J. D. Hinternesch
Pentalpha, No. 23		*P. Reiter, Proxy*	W. A. Kimmel
Arminins, No. 25	J. Toense		
Osiris, No. 26	C. H. Buckler		
King David, No. 28		M. D. Mull	G. W. A. Camp

Past Masters: No. 1, W. H. Proctor, J. S. Tomlinson, W. P. Sheid, R. B. Nixon; No. 4, G. W. Harrington; No. 7, J. H. Tatspaugh, T. H. Young, W. W. Ludlow; No. 9, R. V. Godman; No. 10, Robert Armour, G. W. Linkins, John Breen; No. 11, William H. Douglas, No. 12; Joseph M. Eggleston, W. E. Handy, Charles W. Otis; No. 14, E. C. Elmore, C. H. Smith, H. P. Marshall, J. F. Stewart, W. B. Pettus; No. 15, John C. Chaney; No. 16, John N. Birckhead; No. 17, Lurtin R. Ginn, A. W. Johnston; No. 18, C. J. O'Neill; No. 19, Thomas P. Morgan; No. 20, W. A. Craig, F. P. Hays, J. S. Mills, C. W. Henshaw; No. 23, James C. Johnson, William J. Naylor; No. 24, John W. Ray; No. 29, F. J. Woodman.

Grand Representatives: Myron M. Parker, Delaware, Ireland, Virginia; Harrison Dingman, Georgia, Quebec; James A. Sample, Indiana; M. Seaton, Louisiana; Charles H. Smith, Michigan; Robert B. Donaldson, Mississippi, Victoria; H. S. Merrill, New York; Samuel C. Palmer, New Zealand; William A. Craig, Nova Scotia; William A. Gatley, North Dakota; William G. Henderson, South Australia; E. H. Chamberlin, Scotland, Vermont; John H. Small, Jr., Wisconsin; D. G. Dixon, South Dakota; James A. Wetmore, South Carolina; William R. Singleton, Arizona, Cuba, Federal District of Mexico, Hidalgo, Jacob de Molay, Jalisco,

Lower California, Missouri, Morelas, New South Wales, Vera Cruz, Vincente Guerro.

The Grand Lodge was opened in ample form. Prayer by Rev. and W. Grand Chaplain.

By reason of the fact that Past Grand Master Sample had an important engagement which would prevent his remaining during the session of the Grand Lodge, at his request the regular order of business was suspended, and he was permitted to make a statement respecting the Masonic Temple Association. He, therefore, read a communication addressed to the Grand Lodge calling attention to section three of the charter granted by Congress to "The Masonic Temple Association" of the District of Columbia, approved April 15, 1898, providing that the affairs of said corporation shall be conducted by a board of managers to be selected annually in December by the respective bodies owning capital stock of said corporation to the amount of not less than $500 each. He moved that the Grand Lodge subscribe $1,000, and that an appropriation of ten per cent. of said amount, i. e. $100, be made, and it was so ordered.

The minutes of the Annual Communication, held November 9th, were read and approved.

The following reports from the Committee on Library and the Librarian were received and adopted:

REPORT OF LIBRARY COMMITTEE.

WASHINGTON, D. C., *December 27, 1898.*
To the Grand Lodge, F. A. A. M., of the District of Columbia:

The Committee on the Library submits the report for the year ending this date:

During the year no books were purchased until towards the close, when an opportunity was presented to obtain an excellent collection at a very reduced rate. The amount of funds from the year 1897 on hand, to which was added the regular annual appropriation, has enabled the Committee to add this year more books than for many years, as per report of the Librarian herewith submitted.

NOBLE D. LARNER,
Chairman.

REPORT OF LIBRARIAN.

WASHINGTON, D. C., *December* 27, 1898.

To the Library Committee:

BRETHREN: The following is my report for the year ending this date:

Number of books reported December 27, 1897.................2,990
Number added since...150

Total...3,140

Number of volumes taken out by readers.........640

WM. R. SINGLETON,
Librarian.

REPORT OF COMMITTEE ON JURISPRUDENCE.

The Committee on Jurisprudence requested further time for consideration of certain matters which had been referred to it.

The chairman of the Committee on Accounts, Bro. William A. Craig, P. M., of Hope Lodge, No. 20, presented the following report:

REPORT OF COMMITTEE ON ACCOUNTS.

WASHINGTON, D. C., *December* 27, 1898.

To the M. W. Grand Master, Officers, and Brethren of
the Grand Lodge, F. A. A. M., of the District of Columbia.

BRETHREN: The Committee on Accounts respectfully report that they have examined the books and vouchers of the R. W. Grand Secretary and R. W. Grand Treasurer and have found them to be correct.

The following is a statement of the financial condition of the Grand Lodge during the year ending this date, December 27, 1898, as shown by the books:

Amount received by Grand Secretary from all sources..	$5,000 80
Amount paid to Grand Treasurer..............................	5,000 80
Amount of warrants issued by Grand Secretary............	5,616 60
Amount of warrants paid by Grand Treasurer..............	*5,638 60
Amount received by Grand Treasurer from Grand Secretary	5,000 80

*NOTE.—Warrant No. 74, for $22, unpaid at last report, since paid.

Total receipts during year.............................. $5,000 80
Balance in hands of Grand Treasurer Dec.
    20, 1897.. 6,146 68

    Total amount to be accounted for............... 11,147 48
    Amount disbursed by Grand Treasurer, 1898................. 5,638 60

        Balance in hands of Grand Treasurer........ .... $5,508 88

RECEIPTS IN DETAIL.

Dues from Federal Lodge, No. 1...................................... $249 00
  "   "   Columbia Lodge, No. 3................................. 114 00
  "   "   Naval Lodge, No. 4...... .... 154 00
  "   "   Potomac Lodge, No. 5.. .... 89 00
  "   "   Lebanon Lodge, No. 7................................. 215 50
  "   "   New Jerusalem Lodge, No. 9......................... 322 00
  "   "   Hiram Lodge, No. 10........ .... 168 50
  "   "   St. John's Lodge, No. 11............................. 217 00
  "   "   National Lodge, No. 12 .... 116 00
  "   "   Washington Centennial Lodge, No. 14......... . 269 00
  "   "   Benjamin B. French Lodge, No. 15 .... 370 00
  "   "   Dawson Lodge, No. 16................................. 202 50
  "   "   Harmony Lodge, No. 17...... .... 236 00
  "   "   Acacia Lodge, No. 18...... .... 125 00
  "   "   La Fayette Lodge, No. 19............. .... 442 00
  "   "   Hope Lodge, No. 20.. .... 227 50
  "   "   Anacostia Lodge, No. 21........... .... 145 00
  "   "   George C. Whiting Lodge, No. 22............. ...... 168 00
  "   "   Pentalpha Lodge, No. 23.................... .... 157 50
  "   "   Stansbury Lodge, No. 24......................... ... 57 50
  "   "   Arminius Lodge, No. 25...... 108 50
  "   "   Osiris Lodge, No. 26............................. ..... 137 50
  "   "   Myron M. Parker Lodge, No. 27.................... 168 50
  "   "   King David Lodge, No. 28........................... 46 00
  "   "   Takoma Lodge, No. 29................ .... 42 50

                                                    $4,548 00
Received for calendar.................................... $ 37 80
Interest on investments 415 00   452 80

        Total receipts... $5,000 80

ASSETS.

Masonic Hall stock........ ....—.... $3,000 00
Real estate notes... 7,000 00
Cash on hand............. .... 5,508 88

        Total................. .... $15,508 88

LIBRARY ACCOUNT.

Amount in hands of Grand Treasurer, 1897.......................	$44 40
Amount received during the year.................................	50 00
	$94 40
Expended during the year........	80 00
Balance in hands of Grand Treasurer....................	$14 40

DISBURSEMENTS IN DETAIL.

Rent of hall and library rooms.............	$ 550 00
Salary of Grand Secretary.........	1,000 00
Salary of Assistant Secretary..............................	150 00
Salary of Librarian.........	150 00
Salary of Grand Lecturer..	180 00
Salary of Grand Tiler and extra allowance..........	133 00
Salary of Janitor.......	95 00
Salary of Committee on Correspondence...	50 00
Appropriation for library fund	50 00
Stationery, miscellaneous printing, postage, and type-writing.......	240 25
Masonic publications and advertising.........	15 28
Gas, repairs of fixtures, fuel, ice for two years, washing..	126 34
Carriage hire and funeral....................	43 75
Printing annual proceedings, 1897, and calendar, 1898....	864 00
Printing, advance on proceedings for 1898	200 00
Printing old records, in part......................................	550 00
Repairs of regalia and new......	11 88
Binding annual proceedings of Grand Lodges.....	18 10
Insurance on library and furniture.....	28 50
City directory and expenses of corporator......................	13 00
Jewel of Past Grand Master.........	125 00
Engrossing memorial resolutions.....	15 00
Miscellaneous repairs of furniture and cases.........	7 50
Investments.....	1,000 00
	$5,616 60

All of which is fraternally submitted.

W. A. CRAIG,
CHAS. S. HYER,
Committee.

On motion of Past Master Charles H. Smith, of Washington Centennial Lodge, No. 14, the report was received and adopted.

Past Grand Master Harrison Dingman stated that inability to give the time and attention to the proper performance of the duties pertaining to the position of chairman of Committee on the Celebration of the One Hundredth Anniversary of the Death of Bro. George Washington, to which he had been appointed by the M. W. Grand Master, necessitated his resignation, and he asked that it be accepted. The M. W. Grand Master stated that he learned with great regret the expressed purpose of Bro. Dingman, and that the matter of acceptance of the resignation and the contingent appointment of his successor would be left to the Grand Master-elect.

Past Master William A. Craig, of Hope Lodge, No. 20, moved that an investment be made of $1,000 of Grand Lodge funds, and it was so ordered.

Past Grand Master Henry S. Merrill moved that the R. W. Assistant Grand Secretary be authorized to cast the unanimous ballot of the Grand Lodge for Past Grand Master J. A. Sample as representative of this Grand Lodge on the Board of Managers of "The Masonic Temple Association" of the District of Columbia, and it was so ordered.

By permission of the M. W. Grand Master, Bro. K. Kemper, chairman of the Washington Centennial Committee of the Grand Lodge of Virginia, addressed the Grand Lodge upon the subject of said centennial, presenting a resolution pertaining thereto which he trusted would be adopted by the Grand Lodge.

The M. W. Grand Master stated that he had appointed a committee of five, consisting of Past Grand Masters Harrison Dingman, James A. Sample, Myron M. Parker, and Robert B. Donaldson, and Past Deputy Grand Master L. D. Wine, to act in conjunction with a similar committee appointed by the Grand Lodge of Virginia, as a committee of arrangements for the celebration of said centennial. At the request of the Grand Lodge of Virginia, the committee of this Grand Lodge had been increased to seven; Past Masters

B. W. Murch, of George C. Whiting Lodge, No. 22, and William Brown, of La Fayette Lodge, No. 19, having been added thereto, and the M. W. Grand Master stated that in the absence of objection he would consider that his action met the approval of the Grand Lodge. The M. W. Grand Master stated further that as a special communication of the Grand Lodge would be held in March and semi-annual in May, ample opportunity would be afforded the Grand Lodge and its committee to give the subject careful consideration, and in deference to said committee, he would place the resolution submitted by Bro. Kemper in its hands.

The M. W. Grand Master announced that the time had arrived for the installation of the Grand Officers-elect. He then directed the W. Grand Marshal to present for installation the Grand Master-elect, Bro. John H. Small, Jr., who was duly installed M. W. Grand Master of Masons of the District of Columbia.

The M. W. Grand Master then delivered the following address:

GRAND MASTER'S ADDRESS.

BRETHREN OF THE GRAND LODGE OF THE DISTRICT OF COLUMBIA: In assuming the responsible duties of Grand Master, I extend to you a hearty greeting and congratulations on the peace and harmony which prevail in this Grand Jurisdiction.

The year now drawing to a close has been filled with stirring events, particularly in our own hemisphere, constituting an epoch in the world's history in which the sacred rights of humanity have been protected and upheld and the principles and tenets of Masonry have been exemplified—asserting, as they do, in their broadness and majesty, "the fatherhood of God and the brotherhood of man." While we devoutly render thanks to Almighty God who has been pleased to bring peace out of strife, so also is it our bounden duty to be thankful unto Him that our order has been permitted quietly to cultivate and promote those principles which tend to increase its sphere of usefulness and render its advance steady and certain.

During the past year initial steps were taken toward building in this city a new Masonic Temple—one in keeping with the growth and dignity of our order and the Nation's Capital. The fair and exposition held in April last, to raise funds to this end was a success beyond expectation. The approximate sum of fifty thousand dollars was realized. With this fund as a nucleus, it is hoped and expected that with energy and good judgment the brethren will push the project to a successful termination.

The new Masonic Temple Association, chartered by a special act of Congress, has been organized, and under the able presidency of Past Grand Master Donaldson, will direct to completion the work so auspiciously begun.

I recommend that the Grand Lodge continue to give this undertaking its earnest support and in every way encourage the constituent lodges to unite in a grand effort to build a temple which will be a credit to the fraternity. Complete success can only be obtained by co-operation of all interests involved; every movement being directed by wise counsel along the lines of strict business methods, without unseemly haste or unnecessary delay. The time is now most propitious to secure a suitable site, and, that being accomplished, the building of the temple will be an assured fact.

Your attention is invited to an event of great interest and importance occurring during the coming Masonic year—the celebration of the centennial of the death of George Washington at Mount Vernon. By invitation of the Grand Lodge of the State of Virginia, my predecessor appointed a committee, representing this Grand Lodge, to co-operate with that body in perfecting arrangements. I urge the brethren of this jurisdiction to join, heart and hand, in making those memorial services commensurate in proportion and dignity to the fame of our distinguished brother.

In conclusion, permit me to say that it is my good fortune to have the path in which I am to tread as your Grand Master illumined by the example of distinguished men, who have successively rendered valuable service to the craft. With their example in all instances before me, I shall press toward the high-mark set by them, but with many misgivings of success. May I hope in the end to attain the reward which is theirs—the benedictions of a beloved fraternity.

Relying on the patronage of your good will, I undertake the work which lies before me, trusting that the Grand Master who rules the universe, may vouchsafe to us His leadership in the path of duty, and grant to us favorable issue to our aims and prosperity to our order.

J. H. SMALL, Jr.,
Grand Master.

At the request of the M. W. Grand Master, Past Grand Master Palmer installed the other Grand Officers as follows :

Bro. Wm. G. Henderson, R. W. Deputy Grand Master.
Bro. Harry Standiford, R. W. Senior Grand Warden.
Bro. Malcolm Seaton, R. W. Junior Grand Warden.
Bro. W. R. Singleton, R. W. Grand Secretary.
Bro. C. C. Duncanson, R. W. Grand Treasurer.
Bro. Claudius B. Smith, Rev. and W. Grand Chaplain.
Bro. George H. Walker, W. Grand Marshal.
Bro. James A. Wetmore, W. Senior Grand Deacon.
Bro. Lurtin R. Ginn, W. Junior Grand Deacon.
Bro. Walter A. Brown, W. Grand Sword Bearer.
Bro. F. J. Woodman, W. Grand Pursuivant.
Bro. A. B. Coolidge, W. Senior Grand Steward.
Bro. H. K. Simpson, W. Junior Grand Steward.
Bro. John N. Birckhead, Grand Tiler.

The M. W. Grand Master announced the appointment of the following standing committees:

BY-LAWS:

| W. A. CRAIG. | ADOLPHUS GUDE. | S. M. YEATMAN. |

GRIEVANCES:

| J. A. SAMPLE. | WILLIAM A. DeCAINDRY. | W. W. WETZEL. |

CORRESPONDENCE:

| W. R. SINGLETON. | H. H. GERDES. | J. O. ROLLER. |

LIBRARY :

| N. D. LARNER. | THOMAS H. YOUNG. | LURTIN R. GINN. |

ACCOUNTS:

| CHAS. H. SMITH. | J. R. GARRISON. | J. H. CUNNINGHAM. |

JURISPRUDENCE:

| R. B. DONALDSON. | E. G. DAVIS. | M. M. PARKER. |

WORK AND LECTURES :

| CHARLES BECKER. | W. S. BICKFORD. | WM. J. NAYLOR. |

The M. W. Grand Master also announced the appointment of Bro. William A. Gatley, P. M., of Benjamin B. French Lodge. No. 15, as R. W. Assistant Grand Secretary.

Past Grand Master R. B. Donaldson, chairman of the special committee appointed at the Annual Communication to procure a suitable testimonial to be presented to the retiring ̄and Ma⸺r. then in a very interesting address presented ⸺ P⸺ C⸺d M⸺.

Bro. Arvine W. Johnston, W. Grand Lecturer-elect. declined being installed for good and sufficient reasons assigned by him. Bro. Thomas H. Young was afterwards appointed by the M. W. Grand Master.

WM. R. SINGLETON,
Grand Secretary.

Masonic Board of Relief.

FINANCE REPORT.

WASHINGTON, D. C., *January* 5, 1899.

To the President and Members of the
  Masonic Board of Relief of the District of Columbia.

BRETHREN: Your Auditing Committee has examined the books, accounts, and vouchers of the Secretary and Treasurer and find them correct and accurate in every particular, in so far as they relate to the scope of the Committee's investigation. All the financial transactions of the Board have been properly recorded; all moneys received by the Secretary have been promptly turned over to the Treasurer, as per the latter's receipts on file with the Secretary.

The following is a detailed statement of the receipts and disbursements for the year ending December 31, 1898:

RECEIPTS.		EXPENDITURES.	
Balance on hand Dec. 31, 1897	$196 40	Board and lodging of applicants	$49 90
Received since by— Amounts refunded by lodges to which applicants belonged	43 70	Railroad fares and money advanced applicants	100 40
Amounts refunded by applicants	29 35	Deposit with the W. U. Tel. Co	10 00
One assessment of five cents per capita on lodges	250 40	Dues to General Masonic Relief Association	25 79
		Printing and stationery	38 47
		Postage and incidentals for the year	13 15
Total to be accounted for	$519 85	Repairs to chairs	4 00
Less amount expended	341 71	Salary of Secretary	100 00
Balance on hand Dec. 13, 1898	$178 14	Total	$341 71

The assets of the Board consist of one desk and chairs, valued at $125. There are no liabilities.

Courteously and fraternally yours,

F. J. FOSTER,
W. R. CARVER,
P. J. EDDY,
Auditing Committee.

NOTE.—Less than the usual number of applicants have appeared before the Board during the year. About forty-seven per cent. of those who appeared were found to be unworthy, and no assistance was rendered them. The worthy applicants were assisted to the extent that their several needs seemed to demand, the Board in most instances using its best judgment in what seemed best to do.

There have been numerous requests for employment, especially from the brethren and their dependents of the local fraternity. Owing to the dullness that has prevailed in the business world of this city, the Board has found it absolutely impossible to meet any demands in this direction, but now that business here as elsewhere is again gradually assuming a normal condition, it is earnestly hoped that those who have employment to give will kindly bear in mind that there are those of the fraternity out of employment who will be only too glad for the opportunity to earn an honest livelihood for themselves and families.

If the Board be given a chance in this direction, it will try to recommend none but those who will be honest and faithful, and fitted for the work in hand.

As heretofore, the Board expresses satisfaction at being able to meet and merit the expectations and confidence of the brethren of the lodges. There have been none but the kindest words and assurances, for which the members of the Board are truly thankful.

Courteously and fraternally,

LURTIN R. GINN,
Secretary.

RECAPITULATION showing the numerical condition of the several Lodges in the jurisdiction, the work of the post year, amounts due and paid by each to the Grand Lodge during 1898, and date of charter of each.

Names of Lodges.	Old No.	Present No.	Date of charter.	M. M. last report.	Entered.	Passed.	Raised.	Affiliated.	Reinstated.	Total M. Masons in year.	Gain.	Withd'n.	Died.	Dropped.	Loss.	Present number per M. M.	Exempt.	Amount paid by each to Grand Lodge.
Federal	15	1	Sept. 12, 1793	238	17	17	16	5	2	261	23		5		5	256	5	$249 00
Federal	35		Feb. 19, 1811	141	6	5	5	1	2	149	8	2	3	1	6	143		114 00
Columbia		3	Nov. 8, 1803	183	10	8	6	1	3	195	10	1	4	9	14	181	3	154 00
Columbia	40	4	Feb. 19, 1811															
Washington Naval			Dec. 19, 1805															
Naval	9	5	Feb. 19, 1811	99	8	6	6	4	3	108	9	1	3	2	7	104	6	80 00
Potomac	19	6	Apr. 12, 1789	313	20	9	8	3	3	327	11	3	8	2	14	313	2	215 50
Columbia	43	7	Oct. 22, 1795	356	8	17	16	5	3	378	22	3	21	9	14	364	2	322 50
Potomac		9	Nov. 11, 1811	230	11	6	6	2	4	245	15	2	7	9	9	236	9	168 50
Potomac		10	Feb. 19, 1806	268	18	10	18	1	4	302	19	7	6	4	22	280	1	217 00
Lebanon		11	Oct. 8, 1811	142	17	6	10	5	2	153	11	2	4	5	10	143	5	116 00
New Jerusalem		12	Nov. 2, 1824	250	11	17	18	6	2	289	38	2	7	5	9	271	5	269 00
Hiram		14	Jan. 28, 1828	480	18	13	20	1	5	509	8	6	12	3	14	269	4	370 10
St. John's		15	Feb. 23, 1846	215	17	10	13	7	6	233	28	1	8	6	9	495	2	202 50
National		16	May 7, 1846	316	12	9	8	4	1	338	18	8	8	3	9	224	9	286 00
Washington Centennial		17	Nov. 4, 1852	145	11	7	7	8	3	155	17	4	5	4	12	321		148 00
Benj. B. French		18	Dec. 27, 1853	555	22	21	21	4	1	581	10	10	10	6	26	148	6	442 50
Dawson		19	May 5, 1857	173	18	20	18	8	1	200	30	3	1	4	10	549	3	227 50
Harmony		20	May 6, 1863	92	12	13	18	3	1	108	27	1	2		9	190		145 00
Acacia		21	Dec. 27, 1862	140	12	13	13	1		165	16	1	3	6	9	106	1	168 00
La Fayette		22	Dec. 28, 1865	228	6	7	7	7		235	15	2	1	4	9	152	1	157 50
Hope		23	May 28, 1867	89	7	7	7		1	92	7		3		9	226	6	92 00
Anacostia		24	Dec. 4, 1868	108	7	7	7	2	1	115	12	1	4		4	92	3	108 50
George C. Whiting		25	Dec. 28, 1869	172	14	15	15	5		184	20	1	2		14	111		170 00
Pentalpha		26	Nov. 12, 1873	107	3	3	7	2	3	127	0	2		6	4	170		187 50
Stansbury		27	Oct. 8, 1876	32	3	2	3	2		38	6		4		2	121	1	188 00
Arminius		28	May 14, 1890	53						59		2	2	5	18	38	1	46 00
Osiris		29	May 21, 1891													61		42 50
Myron M. Parker			Nov. 8, 1893															
King David			Nov. 8, 1895															
Takoma																		
Totals				5,142	263	255	253	72	62	5,580	387	67	84	80	253	5,298	75	4,548 00

LIST OF GRAND REPRESENTATIVES
TO AND FROM OTHER GRAND LODGES.

GRAND LODGE.	REPRESENTATIVE FROM—	REPRESENTATIVE TO—
Alabama		Robert B. Webb, Livingston.
Arkansas	Joseph S. McCoy	Isaac C. Casey, Bentonville.
Arizona	W. R. Singleton	G. J. Roskruge, Tucson.
British Columbia	John Lockie	Eli Harrison, Victoria.
California		N. G. Curtis, Sacramento.
Canada	Joseph H. Jochum	H. Robertson, Collingwood.
Connecticut	G. E. Corson	Clark Buckingham.
Colorado	A. H. Holt	Wm. D. Wright, Buena Vista.
Cuba	W. R. Singleton	Antonio Govin, Havana.
Delaware	M. M. Parker	Eugene Massey.
England	N. D. Larner	
Federal Dist. of Mexico	W. R. Singleton	P. J. Senties.
Florida	L. D. Wine	W. E. Anderson, Jacksonville.
Georgia	Harrison Dingman	Charles E. Damon, Macon.
Hidalgo	W. R. Singleton	R. Moreno, Pachua.
Idaho	E. G. Davis	George Ainslie, Idaho City.
Illinois	L. C. Williamson	D. M. Browning, E. St. Louis.
Indiana	James A. Sample	C. W. Prather, Jeffersonville.
Indian Territory	I. L. Johnson	W. A. McBride, Atoka.
Ireland	M. M. Parker	T. A. McCammon, Dublin.
Italy	N. D. Larner	George Vemajo.
Jacob de Molay	W. R. Singleton	D. C. Garcia, Tamaulipas.
Jalisco	W. R. Singleton	F. L. Meldonado.
Kansas	N. D. Larner	George S. Greene.
Louisiana	Malcolm Seaton	Saml. L. Todd, New Orleans.
Lower California	W. R. Singleton	Louis Mendoza.
Maine	George Wallace	Stephen Berry, Portland.
Manitoba	J. F. R. Appleby	Thos. A. Cuddy, Minnedosa.
Maryland	W. H. Orcutt	H. C. Larabee, Baltimore.
Michigan	Charles H. Smith	J. J. Carton.
Minnesota	C. W. Hancock	J. D. Markman.
Mississippi	R. B. Donaldson	Frederick Speed, Vicksburg.
Missouri	W. R. Singleton	J. M. Abraham.
Montana	George H. Walker	Chas. W. Pomeroy, Kalispell.
Morelas	W. R. Singleton	J. A. Cafrera.
Nebraska	F. G. Alexander	B. D. Slaughter, Omaha.
Netherlands		L. Smit, Jr., Rotterdam.
New Hampshire	George W. Balloch	J. F. Webster.
New Jersey	N. D. Larner	Robert S. Gaskill, Mt. Holly.
New Mexico	W. A. DeCaindry	Max Frost.

Nevada............................George W. Baird..........Joseph A. Miller, Austin.
New South Wales............W. R. Singleton........ ..... Thomas Alphen, Sydney.
New York.......................H. S. Merrill.................John H. Cunningham, Utica.
New Zealand....................Samuel C. Palmer.........George Boor.
North Carolina................Jesse W. Lee, Jr...........C. H. Robinson, Wilmington.
Nova Scotia..................W. A. Craig..................James Simmonds, Halifax.
North Dakota..................W. A. Gatley................A. D. Flemington, Ellendale.
Ohio...............................Jose M. Yznaga............A. C. Cable, Covington.
Oregon............................N. D. Larner................Thomas A. McBride.
Oaxaca...J. P. Guzman.
Prince Edward Island.....Matthew Trimble.........John Albert Messervy.
Quebec.......... ....Harrison Dingman......C. R. Jones, M. D.
Rhode Island...................Richard C. Lewis. ....Nelson W. Aldrich, Providence.
South Australia...............Wm. G. Henderson......Ebenezer Cook.
South Carolina...............James A. Wetmore......Charles Inglesby, Charleston.
South Dakota..................David G. Dixon.... ......Henry J. Rice.
Scotland..........................E. H. Chamberlin.........David Reid.
Tasmania........................Edmond Cotterill.........J. T. McDonnell.
Tennessee........................N. D. Larner.................John S. Pride, Culleoko.
Texas.. ....Thos. F. Gibbs.............Wm. Bramlette.
Utah ....Wm. O. Roome............C. S. Varian, Salt Lake City.
Vermont..........................E. H. Chamberlin.........W. N. Kingsley, Middlebury.
Vera Cruz........................W. R. Singleton............J. R. Reys.
Venezuela........................J. M. Yznaga..
Victoria...........................R. B. Donaldson...........George S. Coppin.
Vincente Guerro.............W. R. Singleton..........Jose Montes.
Virginia...........................M. M. Parker...
West Virginia..................Burton R. Ross.............R. C. Dunnington, Fairmount.
Wisconsin.......................John H. Small, jr........Myron Reed West, Superior.

GRAND OFFICERS FOR THE YEAR 1899.

Bro. JOHN H. SMALL, Jr. . M. W. Grand Master.
Bro. WM. G. HENDERSON   . R. W. Deputy Grand Master.
Bro. HARRY STANDIFORD   . R. W. Senior Grand Warden.
Bro. MALCOLM SEATON .   . R. W. Junior Grand Warden.
Bro. WM. R. SINGLETON   . R. W. Grand Secretary.
Bro. WILLIAM A. GATLEY . R. W. Ass't. Grand Secretary.
Bro. CHAS. C. DUNCANSON . R. W. Grand Treasurer.
Bro. THOS. H. YOUNG . . W. Grand Lecturer.
Bro. CLAUDIUS B. SMITH . Rev. and W. Grand Chaplain.
Bro. GEORGE H. WALKER . W. Grand Marshal.
Bro. JAMES A. WETMORE   . W. Senior Grand Deacon.
Bro. LURTIN R. GINN . . W. Junior Grand Deacon.
Bro. WALTER A. BROWN   . W. Grand Sword Bearer.
Bro. FRANCIS J. WOODMAN   W. Grand Pursuivant.
Bro. A. B. COOLIDGE . . W. Senior Grand Steward.
Bro. HENRY K. SIMPSON   . W. Junior Grand Steward.
Bro. JOHN N. BIRCKHEAD . Grand Tiler.

OFFICERS OF THE CONSTITUENT LODGES
FOR THE YEAR 1899.

FEDERAL LODGE, No. 1.

HARRY M. McDADE, Worshipful Master.
HARRY B. MASON, S. Warden.   FRANCIS NYE, J. Warden.
GOODWIN Y. ATLEE, Secretary.   W. S. JENKS, Treasurer.
RICHARD B. NIXON, Past Master.

COLUMBIA LODGE, No. 3.

J. CLAUDE KEIPER, Worshipful Master.
LUTHER F. SPEER, S. Warden.   HERBERT A. GIBBS, J. Warden.
W. S. MACGILL, Secretary.   GEORGE S. KING, Treasurer.
HERBERT WRIGHT, Past Master.

NAVAL LODGE, No. 4.

GEORGE C. OBER, Worshipful Master.
SILAS A. MANUEL, S. Warden.   JOSEPH E. HODGSON, J. Warden.
JOHN SCHULTZ, Secretary.   ADAM GADDIS, Treasurer.
HARRY P. COOK, Past Master.

POTOMAC LODGE, No. 5.

JAMES S. RAEBURN, Worshipful Master.
FRED. W. DAW, S. Warden.   ALPHEUS W. HUDSON, J. Warden.
FRANK THOMAS, Secretary.   WOLF NORDLINGER, Treasurer.

LEBANON LODGE, No. 7.

JOHN E. WALSH, Worshipful Master.
DAN. W. SKELLENGER, S. Warden.   WM. C. FOWLER, J. Warden.
WALTER W. LUDLOW, Secretary.   THOMAS TAYLOR, Treasurer.
JOHN H. TATSPAUGH, Past Master.

NEW JERUSALEM LODGE, No. 9.

EDWARD MATTHEWS, Worshipful Master.
HOWARD D. FEAST, S. Warden.   C. C. COOMBS, J. Warden.
WM. E. DENNISON, Secretary.   ROBT. V. GODMAN, Treasurer.
BENJAMIN PARKHURST, Past Master.

HIRAM LODGE, No. 10.

JOHN T. MEANY, Worshipful Master.
ED. C. BRANDENBURG, S. Warden.   H. C. FRANKENFIELD, J.W.
JAS. W. WRENN, Secretary.   PHILIP H. WARD, Treasurer.
W. F. R. PHILLIPS, Past Master.

SAINT JOHN'S LODGE, No. 11.

REV. CHAS. ALVIN SMITH, Worshipful Master.
CHAS. FERNALD, S. Warden.   ROBERT A. DANIEL, J. Warden.
ROBT. A. DELLETT, Secretary.   CHAS. J. WATSON, Treasurer.
WILLIAM T. JONES, Past Master,

NATIONAL LODGE, No. 12.

FRED. W. BUDDECKE, Worshipful Master.
ABNER P. WILDE, S. Warden.   CHAS. W. BROWN, J. Warden.
HARRY L. WALCOTT, Secretary,   G. TAYLOR WADE, Treasurer.
JOSEPH E. FALK, Past Master.

WASHINGTON CENTENNIAL LODGE, No. 14.

EDSON PHILLIPS, Worshipful Master.
SAMUEL P. JOHNSON, S. Warden.   ERNEST H. DANIEL, J. Warden.
EMMETT C. ELMORE, Secretary.   WALTER S. BARKER, Treasurer.
JOHN H. DAVIS, Past Master.

BENJAMIN B. FRENCH LODGE, No. 15.

ALEX. GRANT, Worshipful Master.
E. St. C. THOMPSON, S. Warden.   JAMES T. GIBBS, J. Warden.
WM. A. GATREY, Secretary.   G. F. JOHNSTON, Treasurer.
JOHN C. CHANEY, Past Master.

DAWSON LODGE, No. 16.

EDWIN S. HOLMES, Jr., Worshipful Master.
BENJ. F. ODELL, S. Warden.   ADDIS D. MERRITT, J. Warden.
RODOLPH WILLIS, Secretary.   SAMUEL H. WALKER, Treasurer.
EDGAR G. HARBAUGH, Past Master.

HARMONY LODGE No. 17.

CHARLES T. CALDWELL, Worshipful Master.
HENRY E. TRIPP, S. Warden.   J. LOUIS WILLIGE, J. Warden.
W. HAMILTON SMITH, Secretary. ORANGE S. FIRMIN, Treasurer.
SHERMAN J. BROWN, Past Master.

ACACIA LODGE, No. 18.

SEWARD T. COVERT, Worshipful Master.
HYLAS T. WHEELER, S. Warden. ULYSSES G. PERRY, J. Warden.
CHAS. J. O'NEILL, Secretary.   GEO. W. KOONCE, Treasurer.
CLARENCE B. LANGAN, Past Master.

LA FAYETTE LODGE, No. 19.

BENJAMIN S. GRAVES, Worshipful Master.
HENRY S. SELDEN, S. Warden.   J. CHESTER BOWEN, J. Warden.
W. H. OLCOTT, Secretary.   A. F. FOX, Treasurer.
THOMAS P. MORGAN, Past Master.

HOPE LODGE, No. 20.

NATHAN S. MEYER, Worshipful Master.
GEORGE A. COHILL, S. Warden. J. D. HINTERNESCH, J. Warden.
WM. A. CRAIG, Secretary.   CHAS. H. DICKSON, Treasurer.
CHARLES C. VAN HORN, Past Master.

ANACOSTIA LODGE, No. 21.

JULIUS W. TOLSON, Worshipful Master.
WM. N. FREEMAN, S. Warden.   SAM'L E. O'BRIEN, J. Warden.
JOHN H. KING, Secretary.   C. B. SMITH, Treasurer.
WILLIAM F. GUDE, Past Master.

GEORGE C. WHITING LODGE, No. 22.

BENJAMIN W. MURCH, Worshipful Master.
B. F. HARPER, S. Warden.   HARRY BECKER, J. Warden.
CHARLES BECKER, Secretary.   W. T. WEAVER, Treasurer.

PENTALPHA LODGE, No. 23.

WILLIAM J. WALLACE, Worshipful Master.
WM. L. PRICE, S. Warden.   WM. A. KIMMEL, J. Warden.
WM. P. H. CREWS, Secretary.   W. K. MENDENHALL, Treasurer.
GEORGE A. TAUBERSCHMIDT, Past Master.

STANSBURY LODGE, No. 24.

HENRY YOST, Jr., Worshipful Master.
CLYDE C. LAMOND, S. Warden. W. H. C. BERGMANN, J. Warden.
W. E. NALLEY, Secretary.   GEO. W. BALLOCH, Treasurer.
GEORGE G. PEARSON, Past Master.

ARMINIUS LODGE, No. 25.

MORITZ GLAESER, Worshipful Master.
WILLIAM BERGER, S. Warden.   CHAS. GERSDORF, J. Warden.
H. H. GERDES, Secretary.   HENRY T. RIES, Treasurer.
WILLIAM F. MEYERS, Past Master.

OSIRIS LODGE, No. 26.

C. HOWARD BUCKLER, Worshipful Master.
WM. H. DE SHIELDS, S. Warden. M. D. BRAINARD, J. Warden.
HERBERT P. GERALD, Secretary. WM. H. BARSTOW, Treasurer.
FRANK A. HARRISON, Past Master.

MYRON M. PARKER LODGE, No. 27.

JOSEPH M. McCOY, Worshipful Master.
JOHN A. MOYER, S. Warden.   THOMAS B. CRISP, J. Warden.
ANDREW K. LIND, Secretary.   J. ELDRIGE BURNS, Treasurer.
THOMAS A. PERRY, Past Master.

KING DAVID LODGE, No. 28.

WILLIAM P. ARMSTRONG, Worshipful Master.
M. D. MULL, S. Warden.   GUY W. A. CAMP, J. Warden.
EBENEZER SOUTHALL, Secretary. JOHN B. LORD, Treasurer.
CHARLES E. BALDWIN, Past Master.

TAKOMA LODGE, No. 29.

H. M. BENNETT, Worshipful Master.
H. M. CAMP, S. Warden.   O. D. SUMMY, J. Warden.
JAMES K. DEPUE, Secretary.   C. M. HEATON, Treasurer.
HORACE J. LONG, Past Master.

APPENDIX.

APPENDIX

REPORT

ON

FOREIGN CORRESPONDENCE,

1898.

————·————

To the Grand Lodge, F. A. A. M., of the District of Columbia:

The Committee on Correspondence presents this report on the proceedings of the various Grand Lodges which have been received since the last report, up to the 1st of November, being the twenty-ninth of the present reviewer.

An index will be found at the close of the report.

WM. R. SINGLETON,

Chairman.

————————

ALABAMA.

The seventy-seventh annual communication was held in Montgomery December 7, 1897.

James A. Bilbro, M. W. Grand Master.

H. Clay Armstrong, R. W. Grand Secretary.

The address of the Grand Master, of twenty-two pages, contains under distinct sub-headings the result of his official actions during the year. He says:

" Desiring to know whether our subordinate lodges observe and practice certain virtues which are essential to true Masonic character, in April last I addressed a letter to each of them, asking to be informed specifically in regard thereto. About one-half of the lodges answered my inquiries; why the others did not I do not know. It may be that a sense of humiliation at their lack of duty and discipline as to the matters inquired about, kept them from doing so. A large majority of those heard from, I am pleased to state, have a membership who are Masons indeed. With them no communication is held at which proper reverence is not shown to God—their members are living in harmony and are ever watchful and prompt to respond to all calls of distress, and among them there are no cases of drunkenness or profanity. Other lodges, however, I regretfully say, are remiss in these matters. Several of them fail to open and close with prayer. Some are powerless for good because of dissension among the brethren, while a large number failed to enforce proper discipline in respect to the vices of profaning God's name and drunkenness.

"How it is, brethren, that a lodge can enter upon its business without invoking the aid of Deity I cannot understand. If God is not in Masonry then I have studied it in vain. Take Him out of it, or cease to honor Him in it, and it is scarcely more than sounding brass or tinkling cymbal. As to the evil of profanity and drunkenness, the unpublished edict of the Grand Lodge is clear and emphatic and should be rigidly enforced. If we expect Masonry to prosper in its mission it should be pure. We will certainly see it die whenever we allow its holy precepts to be trampled under foot. The best and purest of its members will leave it with a sigh that its First Grand Light is so grossly dishonored."

DECISIONS.

"(1) This Grand Lodge has no right to make any suggestions as to the qualifications for membership in the order or society known as the Eastern Star.

"(2) Where one applies for the degrees in Masonry in a foreign jurisdiction, and is rejected, and subsequently moves to this jurisdiction and becomes a bona fide resident citizen of this State, and after twelve months' residence in this State applies to one of our lodges to be made a Mason, it is the duty of such lodge before acting on the petition to correspond with the lodge by whom he was rejected to ascertain if there is any good and sufficient reason known to the lodge why he should not be made a Mason. The lodge of this jurisdiction failing to receive an answer to the inquiry within a reasonable length of time, or after hearing from the rejecting lodge, should proceed to dispose of the petition of the applicant as required by the Constitution of this Grand Lodge, and if applicant should be duly elected and thereafter made a Mason such making would be entirely legal.

"(4) A lodge in this State initiated, passed, and raised two persons who were rejected by a lodge of another jurisdiction about five years ago. Of such rejection the lodge conferring the degrees had no notice until some weeks after the work was done. The applicants did not know it was necessary for them to state in their petition the fact of their rejection. Held: The brethren were legally-made Masons.

"(5) Where a brother is suspended for non-payment of dues and is subsequently reinstated, the lodge does not owe the Grand Lodge dues during the time of such suspension.   -

"(6) Dues continue to accrue against one after his suspension for non-payment of dues."

Now, here is to our view an inconsistency, viz., in decision 8 the dues continue to be charged during suspension, but in decision 5, no tax to the Grand Lodge is to be paid, yet the lodge may get the dues of the suspended brother. Is it fair and reasonable that one who is deprived of his rights as a member should pay for what he does not get by his suspension? Should the Grand Lodge be deprived of *its* tax when the lodge receives the benefit of the suspension? The lodge would be financially benefited by a suspension of *all* its members.

"(20) A person who is crippled in his right leg and has to use a crutch is not thereby prevented from being made a Mason, if his infirmity does not render him incapable of practicing and teaching the ritual of the fraternity.
"(23) One who cannot read or write is not disqualified on that account from holding the office of Worshipful Master."

This latter decision must be peculiar to Alabama. We do not know of any other Grand Lodge having such a law.

"(29) An Entered Apprentice in good standing is entitled to a dismissal certificate for the purpose of joining another lodge which is nearer to his place of residence than the lodge in which he was initiated."

We consider this to be correct.

There were fifty-nine decisions, most of which were in strict accordance with Masonic law generally, and of his jurisdiction. Those copied above were to let our own brethren see what they do elsewhere.

He recommended the co-operation of that Grand Lodge in the centennial memorial service in honor of General Washington in 1899.

MASONIC BURIAL.

"Brother W. W. Daffin, of the Committee on Work, made report on Masonic burial, and the report was adopted, as follows:
"*To the M. W. Grand Lodge, A. F. and A. M., of Alabama:*
"We, the Committee on Work, to whom was referred the following resolution, offered by Bro. William G. Robertson at the last communication of this Grand Lodge, viz.:
"'*Resolved,* That the decision of the M. W. Grand Master on the burial service be so modified that in cases where it is reasonably impracticable and inconvenient to perform such service at the time of interment of a deceased brother, it may be done as soon thereafter as practicable; but that this resolution shall not warrant the willful or careless neglect of performing the service at the time of the burial.'
"Beg leave to report favorably, and recommend the adoption of the same."

Past Grand Master P. J. Pillans, chairman, furnished the report on correspondence, of 150 pages, in which he carefully reviews the proceedings of fifty-six Grand Lodges in his usual exhaustive manner, for the years 1896 and 1897. Two and one-half pages are devoted to our proceedings for 1896.

We are pleased, even delighted, to find that Bro. Pillans agrees with us in many important matters. To have so distinguished a writer on Masonic matters on our side is next to that quotation 'he who thinks his cause to be *just* is doubly armed," and we feel thrice armed when we get the support of able men in our contests for that which we consider "just, right, and true."

James A. Bilbro was re-elected M. W. Grand Master.

H. Clay Armstrong was re-elected R. W. Grand Secretary.

ARIZONA.

The sixteenth annual communication was held in Bisbee November 9, 1897.

William Francis Nichols, M. W. Grand Master.

George J. Roskruge, V. W. Grand Secretary.

Representatives of twelve chartered lodges.

The Grand Secretary is the Grand Representative of the Grand Lodge of the District of Columbia.

The annual address of the Grand Master occupies six pages, and recites the condition of the craft and his official acts during the past year.

He had made fourteen visitations to lodges, which had afforded much pleasure to him, and we are pretty sure they were of benefit to the brethren.

He had convened the Grand Lodge in special session at Nogales in March, and laid the corner-stone of the Masonic temple erected at that place by Nogales Lodge, No. 11, and he says: "To this lodge the credit must be given of having built the first Masonic temple within the jurisdiction." And on September 26 following, he had dedicated the hall in that temple to Masonic purposes.

He recommended that the Grand Lodge recognize the Gran Dieta Simbolica, of Mexico.

The reports of the other Grand Officers show a commendable progress in that young jurisdiction.

There is no report on correspondence.

Joseph Brawner Creamer was elected M. W. Grand Master.

George J. Roskruge was re-elected V. W. Grand Secretary.

ARKANSAS.

The fifty-eighth annual communication was held in Little Rock November 16, 1897.

C. C. Ayers, M. W. Grand Master.

Fay Hempstead, R. W. Grand Secretary.

The Grand Master presented his address, which fills twenty-one pages. Due and fraternal mention is made of the deceased brethren of his and sister jurisdictions.

Two dispensations only were issued to organize new lodges.

Twenty-one decisions made by him are reported, all of which accord with general Masonic usage or the laws of his jurisdiction, and we commend the Grand Master for the display of sound judgment and common sense in his reasoning on many of them.

Three corner-stones of public buildings were laid by himself or proxy.

The temple debt still hangs over them.

The report of the Grand Secretary is an able paper and gives a succinct account of the transactions of his office: receipts, $8,008.60; expenditures, $7,736.86.

The Grand Treasurer also made his report, showing a balance of $140.87.

An address was delivered by the Grand Orator, Bro. S. T. Rowe, on Freemasonry.

A very large amount of local business was transacted at this communication.

From reading the reports of the Committee on Grievances and Appeals we are more and more convinced that in the trials of charges against members of lodges the whole matter should be referred to a regularly-appointed commission, upon whose report the lodge should act, and abolish trials in the lodge itself, as in many of our Grand Lodges. How would it do if in State trials in civil or commercial cases the whole community should be summoned to assemble and listen to and decide upon the testimony and the law in each case?

The report on correspondence, of eighty pages, was prepared by Bro. A. B. Grace, reviewing all the proceedings forwarded to him. The District of Columbia receives a fraternal notice of two pages for 1896, in which the writer concurs in our action on the matter of physical perfection, and we quote his remarks, viz.:

"The writer has a profound respect and veneration for laws founded on reason, consecrated by age, and representing the accumulated wisdom and experience of generations. He is also fully aware of the danger he incurs of being attacked on all sides by those conservative 'Bourbons' who 'forget nothing and learn nothing;' who refuse to recognize the fact that the 'world do move.' Yet, in the face of all this, he ventures to assert that this 'perfect man' idea is being carried to a *reductio ad absurdum*. Common law is common sense, and there is a maxim of the common law to the effect that 'when the reason for a rule ceases, the rule itself ceases also.' There is a reason why a man who has lost an arm or a leg should not be made a Mason. But there is absolutely none why a man otherwise—that is, morally and intellectually—qualified should be denied admission into our ranks because he is 'shy' a little finger, a great toe, or even a pair of ears. Just as well to refuse him because he is bald-headed or suffers from insomnia or rheumatism. In neither case is he a perfect 'youth.' In fact, there never was but one perfect Man on earth. When 'perfect' comes to be understood to mean 'qualified to comply with all the requirements of Freemasonry' we shall enter upon an era of common sense and cease clinging to a shadow after the substance has departed."

*   *   *   *   *   *   *   *   *   *

"The report on foreign correspondence is by Bro. Singleton—his twenty-seventh—and is worthy of more extended notice than our limited time and space admit of here. Arkansas is not mentioned, but under the head of South Carolina, for 1895, he gives liberal extracts from the address of Grand Master Claude E. Sawyer, in which the position of the writer on the 'perfect man' is sustained in vigorous terms. But for the fact that the writer penned his own views before he read those of Brother Sawyer, he would feel subject to a charge of flagrant plagiarism."

J. B. Baker was elected M. W. Grand Master.

Fay Hempstead was re-elected R. W. Grand Secretary.

CALIFORNIA.

The forty-eighth annual communication was held in San Francisco October 16, 1897.

William Thomas Lucas, M. W. Grand Master.

George Johnson, V. W. Grand Secretary.

Two hundred and twenty-seven chartered lodges represented and delegates from six lodges under dispensation.

The address of the Grand Master was only eight pages in length.

He reports his official acts and special communications held for various purposes.

We find nothing of special interest in the address, as it is mostly confined to local matters.

The reports of the Grand Secretary and Grand Treasurer show a favorable condition of finances.

The report on correspondence was made by Past Grand Master William Abraham Davies and appears in its place in the proceedings.

Fifty-nine Grand Lodge proceedings were reviewed, in 128 pages, our own for 1896 receiving two and one-half pages of extracts and fraternal comments. Of our sickness, he says: "We sincerely hope the ruffian has released his 'grippe' on Bro. Singleton and our veteran brother is in the enjoyment of renewed health and strength."

Well! Yes, we are well; so much so that every morning when arising we get tight, or rather, our clothes are so much so that it is a tight squeeze to get into them.

We apologize for the brevity of this report on California. There is much that we could profitably copy and comment upon; indeed, *too much*, for if we began with it we would not find where conveniently to "bring up" we must, therefore, stop just here.

Thomas Flint, Jr., was elected M. W. Grand Master.

George Johnson was re-elected V. W. Grand Secretary.

CANADA.

The forty-second annual communication was held in the city of Brantford July 21, 1897.

William Gibson, M. W. Grand Master.

R. L. Gunn, R. W. Grand Secretary.

Special communications were held August 4 and 24 in 1896, and July 21, 1897, for ceremonial purposes.

At the annual communication Thomas Elliott, mayor of Brantford, delivered an address of welcome to the Grand Lodge, to which the Grand Master made a suitable response. After the opening of the Grand Lodge another address of welcome was presented by the officers of the two lodges in Brantford, to which the Grand Master made a suitable reply.

The Grand Master made his annual address, which occupies over eight pages. From this address we learn that there are on the register 357 lodges (the perfect numbers 3, 5, 7). It would, indeed, be marvelous if every one were in a flourishing state, and still more marvelous if in a membership of 24,000 every member was a model of what a Mason should be.

He is happy to call attention of members of Grand Lodge to their increasing prosperity.

The capital account has reached the sum of $94,202.17. During the past year the receipts of this Grand Lodge have reached the largest amount in its history, viz., $20,828.82, being an increase of $613.65 over last year. From lodges, $17,090.50; investments, $3,738.32; and expenditures, $17,613.03; and now we come to the Masonic part, that the expenditures for benevolence amounted to $9,887.50. This exceeds by far any other instance that we know of among all the Grand Lodges.

He very truly says: "No organization in connection with craftwork has done more good than the General Masonic Relief Association of the United States and Canada."

He had granted dispensations to form three new lodges.

He had made a very large number of grand visitations during the year.

The District Deputy Grand Masters, as usual, made their several reports, which are found in the body of the proceedings to occupy two hundred pages, giving an individual account of all the lodges.

The Board of Jurisprudence on the Maine proposition, viz., limiting the term for rejected candidates to five years, reported: "While they appreciated the effort of that Grand Lodge to obtain uniform legislation in relation to the admission of rejected candidates, they feel that it would at present be undesirable to amend our Constitution, which now provides that rejected candidates cannot be balloted for within twelve months." Such is the law in most Grand Lodges, but this does not touch the Maine question because it does not define whether it refers to rejected candidates in other jurisdictions than wherein the candidate was rejected.

The report on correspondence, of 196 pages, was presented by Past Grand Master Henry Robertson, reviewing the proceedings of fifty-eight Grand Lodges, in his usual exhaustive manner, although he says in his preface, "in order to economize space and to lessen the expense of publication, in accordance with our instructions, our comments will be few." Our own proceedings for 1896 have more than half a page, of which he uses a major part to quote from our report the remarks on those voting in Grand Lodges who, by courtesy and not by *Masonic* right, have membership in some Grand Lodges.

William Gibson was re-elected M. W. Grand Master.

J. J. Mason was elected R. W. Grand Secretary.

COLORADO.

The thirty-seventh annual communication was held in Denver September 21, 1897.

Cromwell Tucker, D. G. M., as M. W. Grand Master.

Edward C. Parmalee, R. W. Grand Secretary.

Eighty-nine chartered lodges; all but two represented.

The acting Grand Master announced that M. W. Grand Master George W. Roe had been very ill since July 27, and while he was now able to sit up, he was not able to be with them.

The first business was to appoint a committee to send a message of sympathy to the Grand Master, which was done and a response secured.

Bro. Wm. D. Wright, our Grand Representative, was present.

The address of the Grand Master was read by Past Grand Master J. H. Peabody, and occupies over eighteen pages.

The condition of the craft he reports to be in a fair state of prosperity; he believes the growth in membership in the past year has exceeded that of the former, with an increase of 170 members.

He reports having issued an edict, in conjunction with the Grand High Priest and the Grand Commander of that jurisdiction, forbidding the use of "keys."

Having been asked "Can we affiliate a brother who has taken the degrees in Masonry in a Scottish Rite Lodge in Mexico," he responded:

"In the first place, we have not been asked officially to recognize that grand jurisdiction, and, of course, until we are, it would seem premature to force recognition upon them. Again, I believe in the theory that if we have a bad law or no law at all, to enforce the law as we find it, to the end that the bad law may be amended or abolished, or a statute formulated to suit the occasion. There is no question in my mind but that the Scottish Rite Masonry is the lawfully-constituted authority in Mexico, and that their action is entirely legitimate; yet, until such time as reciprocal relations are clearly established between that grand jurisdiction and ourselves, I most certainly think that we should withhold Masonic intercourse of every nature, and, therefore feel justified in making the following decision: No lodge shall affiliate or admit as a visitor, a Mason hailing from and made in any lodge chartered by the Gran Dieta of Mexico."

He decided that a candidate who had lost the third finger of his right hand, could be eligible to receive the degrees of Masonry.

An oration was delivered in Grand Lodge by Grand Orator Jasper W. Johnson on the "Antiquity of Masonry."

The Grand Lodge by unanimous vote annulled the charter of a lodge which upon the trial of a brother had almost unani-

mously acquitted him when it was proven that he had been expelled by a lodge in Iowa, of which expulsion he was fully informed, and after which he had petitioned a lodge in Colorado for
affiliation, then petitioned for affiliation in a lodge in New York,
and for the third time petitioned another lodge in Colorado.

Another charter of a lodge was arrested by order of the Grand
Master for the acquittal of a member after trial, wherein it was
clearly proven that he was guilty of gross un-Masonic conduct.
The act of the Grand Master was approved by unanimous vote.

The Committee on the Centennial Memorial Services in commemoration of the burial of Bro. George Washington made their
report, and show that they have received favorable responses to
the invitation sent out from that Grand Lodge to unite together
as Grand Lodges to commemorate the centennial anniversary of
that event in memorial exercises December 14, 1899, and that the
Grand Lodge of Virginia be requested to take charge and formulate
plans for the proper observance of that occasion. The following
letter had been secured from Virginia:

"ALEXANDRIA, VA., *August 30*, 1897.
" DEAR SIR AND BROTHER: Acknowledging the receipt of your
valued letters, with accompanying papers, concerning the proposed memorial exercises in 1899 in honor of Bro. George Washington, and suggesting that the Grand Lodge of Virginia should
assume leadership in the contemplated exercises, I have to make
answer that I seized the first opportunity presenting itself to
confer personally with the M. W. Grand Master of the Grand
Lodge of Virginia, and as the result of that conference I am authorized to accept, for the present committee of our Grand Lodge,
the primacy in this interesting matter, so gracefully tendered by
the Grand Lodge of Colorado, and to say that a full report of the
proposition will be made to our Grand Lodge at its annual communication in December next, at which time, I have no doubt,
a committee will be appointed to take charge of the matter, who
will in due time formulate a programme and take all other steps
needful to carry to a successful completion these exercises, nat-
urally so full of interest to all Americans, especially to ' the Household of the Faithful.' This committee, when appointed, will, I
am sure, gladly avail themselves of your kind offers of assistance.
Reciprocating your kind expressions, I am,
" Yours fraternally,
"K. KEMPER,
"Committee of the Grand Lodge of Virginia."

That jurisdiction has a brother who had passed his centennial birthday seven months before and a committee was appointed to visit him, whose name is Adna A. Treat. To speak
this in Scotch would sound *uncomplimentary*, but I presume it was
really two of them, one to be *found* and the other was to *find* him.

Bro. Greenleaf, one of the committee, verbally reported that about twenty brethren had called upon the venerable brother and tendered him the good wishes and fraternal regards of the Grand Lodge, and that Bro. Treat wished him to convey to the Grand Lodge his deep appreciation of the honor conferred on him for the kindly remembrance on the part of the Grand Lodge.

Two charters were granted to lodges working under dispensations.

Bro. Lawrence Greenleaf presented the report on correspondence, of 157 pages, reviewing the proceedings of fifty-nine Grand Lodges, four pages being devoted to a fraternal notice of our own for 1896, and we thank him for his complimentary reference to our review.

During the meeting in this city last October of the Supreme Council, A. A. S. R., we were very much delighted to meet the Grand Secretary, Bro. Ed. C. Parmalee, and regretted very much that he did not remain longer with us.

Cromwell Tucker was elected M. W. Grand Master.

Edward C. Parmalee was re-elected R. W. Grand Secretary.

CONNECTICUT.

The one hundred and tenth annual communication was held in Hartford January 19, 20, 1898.

George A. Kies, M. W. Grand Master.

John H. Barlow, R. W. Grand Secretary.

M. W. Clarke Buckingham, Grand Representative of the Grand Lodge of the District of Columbia.

The M. W. Grand Master delivered his address, of eighteen pages, which was followed by the reports of the Deputy Grand Master, Grand Treasurer, Grand Secretary, and Grand Trustees.

Reference, in suitable terms of respect, was made by the Grand Master to the brethren who had died during the year.

He had made many official visitations, all of which are specially noted.

Grand Representatives had been nominated by him, and others had been commissioned by him.

Special dispensations to several lodges had been granted for various lodge purposes, and he had been constrained to deny many applications for dispensations.

A few decisions are reported. One, that "non-affiliated Masons are not entitled to burial with Masonic honors." The reports of the other Grand Officers show a very prosperous condition of the craft in that jurisdiction.

The Grand Treasurer reports: balance, June 21, 1897, $7,287.09; received since, $12,441.87; total, $19,738.96.

The report of the Grand Secretary in regard to the Grand Lodge of Peru was reported to the Committee on Jurisprudence, who reported the following, which was adopted:

"*Resolved*, That this Grand Lodge suspends Masonic intercourse with the Grand Lodge of Peru and requires the same of all lodges and Masons in this jurisdiction during the continuance of said edict."

The report on correspondence, of 163 pages, was presented by Bro. Grand Secretary John H. Barlow, in review of the proceedings of sixty-one Grand Lodges, domestic and foreign. One page and a half is devoted to a review of our own for 1896 in a very fraternal spirit, and we are glad that he finds no opportunity for criticism.

Frank W. Havens was elected M. W. Grand Master.

John H. Barlow was re-elected R. W. Grand Secretary.

DELAWARE.

The ninety-first annual communication was held in Wilmington October 7, 1897.

Two special communications were held, viz., October 27, 1896, to lay corner-stone of a church, and September 16, 1897, also to lay the corner-stone of a church.

At the annual communication, October 6, 7, 1897, were present:

J. Paul Leekens, M. W. Grand Master.

Benjamin F. Bartram, R. W. Grand Secretary.

Bro. Eugene Massey, Grand Representative of the Grand Lodge of the District of Columbia.

The Grand Master delivered his annual address, which fills twelve pages, devoted entirely to local matters.

The financial officers rendered their reports, and the condition of their finances appears to be good.

The transactions of the Grand Lodge were local in character.

Brother L. H. Jackson presented the report on correspondence, of eighty pages, embracing forty-nine American, six British

American, two European, and four English colonial Grand Lodges, with several papers on Mexican Masonry, sixty-two in all. Our own for 1896 received a fraternal notice of less than a page.

The proceedings of Delaware always reach us after our report has been made to our Grand Lodge, viz., second Wednesday of November in each year. The proceedings of 1896 were reviewed in our report for 1897. The present copy for 1897 now under review reached us November 23, 1897.

Of Mexico, he says:

"We have received several pamphlets on Masonry in Mexico, with a lot of other literature upon the subject, which we have carefully read, but this writer must still hesitate to encourage the thought of recognition. The difficulties in the way are too great, and it is hard to see how they can be overcome unless some method of regeneration is devised."

  *   *   *   *   *   *   *   *   *   *

"All the lodges now existing in Mexico are derived from the Supreme Council of the Ancient and Accepted Scottish Rite, and should not be recognized as a lawful basis for a legitimate Grand Lodge."

We are sorry to hear that from you, my brother. Now, what will you do with the Grand Lodge of Cuba, which we find in your list, 102, with your Grand Secretary as your Grand Representative? Nearly every lodge in the Grand Lodge of Cuba, if not every one, was derived from the Supreme Council, A. A. S. R. No. It has been well settled by our very best Masonic authorities that the symbolic degrees of the A. A. S. R. are legitimate bodies.

James E. Dutton was elected M. W. Grand Master.

Benjamin F. Bartram was re-elected R. W. Grand Secretary.

FLORIDA.

The sixty-ninth annual communication was held in Jacksonville January 18-20, 1898.

James M. Hilliard, M. W. Grand Master.

Wilber P. Webster, R. W. Grand Secretary.

Past Grand Master Wm. E. Anderson, Grand Representative of the Grand Lodge of District of Columbia.

Twenty-one pages are filled with the annual address of the Grand Master. He pays suitable memorial tributes to the distinguished brethren who had died during the year. He had

granted dispensations to organize two new lodges and a very large
number of special dispensations to various lodges for miscella-
neous purposes.

In his report of " decisions " we find the same old question coming up as to when the " dimit " of a member is effectual, and his
answer very properly is: " The action of the lodge is the dimit,
and the document itself is simply a certificate showing the action
of the lodge."

Eleven questions were answered by him, all in accordance with
Masonic law and the rules of his jurisdiction.

He had laid the corner-stone of a new Masonic temple in the
city of Pensacola.

He had made many official visits to the lodges during the year
and conferred the degrees in many of them.

The reports of the several Grand Officers give encouraging accounts of the prosperity of the craft.

Four lodges had charters issued to them.

Bro. R. H. Weller, Grand Orator, delivered the annual address.

We regret the absence of a report on correspondence.

James M. Hilliard was re-elected M. W. Grand Master.

Wilber P. Webster was re-elected R. W. Grand Secretary.

GEORGIA.

The one hundred and eleventh annual communication was held
in Macon October 26, 1897.

The Grand Lodge was opened with a characteristic prayer
offered by the Grand Chaplain, Rev. and Worshipful Robert W.
Hubert.

James W. Taylor, M. W. Grand Master.

William A. Wolihin, R. W. Grand Secretary.

We notice that the several lodges were represented by the Worshipful Masters and proxies. There were no wardens present.

The Grand Lodge of the District of Columbia was represented
by Grand Representative Charles E. Damour.

The Grand Master read his annual address, of sixteen pages.

He refers to the death of the Grand Secretary, Bro. Andrew M.
Wolihin, of whom he says:

"Among those who have left their imprint upon the cause in
our jurisdiction, whose face we now miss, whose voice is stilled in
death, whose friendly grasp we will never again feel this side of

the home of the good, whose body lies buried in the silent city of the dead, whose words of welcome and encouragement we will never hear in this hall, whose great and noble heart prompted the fertile brain to conceive plans for our good and the benefit of the craft is Andrew M. Wolihin, Grand Secretary of the Grand Lodge of Georgia."

Thirteen decisions are reported.

He decided that a lodge in Georgia cannot waive jurisdiction to a lodge in Mexico. The Grand Lodge of Georgia does not recognize the Grand Lodge of Mexico. We presume he referred to the *Gran Dieta;* there is no Grand Lodge of Mexico.

All the decisions are according to general Masonic law and usage.

Six new lodges had been constituted by proxies duly appointed by him.

Twelve corner-stones of public buildings had been laid; seven had been laid by proxies for him and five by himself.

Three dispensations for new lodges had been issued.

Prosperity has, at last, reached Georgia.

"The development of our grand old State is very rapid. Waste places are being built up, new industries being introduced, towns and villages springing up in sections which only a few years ago were but a wilderness. Many of the inhabitants being Masons from other jurisdictions and being desirous of enjoying the social and fraternal privileges peculiar to Masonic organizations render it very necessary that in the near future many new lodges be organized within our limit, and the old ship of Masonry continue on her voyage on the ocean of prosperity, dispensing charity and brotherly love to the inhabitants of earth."

He had utilized his time in visiting lodges which he thought needed help and encouragement, and found everywhere a great desire for more light, and had endeavored to inform the brethren to the best of his ability.

The report on correspondence, of ninety pages, was furnished by Bro. W. S. Ramsay, chairman, reviewing nearly all of the American and a few foreign Grand Lodges. We find nearly two pages devoted to our proceedings for 1896, with complimentary reference to our report, for which we tender our sincere and grateful thanks.

In reference to Mexican, so-called, Masonry, we are yet seeking more light, dear brother.

James W. Taylor was re-elected M. W. Grand Master.

William A. Wolihin was re-elected R. W. Grand Secretary.

IDAHO.

The thirtieth annual communication was held in Boise September 14, 1897.

Fred. G. Mock, M. W. Grand Master.

Charles C. Stevenson, R. W. Grand Secretary.

Bro. George Ainslee, P. G. M., Grand Representative of the Grand Lodge of the District of Columbia.

Twelve pages occupied with the address of the Grand Master. Notice is taken of the deceased brethren of the past year.

One lodge was consecrated and dedicated, and a new temple was dedicated.

Ten decisions were reported, all in accordance with general usage. During the year he had made an official visitation to every lodge in the jurisdiction. (Well done, thou good and faithful servant, we trust thou shall enter into the joy of thy Lord.) As we have no doubt from his remarks, it was a joy to himself in these several visitations.

A very excellent report was made by the Grand Secretary.

The R. W. Grand Secretary of the Grand Lodge of Utah, Bro. Christopher Diehl, being present, was formally introduced and received with the grand honors of Masonry.

The Grand Secretary, Bro. Charles C. Stevenson, presented the report on correspondence, of eighty pages, reviewing for the tenth time the proceedings of the various Grand Lodges. The District of Columbia is indebted for one page and a half of fraternal notice, and special mention of this writer, and we thank him for his sympathies in our recent affliction, and say that we are now all right and have been for several months.

George M. Waterhouse was elected W. M. Grand Master.

Charles C. Stevenson was re-elected R. W. Grand Secretary.

NOTE.—Since writing the above we have had official notice of the death of the Grand Secretary and the appointment of his successor.

KANSAS.

The forty-second annual communication was held in Wichita February 16, 17, 1898.

Wm. M. Shaver, M. W. Grand Master.

Albert K. Wilson, R. W. Grand Secretary.

The Grand Master's address, of twenty-six pages, is a complete statement of the affairs of the grand jurisdiction and a report of his official acts.

Two lodges chartered at the preceding communication had been duly constituted by his duly commissioned deputies.

Four lodges had been working under letters of dispensation during the year and their petitions for charters would come before the Grand Lodge.

Thirteen decisions are reported, but the first three are not published.

The reports of the other Grand Officers indicate progress and prosperity in that jurisdiction.

There was an address delivered by the Grand Orator upon the "Fundamentals of Freemasonry."

The report on correspondence, of 132 pages, was presented by Bro. John C. Postlethwaite.

Our proceedings for 1896 received a fair review of two pages, with very complimentary notice of our own report, for which we have sent our thanks.

Maurice L. Stone was elected M. W. Grand Master.

Albert K. Wilson was re-elected R. W. Grand Secretary.

KENTUCKY.

The ninety-eighth annual communication was held in Louisville October 19-21, 1897.

Robert Francis Peak, M. W. Grand Master.

Henry Bannister Grant, R. W. Grand Secretary.

The Grand Master's address is not as long as usual for so large a jurisdiction, six pages only containing all he has to report of his official actions, &c.

He is gratified to announce that Masonry in that jurisdiction has prospered, notwithstanding the hard pressure in the business world.

He deemed eight decisions of sufficient importance to report them to Grand Lodge, all of which are in accordance with Masonic law and usage.

He had granted four dispensations to form new lodges.

The reports of the Grand Secretary and Grand Treasurer show a good financial condition.

Balance, last year, $8,142.32; received since, $11,866.85; total, $20,009.17; disbursements, $10,117.27; cash on hand, 1897, $9,891.90.

Charters for nine new lodges were granted.

One dispensation was continued and two dispensations were to be issued for new lodges. Four new charters to be granted to lodges whose charters had been destroyed by fire.

Past Grand Master Frederick Speed, of the Grand Lodge of Mississippi, was present and was received with the grand honors, and addressed the Grand Lodge as follows:

"MOST WORSHIPFUL SIR AND BRETHREN: While I am conscious that your very kind reception is not due to any merit of my own, but is rather to be taken as a welcome home from the mother to the daughter, in the name of that child of Kentucky, I thank you with equal heartiness, and beg to assure you that she traces her lineage with the utmost pride and satisfaction. In the sunrise of the century, when the Anglo-Saxon civilization was beginning to crowd back the Latins and to plant on the shores of the great Father of Waters the never-dying spirit of liberty, which characterizes and makes us one people from the Aroostock to the Rio Grande, ere the lilies of La Belle France had been replaced by the 'flag of the free hearts, hope and home,' Kentucky lighted the fire upon a Masonic altar at Natchez, and it is my proud privilege to say to you to-day that it has never ceased to burn there with effulgent splendor, and we trust has reflected credit and honor to the source from which that fire came. But as Kentucky gave much to Mississippi, she gave much in return when she made a Mason of dear Robert Morris, and sent him back to the loving arms of Kentucky, and I am sure that I cannot win a way closer to your hearts than to say that I am the privileged custodian of his petition for initiation in a Mississippi lodge. All hail to the stately matron whom we are so proud to call by the endearing term of mother, is the message which I bring from every Masonic heart in Mississippi. God guide the Grand Lodge of Kentucky, first in every good work, and preserve her unto the latest generations."

Past Grand Master W. W. Clark prepared the report on correspondence, of 104 pages, reviewing the proceedings of fifty-one Grand Lodges, our own for 1896 receiving a fraternal notice of three pages.

Commenting upon the action of our Grand Lodge in the matter of a member dropped for non-payment of dues and who has been rejected for reinstatement, he says:

"From the foregoing it appears that the rejection of the petition for reinstatement in the first place makes the petitioner a non-affiliate, and thereby increases the difficulty of his regaining membership in the lodge of which he was a member, and in the second place, obliges the lodge that refused him membership to issue to him a certificate on which he may gain membership in another lodge—a certificate of character to one to whom it will not grant membership."

What sort of certificate is it? Wherein does the *character* consist? It says "that he has paid all indebtedness to the lodge and has ceased to be a member thereof." This is the usual, nay the universal form of a certificate of a regular "dimission" from a lodge, which also recommends the dismissed brother to the favorable consideration of the craft wherever he may sojourn. Why have not your criticisms, dear brother, been launched against the great ship, "New York," which has the same law and very same certificate, which we have simply copied. Moreover, our rule gives the brother applicant a fair chance of re-instatement, as it requires a majority vote on his application instead of a single black ball, and if he cannot get in under such favorable circumstances on the first trial we scarcely think any one would attempt it the second time. The object of the law and the certificate is to allow such an one a good opportunity to go to some other lodge if it be possible to gain admittance therein.

Reginald H. Thompson was elected M. W. Grand Master.

H. B. Grant was re-elected R. W. Grand Secretary.

LOUISIANA.

The eighty-sixth annual communication was held in New Orleans February 14, 1898.

Albert G. Brice, M. W. Grand Master.

Richard Lambert, R. W. Grand Secretary.

Past Grand Master Samuel M. Todd, Grand Representative of the Grand Lodge of the District of Columbia.

The address of the Grand Master occupies thirty-three pages and is a report of his official actions and the conditions of the craft during the year.

In view of the general depressed condition of the business affairs of the country and diseases which become pestilential we record from this address that the losses exceeded the additions by only five.

Announcement of the death of Past Grand Master J. Q. A. Fellows, which occurred November 28, 1897, in the seventy-third year of his age, and forty-eighth of his Masonic life.

This lengthy address, while almost entirely local in its character, is yet a fine State paper and worthy of perusal, and we have been much gratified in its consideration. The various topics are well handled and his conclusions and decisions well matured and concisely stated. The reports of the Grand Secretary and Grand Treasurer show a fair condition in membership and finances.

There is no report on correspondence, which we regret.

A. C. Allen was elected M. W. Graud Master.

Richard Lambert was re-elected R. W. Grand Secretary.

MARYLAND.

The two hundred and twenty-first stated communication, which was the semi-annual, was held in Baltimore, May 11, 1997.

Thomas J. Shryock, M. W. Grand Master.

Jacob H. Medairy, R. W. Grand Secretary.

The M. W. Grand Master congratulated the Grand Lodge on the prosperous condition of the lodges in Maryland, and so far as he could learn the prospect was most encouraging to the craft, as the zeal and interest manifested by the members was unabated. He regretted to announce the death of brother Sylvester L. Stockbridge, P. D. G. M., P. D. G. H. P., on the morning of February 11, 1897.

The current business was transacted.

A charter was granted to Kensington Lodge, Montgomery County, to be numbered 198.

This lodge is located at Kensington near the northeast boundary line of the District of Columbia, and is easily reached by the street railways of our city of Washington, and we are pleased to learn is quite a success. In that immediate vicinity there are three other lodges of very recent organization, which demonstrates the spread of Masonry in the vicinity of Washington City, Stansbury Lodge, No. 24, of our jurisdiction, having initiated the movement in 1873, followed by Chillum Castle Lodge, in Maryland, and Takoma Lodge, No. 29, of the District of Columbia.

Past Grand Master John M. Carter, for the Grand Lodge, presented to Bro. William H. Shryock, P. G. T., a very handsome memento of the sincere regard and affection of the Grand Lodge in an appropriate Past Grand Treasurer's jewel, to which Bro. Shryock made a suitable response.

The one hundred and eleventh annual communication was held November 16.

The same Grand Officers presiding and Bro. Henry C. Larrabee the Grand Representative of the Grand Lodge of the District of Columbia.

The Grand Master delivered his address. He refers to the Grand Convocation of the General Grand Chapter of the United States which convened in Baltimore in September, 1897, and we heartily concur in what he says of them:

"I refer to the General Grand Chapter of Royal Arch Masons of the United States, a body of representative men, not only in Masonic, but in all the walks of life, and indeed it was a most agreeable pleasure on behalf of the Masons of Maryland to entertain them as well as it lay in our power to do. The committee appointed by the Grand Lodge performed their duty well and did everything to uphold and maintain the reputation of this grand body. They acted in harmony with the committees of the other grand bodies, and I have, as your representative, received many letters of thanks from distinguished men all over the country, thanking the Grand Lodge and the brethren for the courtesies extended to them."

In justice to Grand Master Shryock we quote his remarks on the matter of making a Mason at sight.

"By virtue of the authority in me vested as your Grand Master I convened an emergency lodge, and made 'at sight,' his excellency, Lloyd Lowndes, governor of Maryland, a Mason. An erroneous idea has arisen in the minds of many of the fraternity as to the ceremony of making a Mason 'at sight,' and to erase the wrong and perhaps damaging impression I deem it but proper to say that, in the making of a Mason 'at sight' by the Grand Master the candidate is required to pass through all the forms and ceremonies incident to conferring of the three degrees, in the same manner that an applicant does in applying to a subordinate lodge. The impression of some, that the Grand Master, by virtue of his authority, touches a man on the shoulder and creates him a Mason is entirely erroneous, and as I know this impression does exist to a certain extent, I think it proper to here state, so that the craft may understand it throughout our jurisdiction, that such is not the case. The making of a Mason at sight is one of the landmarks of the fraternity, the prerogative of the Grand Master, and I have on two occasions exercised that prerogative, as much for the purpose of not allowing it to become dormant as for any other reason."

We regret very much the necessity for the following:

"One of the saddest duties of my long term of office is to read to you a communication from Bro. Edward T. Schultz, who for so many years acted as chairman of the Committee on Correspondence. I can assure you when I read it my heart went out in sympathy to our well-beloved brother, and feel satisfied yours will also. He has been sorely afflicted by the Great Giver of all Good for some wise and unforseen reason which is incomprehensible to us, but I have no doubt that you, with me, indulge the hope that it will not be as serious as our brother indicates his belief it will be. Brother Schultz has been one of the most untiring, unselfish, and devoted workers in this Grand Lodge for many years back; indeed, before many of us had seen the light of Freemasonry, and his record will live in the annals of this Grand Lodge as long as memory lasts. When all of us present have passed the Jordan of death and others have taken our place in the ranks, the name of

Schultz will still be upheld in remembrance; aye, in reverence, by those who come after us.

"I recommend that a suitable resolution be passed by the Grand Lodge of sympathy for our sorely-afflicted brother."

The letter follows:

"BALTIMORE, *November* 13, 1897.
"MOST WORSHIPFUL THOMAS J. SHRYOCK,
    "*Grand Master of Masons of Maryland.*

"M. W. SIR AND BROTHER: As chairman of the Committee of Correspondence I beg to report:

"About the time I should have commenced the preparation of my review of the proceedings of other Grand Lodges with which we are in fraternal correspondence my eyesight failed to such an extent that I was unable to read, and I was prevented from preparing and printing the usual report of correspondence for distribution at the coming communication of our Grand Lodge.

"The hope was indulged that my sight would sufficiently improve to enable me to prepare, with the aid of a stenographer, something in the nature of a brief report for the occasion, but my general health has declined to such an extent, with my loss of vision, that it has been quite impossible for me to do so. I am still encouraged to hope for an improvement in my condition, which now amounts to almost total blindness, but there is no reasonable probability of my regaining sufficient vision to enable me to examine the proceedings of other Grand Lodges and report upon them as heretofore.

"With great reluctance, therefore, I am compelled to ask to be relieved from the post which has been most agreeable to me, and which I trust I have succeeded in filling to the satisfaction of the brethren.

"I am loath to relinquish the duties which have afforded me so much pleasure without a parting word to the brethren at home and correspondents elsewhere, and with your kind permission I would be much gratified to prepare, with the aid of a stenographer, a brief paper in the nature of personal reminiscences, reports, and reporters of Masonic correspondence for publication with the proceedings of the coming annual communication.

"I beg to acknowledge most gratefully the unvarying courtesy and kindness I have enjoyed at the hands of yourself and the brethren of the Grand Lodge, and also of the whole corps of reporters with whom I have had such pleasant relations.
            "Fraternally,
                    "EDWARD T. SCHULTZ."

The committee on Grand Master's address made suitable reference to the above and extended their sympathy to Bro. Schultz.

The Grand Secretary notified Bro. Schultz that the printer was ready for his promised paper, and Bro. Schultz responded that he had been unable to comply with his promise, owing to continued ill health. We very much regret the failure of the brother to let us hear from him, as it would be most gratifying to have from him such reminiscences as we feel well assured he could prepare for publication, and we close this notice of him with our most sincere condolence and sympathy for his great affliction.

Thomas J. Shryock was re-elected M. W. Grand Master.

Jacob H. Medairy was re-elected R. W. Grand Secretary.

MICHIGAN.

The fifty-fourth annual communication was held in the city of Grand Rapids January 25, 1898.

Lou B. Winson, M. W. Grand Master.

Jefferson S. Conover, R. W. Grand Secretary.

John J. Carton, P. G. M., Grand Representative of the Grand Lodge of the District of Columbia.

Seventy-two pages contain the annual address of the Grand Master, who very carefully and succinctly gives an account of his official acts, and a statement of the condition of the craft in his jurisdiction. After his introduction he mentions in suitable terms the deaths of distinguished brethren at home and abroad. This is the longest address we remember to have had the pleasure of reviewing.

Five new lodges chartered at the last Grand Lodge he had constituted, either in person or by proxies duly appointed.

Three new lodges had been granted dispensations to organize.

As an evidence of the substantial prosperity of the institution of Masonry in that grand jurisdiction during the past year, nineteen new, beautiful, and magnificent halls and temples had been dedicated to Masonic uses, eight of them owned by the fraternity and devoted solely to the uses of Masonry.

Three corner-stones of public buildings had been laid with Masonic ceremonies.

He had had propounded to him during the year 372 questions on Masonic law. Law, me !! What a questionable membership ! And he found it necessary out of this entire number to report less than thirty for the consideration of the Grand Lodge, and that is a *considerable* number. He is exercised as to the best mode of educating the Worshipful Masters up to a proper standard in Masonic jurisprudence, and suggests that the Grand Lecturers set apart a portion of the time for an examination of the Worshipful Masters by a catechism on Masonic law. Well, according to our experience, the Grand Lecturers are illy qualified for this task.

Memory, memory is the special function of a Grand Lecturer, and those who possess the best memories are the worst interpreters of law of any kind.

Fifteen pages are filled with his decisions on twenty-five questions. We have carefully read all of these decisions and find they are all in accordance with general Masonic usage exept a few, and they are according to the statutes of that jurisdiction, so decided by the Grand Master.

A very lengthy, but interesting and instructive, report was made by the Grand Secretary, prefaced by a very excellent picture of the brother, who appears to be looking for the "go-it" referred to in his report on correspondence, page 42, the same which rhymes with "poet," q. v.

Bro. Grand Secretary Jefferson S. Conover furnished the report on correspondence, which is extended "promiscuous like" over 302 pages, and he treats the District of Columbia to over three of these, with fraternal notice and many extracts, and copies our "poortry," and adds thereto:

> "That's very true and we both know it,
> And my crude verses plainly show it."

"*Verbum Sap.*"

James Bradley was elected M. W. Grand Master.

Jefferson S. Conover was re-elected R. W. Grand Secretary.

MINNESOTA.

The forty-fifth annual communication was held in St. Paul January 12, 1898.

James F. Lawless, M. W. Grand Master.

Thomas Montgomery, R. W. Grand Secretary.

Bro. James G. Markham, Grand Representative of the Grand Lodge of the District of Columbia.

The Grand Master's address fills eighteen pages.

Four lodges had been constituted.

He was able to answer all questions propounded to him during the year by referring the questioners to the Digest, with one exception only, which was that a Mason who resided out of their jurisdiction, having been expelled, but subsequently restored to all his rights as a Mason, could be elected to membership upon the ground that a Mason had the right to select his own Masonic home. In violation of this rule, one at least, of our Grand Lodges requires a member of a lodge to be a resident of its jurisdiction ! ! !

He refers to the deaths of distinguished brethren of sister Grand Lodges, and makes special mention of those of his own jurisdiction who had died during the year.

The Grand Secretary submitted his report, which is his ninth, and which is a thorough statement of all the transactions of his office during the year.

Returns had been received from all the lodges. Gains have been 1,069; losses, 859; net gain, 210; total membership, 15,691.

The Grand Treasurer's report shows: on hand, 1897, $11,863.13; received since, $8,128.75; total, $19,991.88; total paid out, $7,987.97; cash on hand, $12,003.91.

The following was adopted:

" *Resolved*, That it shall be deemed un-Masonic for any Mason within this jurisdiction to hereafter become a member of any insurance company having or using Masonic insignia, or the term Masonic, or referring to the Masonic fraternity in its title, or using illustrations or representations of Masonic emblems on its business cards, circulars, or correspondence, and it shall be deemed un-Masonic for any Mason to hereafter solicit any person in this jurisdiction to become a member or beneficiary in any such organization using title or emblems indicated; *provided*, that this resolution shall not take effect until March 31, 1899."

Here comes in a question: Who is to reimburse all those Masons who are now beneficiaries or members and have hitherto paid large sums for benefits should they withdraw from such companies? The *hereafter* inserted in the beginning of this resolution separates the Masons in that jurisdiction into two classes; is that correct?

We have always objected to the word "Masonic" in these insurance companies unless they were strictly Masonic in their organization and regulations, viz.; every Mason being a member of some lodge in good standing, however old or whatever may be his condition physically, &c., and added to this, every member of a lodge should be required to become a member of such insurance company.

This at once brings it back to the plan of the Independent Order of Odd Fellows of fifty years ago. After many years the "widows' dollar" plan, *i. e.*, each individual member being responsible for the dollar, we believe, was changed, and the lodge became responsible for the dollar of each member.

The Grand Lodge adopted the following:

"*Resolved*, That all Masonic intercourse between this Grand Lodge and the lodges and Masons of its obedience and the Grand

Lodge of Peru, and any man or body of men claiming or professing to be Freemasons acknowledging any allegiance to said Grand Lodge of Peru is hereby prohibted."

A very excellent address was delivered by the Grand Orator, Bro. Robert C. Hine, upon Masonry, in which several anecdotes are related illustrating the value of Masonry, particularly to those who may be travellers in strange countries and among strangers.

The report on correspondence is by Bro. Irving Todd, P. G. M , for the committee. Ninety-six pages are occupied with his review. Of these our own proceedings for 1896 have one page, *and we repeat* about as much as we are entitled to. Thanks.

Alonzo T. Stebbins was elected M. W. Grand Master.

Thomas Montgomery was re-elected R. W. Grand Secretary.

MISSISSIPPI.

The eighteenth annual communication was held at Water Valley February 10, 1898.

John S. Cobb, M. W. Grand Master.

John L. Power, R. W. Grand Secretary.

Fred. Speed, P. G. M., Grand Representative of the Grand Lodge of the District of Columbia.

Two hundred and thirty-eight lodges were represented.

The Grand Master's address occupies thirteen pages, and gives a succinct account of his official acts and the condition of Masonry in that jurisdiction.

Under dispensations, he had granted nine for various lodge purposes and refused to grant thirteen.

Under decisions, quite a number had been rendered but not necessary to enumerate most of them. Several are reported, which are in accordance with general Masonic law.

Five charters had been signed for new lodges.

He had issued dispensations to form six new lodges.

He refers to the Peru Grand Lodge matter and recommended that all fraternal relations with said "so-called Grand Lodge of Peru" be declared at an end. (The Grand Lodge adopted a resolution to that effect.) Three corner-stones had been laid. He had visited officially but few lodges.

Under "Grand Secretary's Salary," he says:

"It will be remembered that at the communication of Grand Lodge in Holly Springs in 1894, our Grand Secretary submitted his twenty-fifth annual report. Such a record as he had made prompted the surviving Past Grand Masters to propose that he be created an 'honorary Past Grand Master of the Grand Lodge of Mississippi.' This was approved by a unanimous rising vote, and many of our sister grand jurisdictions said that the Grand Lodge of Mississippi had done a most unusual but most proper thing."

It is very true that it has been very unusual in the Grand Lodges in the United States, but has frequently occurred in Europe. If we remember correctly, when the Grand Lodge of England learned that Prince Albert Edward had been made a Mason in Sweden, they at once elected him Past Grand Master.

We do not remember all the instances of such action by several Grand Lodges, but we feel sure that such action is justifiable when the recipient has by a long series of years devoted his whole time and services for the benefit of Masonry, as in the case of Bro. Power.

The report of the Grand Secretary shows increased prosperity. There were initiated in the past year, 539; raised, 484; affiliated, 297; reinstated, 178; dimitted, 307; died, 240.

The Grand Treasurer's report shows a good financial condition.

Nine charters were granted to constitute new lodges.

Bro. Past Grand Master A. H. Barkley again presents the report on correspondence, of 108 pages, our own Grand Lodge proceedings for 1896 receiving nearly one page of fraternal review with a complimentary notice of ourself. Thanks, dear brother, for your franal notice.

John M. Stone was elected M. W. Grand Master.

John L. Power was re-elected R. W. Grand Secretary.

NEW BRUNSWICK.

The thirtieth annual communication was held at St. John August 24–25, 1897.

Julius T. Whitlock, M. W. Grand Master.

J. Twining Hartt, V. W. Grand Secretary.

Fifteen lodges represented.

The address of the Grand Master, of nearly seven pages, reviews the conditions of Masonry in his jurisdiction and his official acts for the past year. He refers to the deaths of those of his jurisdiction and also of sister Grand Lodges.

During the delivery of the address, the M. W. Grand Master of Nova Scotia with several other distinguished Masons were in waiting, who were most cordially welcomed by the Grand Master and conducted to the East. The M. W. Grand Master of Nova Scotia addressed the Grand Lodge in acknowledgment of the fraternal reception.

The usual current business was transacted.

There is no report on correspondence.

Thomas Walker was elected M. W. Grand Master.

J. Twining Hartt was re-elected V. W. Grand Secretary.

NEBRASKA.

The proceedings for 1897 were not received until December 20, 1897, hence were not reviewed in our last report for that year. This was owing to a fire which occurred in the office of the printing company which delayed the issuance of the proceedings and prevented the publication of the usual review on foreign correspondence.

The fortieth annual communication was held in the Capitol at Lincoln June 16, 1897.

Charles J. Phelps, M. W. Grand Master.

William R. Bowen, R. W. Grand Secretary.

Two hundred and twenty-one of two hundred and twenty-eight lodges were duly represented.

The address of the Grand Master is found in eighteen pages. Notice is taken of the deceased brethren in his own and sister jurisdictions.

Forty-one decisions are reported, all of which are conformable to general Masonic law and the laws of that jurisdiction.

Eight new lodges to which charters had been granted had been by his authority duly constituted.

Two corner-stones of public buildings had been laid. One of them was for a building to remain permanently upon the grounds to be used for the coming "Trans-Mississippi and International Exposition" at Omaha early in the summer of 1898.

He reports that after careful examination of the prerogative of a Grand Master to "make a Mason at sight," he had used that privilege and had made his son a Mason, he having observed all due precautions in the premises, and followed out the usual method of holding an "occasional lodge." In this we concur.

One dispensation had been issued for a new lodge.

The usual transactions were pursued in which, although very interesting to the brethren of that jurisdiction, we find nothing of importance to others.

There is no report on correspondence by reason of the fire as stated in our preface.

John B. Dinsmore was elected M. W. Grand Master.

William R. Bowen was re-elected R. W. Grand Secretary.

NEW JERSEY.

Emergent communications were held February 15 and March 18, 1897, and the one hundred and eleventh annual grand communication was held at Trenton January 26–27, 1898.

George W. Fortmeyer, M. W. Grand Master.

Thomas H. R. Redway, R. W. Grand Secretary.

James H. Durand, P. G. M., Grand Representative of the Grand Lodge of the District of Columbia.

One hundred and sixty-three lodges represented.

This volume is interspersed with very well executed pictures of the Masonic home, and adds greatly to the artistic appearance of the book, which is the largest we have ever seen of the Grand Lodges.

Nineteen pages contain the excellent address of the Grand Master, who presents the results of his year's work and the condition of the craft. Seven pages occupied in his special mention of brethren who had died during the year past.

Under foreign jurisdiction, besides other questions, he says sixty-nine requests for waiver of jurisdiction had been disposed of and five were pending. "His own jurisdiction" receives due consideration.

Under Masonic law he reports four answers to as many questions, all in accordance with Masonic law.

Dispensations and permission had been granted to lodges for various purposes in the interest of Masonry.

Under territorial jurisdiction, two requests for the establishment of a definite boundary line of jurisdiction between lodges had been received and referred to the appropriate committee.

At the emergent communications of February and March two lodges had been constituted.

"Masonic Home." This subject receives proper notice from the Grand Master.

At the outset, the committee resolved that nothing should be done in prosecution of the work assigned to it that would impair the welfare and prosperity of the Grand Lodge, and hence the determination that no home should be procured unless the funds were available to pay for it. The wisdom of the plan has been proven, the full details of which were presented in the report of the committee.

"Improper publications" in the newspapers of the proceedings within the lodges. He refers "particularly to allusions to the work in conferring the degrees and details of style," which he condemns.

"Improper use of the ballot." This he also deprecates, and so does every good Mason of whatever rank, but how are we to prevent it?

The report of the committee on the "Home" made a very interesting report occupying thirty pages, with many illustrations of the buildings, &c., copies of deed and papers explanatory, and a map of the land.

The Grand Lodge adopted the following resolution recommended by the Committee on Jurisprudence:

"Your Committee on Jurisprudence respectfully report upon the recommendation of the Grand Lodge of Maine that 'the effect of a rejection should be limited to five years.' That they see no good reason why any lodge in this grand jurisdiction should be called upon to surrender, after the lapse of any specified or limited time, its jurisdiction over rejected material."

This appears to us to be very remarkable:

"Your Committee on Masonic Jurisprudence make reply to the question submitted by Worshipful Bro. Fithian that a motion, instructing the representatives of a lodge to vote for or against a proposition pending before this Grand Lodge, would be out of order, and should, therefore, be not entertained by the Master."

In Section 10 of Anderson's regulations of 1721, is the following:

"The *majority* of every particular *lodge* when congregated, shall have the privilege of giving *instructions* to their *Masters* and Wardens before the assembling of the *Grand Chapter* or *Lodge* at the three *quarterly communications* hereafter mentioned, and of the annual Grand Lodge too, because their *Master* and Wardens are their representatives and are supposed to speak their mind."

Bro. George B. Edwards again presents the report on correspondence, which is an extended review in 154 pages of the proceedings of sixty-one grand jurisdictions, those of our own Grand Lodge for 1896 receiving two pages.

He says of our own report: "It is very brief, covering about the half of one page."

Well, Brother Edwards, the present report on New Jersey is somewhat longer, as we found more matters to engage our attention.

Josiah W. Evans was elected M. W. Grand Master.

Thomas H. R. Redway was re-elected R. W. Grand Secretary.

NEW MEXICO.

The twentieth annual communication was held at Albuquerque October 4, 1897.

Charles Bowmer, M. W. Grand Master.

Alpheus A. Keen, R. W. Grand Secretary.

Fourteen chartered lodges represented, out of twenty on the rolls.

Twelve pages given to the address of the Grand Master. Dispensations granted for various lodge purposes. Some asked for and not granted. Not one decision asked for. Grand Representatives' commissions forwarded and received. Ritual revision discussed. Trials had been had. Grievances under all of these headings, which were strictly local. He deals very justly upon each and we presume satisfactorily to the brethren of his Grand Lodge.

The reports of the other Grand Officers show a commendable progress and somewhat prosperous condition in Masonic affairs.

The chairman, Bro. Max Frost, of the Committee on Correspondence being absent from illness, the other two members made their report of the proceedings committed severally to them. The chairman, however, has furnished the completed report, which appears in the proceedings.

Forty-nine domestic and fourteen foreign Grand Lodge proceedings are reviewed in ninety-five pages.

The District of Columbia proceedings for 1896 have over a page. He makes one extract, viz., under Mississippi, on the "liquor question," and he concurs therein.

John W. Poe was elected M. W. Grand Master.

Alpheus A. Keen was re-elected R. W. Grand Secretary.

NORTH CAROLINA.

The one hundred and eleventh annual communication was held at Oxford January 11-13.

Walter E. Moore, M. W. Grand Master.

John C. Drewry, R. W. Grand Secretary.

Eight pages contain the address of the Grand Master.

In his preface he refers to the fact that "for the first time in its history the Grand Lodge of Ancient Free and Accepted Masons in North Carolina, at its annual communication in Raleigh in January, 1897, conceived the idea that in January, 1898 (the date of its regular annual communication), would be a proper time to pay its visit to its institution at Oxford, and for a brief season visit the children at their home, and with them have a pleasant time around the fireside and over the farm, and see for themselves what is being done by the Grand Lodge in the interest of and for the protection, care, and maintenance of those otherwise unable to care for themselves."

He says:

"The brightest page in the history of Masonry in North Carolina was written when the Grand Lodge established this institution for a home for the homeless, the fatherless, and motherless within the bounds of this grand jurisdiction, and that 'page' grows brighter as we see the Masons year after year striving to maintain it, to increase its capacity, and thereby its usefulness; and while we, as Masons, are doing this, we must not be unmindful but ever grateful to those (who are not Masons) who have so liberally contributed of their means with which God has blessed them to aid us in this great work."

He recommended that the Grand Lodge do not establish any fraternal communication with the Grand Lodge of Peru in consequence of the recent movements of that Grand Lodge in relation to the removal of the Great Light from the lodge room, which, upon report of committee, was adopted.

Of the fraternal dead he makes due notice.

He had granted nine dispensations to form new lodges.

A great many questions had been decided; a great many more than necessary if the brethren had only consulted the code and proceedings of the Grand Lodge.

This is inevitable in every jurisdiction, for even by examination of the code, from the often vagueness and paucity of expressing the meaning, even lawyers differ in many cases as to what was the real meaning of the code, and we have an evidence in the "decisions" of the Grand Master himself, where he says: "I am fully aware that this decision runs counter to the decision of Past Grand Master Gudger in proceedings of 1892, page 12. I have construed this section strictly, and take it that if the Grand Lodge intended it to apply to Entered Apprentices, it could easily have inserted the word 'initiation.'" There it is. When Grand Masters differ, how can you expect the "laity" to agree?

The reports of the Grand Secretary and Grand Treasurer show increased prosperity in that jurisdiction.

The report on correspondence was prepared by Bro. John A. Collins for the committee, of ninety-five pages. Among the reviews we find our own proceedings for 1896 with nearly two pages of fraternal comments and extracts.

Walter E. Moore was re-elected M. W. Grand Master.

John C. Drewry was re-elected R. W. Grand Secretary.

PENNSYLVANIA.

A Grand Lodge of emergency was held at Philadelphia January 29, 1897.

The Grand Master stated that he had called this communication for the purpose of exercising his prerogative by making Masons at sight.

The several lodges of Entered Apprentice Masons and Fellow Craft were successively opened, and these degrees were conferred in a regular manner upon two candidates separately. The Fellow Craft Lodge was closed and these candidates separately introduced for the third time and raised to the sublime degree of a Master Mason. The Grand Lodge was then closed.

The constitution of Pennsylvania, called the Ahiman Rezon, provides for this proceedure.

The quarterly communication was held at Philadelphia March 3, 1897.

William J. Kelly, M. W. Grand Master.

William A. Sinn, R. W. Grand Secretary.

One hundred and twenty-six lodges represented.

The quarterly communication was held same place June 2, 1897. Same officers.

One hundred and sixteen lodges represented.

The special committee appointed on the German Empire recognition question reported:

"The special committee appointed by the R. W. Grand Master for 'the purpose of ascertaining what differences exist, if any, which prevent Masonic brethren connected with the lodges in the various German States forming the German Empire, from visiting the lodges in the jurisdiction of Pennsylvania, and also the causes which have made it impossible for brethren hailing from our jurisdiction visiting the lodges in the jurisdiction above mentioned,' respectfully report that they have given the subject full and careful consideration, and are unanimously of the opinion that no differences exist which prevent Masonic brethren connected with the lodges in the various German States forming the German Empire from visiting the lodges in the jurisdiction of Pennsylvania, and that no causes make it impossible for brethren hailing from our jurisdiction visiting the lodges in the jurisdiction above mentioned."

The report was adopted.

In view of this report and its adoption it is well to refer to the report on correspondence by Bro. Vaux, made in 1876.

Quarterly communication, March 1, 1876, pages five to fifteen.

The whole report should be carefully *studied* to appreciate the following extract found on pages thirteen to fifteen.

"There appears from the elaborate, most masterly, and able reports of Bro. James Gibson, Chairman of the Committee on Correspondence of the Most Worshipful Grand Lodge of New York, presented to that Grand Lodge on the 4th of June, 1874, and that of Bro. Henry L. Dechert, Chairman of the Committee on Correspondence of the Grand Lodge of Pennsylvania, presented St. John's Day, 1872, that a most unfortunate state of affairs exists in some of the so-called Grand Lodges in Europe and elsewhere. These brethren have devoted great care and exhaustive examination into the facts they developed. From the evidence they present there is an inherent confirmation of the conclusions they reached from the facts themselves. It would be too tedious to recount all the heresies that are now existing in many of the so-called Grand Lodges or Orients on the continent of Europe. It would appear from a careful reading of the proceedings of most of them that the essential principles of Freemasonry are ignored, or so mutilated or watered with isms that they can with difficulty be recognized.

"Eight bodies claiming to be Masonic Grand Lodges in Europe have formed a Masonic Diet or grand governing national Masonic authority, which assumes power over and regulates the rights and privileges of the inferior bodies that have surrendered these rights to this Diet. Among the extraordinary powers claimed by this German Masonic Diet or League is 'the right of jurisdiction,' or a control over it. This Diet has the disposition, it would seem, to go into any Grand Lodge jurisdiction of the United States and set up lodges under the plea of nationality, that Masons so organized into a lodge are Germans, or work in the German tongue, and, therefore, owe allegiance to this German Grand Diet. This appears to be the logical deduction from a claim of the 'right of jurisdiction.'

"It is also claimed by this Diet that 'the object and aim of this league is to secure and promote the unity and Masonic joint action of the lodges in Germany, and to assume in common a Masonic attitude toward the Grand Lodges outside of Germany;' that 'it is exclusively the business of the German Grand Lodge League to determine whether new alliances shall be formed with Grand Lodges outside of Germany, and whether those already formed are to be dissolved.' The Grand Lodge Diet is the organ of the Grand Lodge League, and this Grand Lodge Diet consists of the eight

Grand Masters and the two Master Masons elected by each Grand Lodge.

"The Grand Lodges which are assumed once to have been supreme and sovereign bodies, but have now surrendered some of their inherent powers which are inseparable from Masonic Sovereignty, are:

"I. The Grand National Mother Lodge of the Prussian States, zu den drei Weltkugeln, at Berlin.

"II. The Grand Lodge of Saxony, at Dresden.

"III. The Grand Lodge of Hamburg, at Hamburg.

"IV. The Grand Lodge of the Eclectic Union at Frankfort-on-the-Main.

"V. The Grand Lodge of Freemasons of Germany, at Berlin.

"VI. The Grand Lodge of Freemasons zur sonne, at Bayreuth.

"VII. The Grand Lodge of Prussia, called Royal York, zur Freundschaft, at Berlin.

"VIII. The Grand Lodge zur Eintracht, at Darmstadt.

"Whatever may be the future relations of this Diet with lawfully organized Grand Lodges, it is very evident to every member of our Grand Lodge that there can be no longer any Masonic intercourse with, or recognition by, the Right Worshipful Grand Lodge of Free and Accepted Masons of Pennsylvania and the Masonic jurisdiction thereunto belonging, of either this Diet or the emasculated Masonic bodies that are its present constituents during the existence of this Diet with its present character.

"The Grand Lodge of Pennsylvania is old enough and wise enough to understand her own duty, and no greater benefit can be conferred by her on her sister Grand Lodges, both in the States of our Union and wherever Masonry is to be maintained on the landmarks, than by declaring in her conservative action that no recognition can be given to this Diet or its constituents. All time has proven that the abandonment of Masonic law brings its own condemnation.

"Your committee have also to report that the so-called Grand Orients of Italy, France, Brazil, Portugal, Hungary, Egypt, the Association called the Grand Lodge of Polynesia, the so-called Grand Lodge of Indian Territory (U. S.), the several associations called Lodge of Memphis, the Grand Lodge of New South Wales, and Grand Lodge of Australia, are not in such a Masonic condition as to justify the Grand Lodge of Pennsylvania recognizing them as Masonic Grand Lodges, and such recognition is hereby withheld. Your committee offers the following resolution:

"*Resolved*, The report be accepted, approved, and printed.

"Respectfully submitted,

"RICHARD VAUX,

"*Past Grand Master and Ch'r. Com. on Correspondence.*

"MARCH 1, 1876."

It has not come to our knowledge that there has been any change in the status of the Grand Lodges comprising the Grand Lodge League or Diet of Germany. Morever, one of these German Grand Lodges, viz., the Grand Lodge of Hamburg, did issue charters to various lodges in several of our grand jurisdictions; notably, in

New York, Missouri, and California, and we think those lodges are yet in existence.

Quarterly communication was held September 1, 1897.

The same Grand Officers.

One hundred and eleven lodges represented.

Quarterly communication held December 1, 1897.

Same Grand Officers.

At this communication it appears that most of the annual business was transacted.

The annual communication was held on St. John the Evangelist Day, December 27, 1897.

The same Grand Officers.

The R. W. Grand Master presented his annual address, of fourteen pages, relating succinctly all of his official acts during the year.

He refers to his having directed the Worshipful Master of Lodge No. 398 to bury a brother in response to the request of New Jerusalem Lodge, No. 9, Washington, D. C., for which the lodge, as well as our Grand Master, were very grateful.

The Grand Officers were duly installed, Bro. William J. Kelly having been re-elected.

The report on correspondence, of 198 pages, was the product of the whole committee.

"The work of reading and digesting the reports of the several Grand Lodges was divided into four parts and assumed by Bros. S. Kingston McCoy, William H. Whitty, Bushrod W. James, and Charles J. McClary, the chairman being unable to digest more than one of the reports, but he read and reviewed all the matter prepared by the other members of the committee, and now the whole committee make the following report, which it is hoped will be interesting to the brethren."

William J. Kelly was re-elected M. W. Grand Master.

William A. Sinn was re-elected R. W. Grand Secretary.

PRINCE EDWARD ISLAND.

The twenty-third annual communication was held at Summerside June 24, 1897.

An emergent communication was held at Charlottetown Octo-15, 1897, for the purpose of participating in the celebration of the centennial of St. John's Lodge, No. 1.

At the annual were present:

Leonard Morris, M. W. Grand Master.

Neil Mackelvie, R. W. Grand Secretary.

R. W. John A. Messervey, Grand Representative of the Grand Lodge of the District of Columbia.

Twelve lodges were represented.

Ten pages occupied with the address of the Grand Master.

Peace and harmony prevail throughout the jurisdiction.

Reference is made to the deceased brethren. None of his own Grand Lodge had died. Some of the members of the subordinate lodges, however, had "exchanged worlds." He reports the names of distinguished brethren of sister jurisdictions who had died.

He had made some official visitations to a few of the lodges.

One dispensation had been issued to form a new lodge.

Finances are reported as being in better shape than for some time.

Membership had not materially increased, and yet they were holding their own.

The reports of the other Grand Officers show the condition of Masonry to be fairly good.

There is no report on correspondence.

Leonard Morris was re-elected M. W. Grand Master.

Neil Mackelvie was re-elected R. W. Grand Secretary.

QUEBEC.

The twenty-eighth annual communication was held at Montréal January 26, 1898.

E. T. D. Chambers, M. W. Grand Master.

J. H. Isaacson, R. W. Grand Secretary.

The address of the Grand Master occupies twenty-one pages.

He says: "Much of the recent growth of the order, especially in the city of Montreal, I attribute to the influence of this splendid home of Masonry in which we are now assembled."

He proclaims " peace at home."

Of those "at rest," he refers to those in sister jurisdictions as well as his own.

He had constituted one lodge under dispensation and issued a dispensation for the formation of another lodge.

The reports of the other Grand Officers and Past Deputy Grand Masters show an increased interest in Masonry in that jurisdiction.

The report on correspondence, of 122 pages, was made by Bro. Will H. Whyte, in which he reviews the proceedings of Grand Lodges, viz., forty-eight American, two British, six Canadian, three Australian, German, and Swedish, in a very satisfactory manner. The District of Columbia is honored with two pages of fraternal remarks and several extracts.

We thank him for his personal reference to our illness of last year and respond to his trust of our soon restoration to health, that we are now in good and sound condition, for which we render daily thanks.

E. T. D. Chambers was re-elected M. W. Grand Master.

J. H. Isaacson was re-elected R. W. Grand Secretary.

SOUTH CAROLINA.

The one hundred and twenty-first annual communication was held at Charleston December 14-15, 1897.

Jacob T. Barron, M. W. Grand Master.

Charles Inglesby, R. W. Grand Secretary.

The Grand Secretary being Grand Representative of the Grand Lodge of the District of Columbia.

Bro. J. Adger Smith, Past Grand Master and Mayor of the City of Charleston, ascended the dais and in fitting and eloquent terms extended a hearty welcome to his Masonic brethren.

The M. W. Grand Master in chosen and feeling terms responded on behalf of the Grand Lodge, and accepted the hospitality and welcome so warmly tendered to them.

Special communications had been held:

At Spartanburg July 9, 1897, to lay the corner-stone of a public school building.

At Bamberg August 10, 1897, to lay the corner-stone of a court-house.

At Greenwood September 7, 1897, to lay the corner-stone of a courthouse.

At Anderson October 20, 1897, to lay the corner-stone of a court-house.

At all of these ceremonies the M. W. Grand Master presided.

The Grand Master's address, of nine pages, gives an account of his official actions during the year and the state of the craft.

He states that in his judgment, based on personal observation and the opinions of the District Deputy Grand Masters, the general condition of the craft is fairly good, and that in many lodges there exists an intelligent appreciation of Masonry and a satisfactory enthusiasm and activity in the work of the order. Some seem to be "holding their own" and to be entirely satisfied with that degree of success, other lodges are too weak numerically and the constant struggle for a bare existence discourages the members and deters good men from seeking Masonic light, and finally, there are some lodges which should be prosperous and yet are no credit to themselves or this Grand Lodge.

These last, in our judgment, are like balky mules—would be improved by having some fire put under them to "make them go," and we think the Grand Master and other drivers of the Grand Lodge could do it by paying such lodges fraternal visits and put the fire of enthusiasm into them. Try it, brethren, and you will be surprised at the beneficial results.

He had the pleasure of visiting eleven lodges, being uniformly received with all the courtesy and respect due the Grand Master, and we venture to say these lodges will be greatly benefited by his visits.

He reported his official actions in laying the corner-stones of public buildings above enumerated.

He had granted a dispensation to revive a lodge which had ceased to work.

He had made quite a number of rulings, and recommended:

"That the article in the Constitution be so amended as not to require physical perfection in all cases, but to permit the Grand Master to grant his dispensation to receive such candidates as in his judgment can literally comply with all the requirements of the ritual. There seems to have been an erroneous impression prevailing in this State that physical perfection is one of the landmarks of the fraternity. Such is not the case. This 'perfect youth fad' is not in touch with the spirit of Masonry as generally interpreted and understood throughout the world, and I am convinced the sooner we pay less attention to physical qualification the better it will be for the prosperity of the craft and the good of mankind. Again, an opportunity will thus be given for members of Entered Apprentice's and Fellow Craft's who have been stopped for slight defects to receive more light in Masonry, and the opportunity given us to do simple justice to them."

In all of which enlightened remarks we heartily concur, for it has been our decided opinion ever since we were made a Mason "that it was the *internal* and not the external qualifications which entitled *us* to be made a Mason."

The Committee on Jurisprudence did not concur with the Grand Master's recommendation as to the proposed amendment, and the

Grand Lodge sustained the report of the committee. There needs to be "more light" among the brethren of that Grand Lodge.

There is no report on correspondence, owing to heavy expenses in printing a new Grand Lodge Code, which omission we regret as we have always appreciated and enjoyed the reports of Bro. Grand Secretary Inglesby.

Jacob T. Barron was re-elected M. W. Grand Master.

Charles Inglesby was re-elected R. W. Grand Secretary.

TENNESSEE.

The eighty-fourth annual communication was held at Nashville January 26, 1898.

A. N. Sloan, M. W. Grand Master.

John B. Garrett, R. W. Grand Secretary.

The Grand Master's address occupies ten pages, in which he refers to the various subject-matters as our dead, official acts, dispensations, new lodges, removal of lodges, appointments, appeals, official rulings, of which there are twenty-one, all being strictly in accordance with Masonic law; official visitations, foreign relations, Masonic Widows' and Orphans' Home, recommendations under five sections, exemplification, and conclusion.

The reports of the other Grand Officers show a fair condition of Masonry in that jurisdiction.

The report on correspondence was submitted by Bro. George H. Morgan for the committee, which is his second, and in his conclusion says: "Much of it has been prepared under circumstances of great tribulation. My old affliction, rheumatism, of which the brethren in Tennessee are aware, has had its clutches on me much of the time during its preparation," &c.

We can sympathize with our brother, as during the last year we too, had that complaint, added to the one which laid us up from January 3 to about October 1st. During the two months of August and September, twice each day, we had an electrical charge sent through the left leg; it *cured* the complaint, and we have not been troubled with it since. "Go thou and do likewise."

Due notice is taken of our own proceedings for 1896, giving nearly two pages of extracts and comments thereon.

We were recently gratified by a social visit to us in our *sanctum* by Most Worshipful Brother H. H. Ingersoll, Past Grand Master, and regret that the visit was so brief.

William H. Bumpas was elected M. W. Grand Master.

John B. Garrett was re-elected R. W. Grand Secretary.

TEXAS.

The sixty-second annual communication was held at Houston
December 7–10, 1897.

A. B. Watkins, M. W. Grand Master.

John Watson, R. W. Grand Secretary.

William Bramlette, P. G. M., Grand Representative of the
Grand Lodge of the District of Columbia.

The address of the Grand Master, of fourteen pages, after the
salutatory paragraph, says:

"Another has been added to the unnumbered years of our
immortal order. It has been one of peculiar peace and quietude
to the craft. From almost every district comes the cheering news
of brotherly affection and good will. No great disaster calling for
special aid has anywhere occurred, and while we for months past
have rested under the shadow of a great plague 'He has made His
face to shine upon us,' and the danger is passed.

"The first thought that meets us here is, have we as Masons
progressed with the passing year? Have we kept step with that
vanguard of honor, leading men up to higher things? Is there
yet a place and a need for Masonry in our civil and social life?

"It is not enough that we as Masons point to our acts of charity
and benevolence and answer that in the year that has passed we
have relieved the distressed, comforted the sick, provided for the
needy, and buried the dead."

The thought has passed through our mind that in just such
language do all the annual addresses of our Grand Masters appeal
to the hearts of the entire craft in each grand jurisdiction, remind-
ing the members of the great duties incumbent upon us as Masons,
and this has been the ever-continued appeal from the Grand East
of every Masonic grand body, to our certain knowledge, for the
past fifty years or more, and yet we can find those who oppose
Masonry as an irreligious and immoral institution, and one de-
nomination of so-called Christians setting itself up as the only
Church of Jesus Christ, all others being heretics, and that Masonry
is the child of the devil. If the last be true, then the devil can
produce good fruit such as can be imitated even by that church
and never detract from the principles of the "*Word of God*"
which they, the Hierarchy, will not permit to be read by the
laity. Read now the following paragraph of the address of the
Grand Master.

"We may recall with just pride that the Masonic lodges in
Texas have expended more money in the actual relief of the needy
and distressed than any other organization in the State, that the
interests and rents of our magnificent properties are perpetually

dedicated to charity alone, and that we will shortly begin building a home for orphans commensurate with the demands of our great State."

There were constituted during the year nineteen new lodges under charter.

Dispensations had been granted to organize three new lodges, and dispensations had been issued to continue two lodges which had forfeited their charters. Other dispensations had been issued for various purposes to lodges. Dispensations had been issued to eight lodges to lay corner-stones.

Two duplicate charters had been issued to replace charters which had been lost.

A large number of dispensations had been refused for good and sufficient reasons.

Four decisions were reported, all *sound* and according to Masonic law.

Other matters referred to were altogether local in character.

A short report was made by the Deputy Grand Master on three new lodges constituted by him by deputation to other brethren.

Six decisions were reported, all in conformity to Masonic law.

He had granted five dispensations for public installation of officers.

He had also granted a dispensation to a lodge to lay a corner-stone.

The reports of the Grand Treasurer and Grand Secretary show a favorable condition of finances and work.

Bro. Thomas M. Matthews again presented the report on correspondence, of 111 pages, in review of the various Grand Lodge proceedings, in which we find about two pages given to our own for 1896, doing ample justice to our little District. He commends some of our remarks on several topics.

What we meant by "demand," was not a peremptory act, but simply to ask in a *Masonic* manner, which means, of course, in a *courteous* manner. When we were made a Mason in 1840 we were instructed that it was a *right* to ask to see the charter and unless *certain* that the lodge was a regularly chartered body it was a *duty* to do so. See ye there, now.

Many thanks to Bro. Matthews for his commendations.

John L. Terrell was elected M. W. Grand Master.

John Watson was re-elected R. W. Grand Secretary.

UTAH.

The twenty-seventh annual communication was held at Salt Lake City January 18–19, 1898.

Abram Gale Gash, M. W. Grand Master.

Christopher Diehl, R. W. Grand Secretary.

Charles S. Varian, P. S. G. W., Grand Representative of the Grand Lodge of the District of Columbia.

The Grand Master delivered his annual address, of eleven pages.

He says: "In spite of the dull times which have been upon us during the year the craft has been prosperous, and we have gained in membership. This gain has been of proper material, brought up, inspected, and declared sound and fit material for the builder's use."

The address is mostly upon local matters, but we can commend it for its sensible views of all matters entertained, especially his remarks under the head of decisions.

Bro. Grand Secretary Christopher Diehl, chairman, continues to write the reports on correspondence. This is his twenty-second in course and comprises a review of the proceedings of the fifty-six American Grand Lodges, and we find our own for 1896 having about one page. We regret that we did not find in this last review matter enough to see his one and go one better, without raising too high, which we could have done very easily; but here was the difficulty, we did not dare to draw on the bank for fear we should exceed our lawful limits. Like the game we have drawn on for illustration, which we have often seen played "for fun," but in which we never even took a hand, nor ever could understand, we are often tempted to extend our comments, but found we were apt "to bite larger than we could chew," so have been compelled to a "sudden bring up" as old Mr. Weller said to Samuel his son.

John Francis Hardie was elected M. W. Grand Master.

Christopher Diehl was re-elected R. W. Grand Secretary.

VICTORIA.

Quarterly communication held at Melbourne March 17, 1897.

Lord Brassey, M. W. Grand Master.

John Braim, V. W. Grand Secretary.

The Grand Master, Lord Brassey, was unanimously elected.

The grand anniversary festival was held at Melbourne May 19, 1897.

The same Grand Officers present.

Most Worshipful G. S. Coppin, Grand Representative of the Grand Lodge of the District of Columbia.

The appointed Grand Officers were installed and invested.

A quarterly communication was held at Melbourne June 16, 1897.

George Baker, P. G. M., as Grand Master.

John Braim, V. W. Grand Secretary.

A quarterly communication was held at Melbourne September 15, 1897.

George Coffin, P. G. M., as Grand Master.

John Braim, V. W. Grand Secretary.

At these several communications the regular business was transacted.

The Grand Officers continued.

VIRGINIA.

The one hundred and twentieth annual communication was held at Richmond December 7–9, 1897.

Alfred R. Courtney, M. W. Grand Master.

George W. Carrington, R. W. Grand Secretary.

Grand Chaplain George H. Ray, Grand Representative of the Grand Lodge of the District of Columbia.

The Grand Master's address, of fifteen pages, gives a full account of his official acts and the state of affairs during the year.

He had issued dispensations for eight new lodges during the year.

He had laid many corner-stones of public buildings and dedicated several Masonic halls, and says:

"I declined to call the Grand Lodge to lay the corner-stone of the Presbyterian church in Charlottesville   *   *   *   * because I did not consider that that was a building of such general and public character as to justify the performance of the ceremony by the Grand Lodge.   The subordinate lodges may with propriety, and frequently do, lay the corner-stones of churches, but I do not think it would be becoming in the Grand Lodge to do so."

This, of course, is his individual opinion, but it is not the opinion generally entertained by Masonic authority. In some jurisdictions it is the province of the Grand Master only or by his dispention to someone else.

He had visited as many lodges as his business engagements would permit, but not nearly so many as he would have liked to visit, nor as many as needed the attention of the Grand Master.

Under the heading of Masonic Home of Virginia he furnished a tabular statement of the amounts given by the several lodges, aggregating the sum of $2,190.62.

He recommended the recognition of the *Gran Dieta* of Mexico, for reasons good and sufficient to him. The committee recommended that no action be now taken looking to its recognition. Adopted. (Hasten slowly.)

Five decisions were reported, all conformable to Masonic law, one of which we quote as it is of general interest.

"I decided that where the by-laws of the lodge were in conflict with the law, as laid down in the digest, the by-law was inoperative, even though it had been regularly approved by the Most Worshipful Grand Master at the time it was adopted."

This question was thus decided in our own Grand Lodge many years since.

A very large amount of local business was transacted at this communication, much of it quite interesting to the general reader, but our limits do not permit of our introducing the same into these pages.

Owing to the feeble health of M. W. William F. Drinkard and M. W. William B. Taliaferro, the work of reviewing the proceedings of other Grand Lodges was performed by the junior member of the committee, R. W. J. E. Alexander, who furnishes the report, of 142 pages. Three and one-half pages contain a very fraternal review of our own proceedings for 1896.

The reviewer, taking the last number of our lodges, viz., No. 29, gives our jurisdiction credit for that total of lodges. We are minus four, of which three have gone out of existence and one, No. 13, became No. 1 of the Grand Lodge of California in 1849.

He refers to our annual grand visitations by the Grand Master accompanied by the other Grand Officers. That "the custom has prevailed for some years." We state that it was by constitutional provision in 1813 and has invariably been observed ever since, and to its observance we may trace mainly the continued advancement and prosperity of Masonry in this jurisdiction.

The late esteemed Bro. William B. Isaacs, the Grand Secretary of Virginia, happened to be present at a grand visitation to Lafayette Lodge, No. 19, and he then stated that our proceedings on that occasion were a "revelation" to him.

R. T. W. Duke, Jr., was elected M. W. Grand Master.

George W. Carrington was re-elected R. W. Grand Secretary.

WEST VIRGINIA.

The thirty-third annual communication was held at Charleston November 9-10, 1897.

Thirteen special communications were held for special purposes.

At the annual communication were present:

B. D. Gibson, M. W. Grand Master.

George W. Atkinson, R. W. Grand Secretary.

The Grand Master delivered his address, which occupies thirty-four pages.

He reports that the condition of the craft is very good.

He had issued charters to four new lodges and duplicates to two others.

Three dispensations had been granted to form new lodges.

Grand Representatives had been commissioned to other Grand Lodges and he had recommended others for appointment near his own Grand Lodge.

Sixteen decisions are reported.

The reports of the other grand officers show a steady growth and improvement in all Masonic matters in that jurisdiction.

The R. W. Grand Secretary, George W. Atkinson, besides being the present Governor of the State can find time to act as Grand Secretary and write the report on correspondence, which this time comprises 175 pages, with an addenda of five pages obituary notice of our deceased Bro. Past Grand Secretary Odell B. Long, who died in December, 1897.

S. N. Meyers was elected M. W. Grand Master.

George W. Atkinson was re-elected R. W. Grand Secretary.

BRITISH COLUMBIA.

The twenty-seventh annual communication was held at New Westminster June 25, 1898.

Rev. E. D. McLaren, M. W. Grand Master.

W. J. Quinlan, V. W. Grand Secretary.

Twenty-three lodges represented.

Six pages contain a very excellent address of the Grand Master.

The fraternal dead are duly and appropriately remembered.

He had visited officially eighteen of the twenty-four lodges, and says, "I cannot speak too highly of the abounding kindness I everywhere experienced."

Masons everywhere are like the bees and pay due respect to their "sovereign" for the time being.

The Deputy Graud Master also presented his address, giving an account of his official acts and visitations.

The Grand Secretary's and Grand Treasurer's reports show a very good condition of affairs in their departments.

The several District Deputy Grand Masters also reported the affairs in their districts as being very favorable, and from what we observe in all the proceedings Masonry in that jurisdiction is steadily advancing.

As usual, a sermon was delivered by J. A. Logan, V. W. Grand Chaplain.

The report on correspondence, of 190 pages, was prepared by Bro. W. A. De Wolf Smith. The proceedings of our own Grand Lodge for 1897, have a very fair and fraternal notice of over three pages, and we return our thanks for his remarks as to ourself.

In regard to the question of reinstatement of those dropped for non-payment of dues we personally agree with him as to how one dropped should be reinstated, and when our last rule was adopted we made an effort to so state the case, but our motion was rejected because the "old rut" was so deep our brethren could not get the wagon out of it. We hope sometime justice will be done and the rule of New Brunswick will be adopted, viz: that when a dropped member is willing to pay all dues and applies, he shall be reinstated without a vote.

David Wilson was elected M. W. Grand Master.

W. J. Quinlan was re-elected V. W. Grand Secretary.

INDIANA.

The seventy-seventh annual communication was held at Indianapolis May 24-25, 1898.

Mason J. Niblack, M. W. Grand Master.

William H. Smythe, R. W. Grand Secretary.

Four hundred and eighty of the 489 chartered lodges were represented.

The Grand Master's address, of eleven pages, refers to official acts and the condition of the craft during the year. He says, after referring to the act of the Grand Lodge of Peru in removing the Bible from the altar:

"We can no longer hold communication with the Grand Lodge of Peru, as such action robs Masonry of its very foundation. I, therefore, recommend that such action be taken by this Grand Lodge as will be necessary to terminate and absolve all relations with that Grand Lodge."

Under "necrology" he refers to the deaths of the distinguished brethren of his own and seven sister jurisdictions.

Six new lodges had been constituted under charters and six dispensations had been issued to form new lodges. Special dispensations had been issued to various lodges, subjects not mentioned.

Six duplicate charters had been issued because the originals had been destroyed by fire.

Two corner-stones of public buildings had been laid, one by his proxy and one in person.

Two Masonic halls had been dedicated, one by himself and one by proxy.

He had approved of the by-laws of very many lodges duly specified.

He had appointed Grand Representatives to several Grand Lodges and had recommended Grand Representatives of three other Grand Lodges.

Matters of local interest connected with several lodges are reported.

He says begging circulars are not permitted within that grand jurisdiction. He had occasion to deny several requests for permission to send such circulars to the various lodges.

He refers to the Washington memorial and recommends that suitable arrangements should be made to have that Grand Lodge properly represented upon the occasion. Reference is made to the "history of Masonry in Indiana" by the historian, Past Grand Master Daniel McDonald, which we trust will soon be published.

He reports that, accompanied by the R. W. Grand Secretary, William H. Smythe, he visited Cape Girardeau, Mo., and assisted in removing the remains of Past Grand Master Alexander Buckner from the unmarked and lonely place where they had laid for sixty-four years to the old and beautiful cemetery in the city of Cape Girardeau.

We are pleased to learn that the book which Bro. Grand Secretary Smythe proposes to prepare and publish, and which is to contain "the latest, best, and most authentic decisions of that Grand Lodge as shown by the records thereof," may be completed in a short time.

The reports of the other Grand Officers show a very favorable condition, with a balance in the treasury of $4,239.68.

The report on correspondence, of 135 pages, was presented by Bro. Past Grand Master Nicholas R. Ruckle, reviewing the proceedings of fifty-four Grand Lodges (English-speaking) and the account of non-English speaking Grand Lodges, condensed from the New York report.

We presume that the copies of our proceedings for 1897 had not been received prior to printing this report, as no notice is taken of them. They were regularly forwarded.

Simeon S. Johnson was elected Grand Master.

William H. Smythe was re-elected R. W. Grand Secretary.

Since the above was written it has been our great pleasure to meet Bro. Smythe and his estimable wife at the session of the O. E. S.—in Washington, September 27-30.

MAINE.

The seventy-ninth annual communication was held at Portland May 3-5, 1898.

Joseph A. Locke, M. W. Grand Master.

. Stephen Berry, R. W. Grand Secretary.

Number of chartered lodges, 192; represented, 177; delegates, 240; represented by proxy only, 59.

The Grand Secretary, Grand Representative of the Grand Lodge of the District of Columbia.

The Grand Master delivered his address, which is thirty-two pages in length.

During the year peace and harmony had prevailed. Not a single complaint had been made to him, nor a charge preferred. He says:

"We are also in cordial and fraternal touch with all the Grand Lodges throughout the world with whom we have heretofore held fraternal relations, excepting the Grand Lodge of Peru, with which I was much grieved to be obliged to sever Masonic communication, as more fully hereinafter stated."

Due reference is made to the deceased brethren in his own and sister jurisdictions.

Differing from the Grand Master of another jurisdiction he had granted, very properly and according to ancient Masonic usage, several lodges to appear in public for the purpose of attending divine service.

Three dispensations had been issued to form new lodges.
He had dedicated two new Masonic halls.

"From reports received from the District Deputy Grand Masters and from information received otherwise I learn that our lodges are generally prosperous and the brethren more attentive upon the meetings."

He reports, 774 initiated, last year, 746; 768 raised, last year, 721; 54 reinstated, last year, 59; 407 died, last year, 339. Now a membership of 22,191; gain of 106.

We are pleased to read the following decision.

"A brother suspended from membership for non-payment of dues, on payment of his dues is restored to all the privileges of Freemasonry, as though he had not been suspended, and without a vote of the lodge. When paid, if the records show his suspension, as I presume they do, a minute should be made thereon by order of the Worshipful Master that Brother ———, having paid his dues, is restored to membership."

We regret that our own constitution does not go as far as that of Maine. We only allow one year for such self reinstatement. After that, the one dropped must subject himself to investigation by a committee, and a *majority vote*. We have always held that as a *majority* of brethren are dropped from inability to pay dues that should they at *any future time* come forward and pay the amount of indebtedness, that by such act, having fulfilled their obligations, they should be reinstated.

If common fame or any good reasons can be assigned why a brother should not be a member, then charges should be preferred against him and a trial had, and, if convicted, he should be either suspended or expelled, as the case may require.

Being dropped and afterwards excluded is not Masonic in its character and is anomalous.

The Grand Master submitted a full statement of the matter connected with the action of the Grand Lodge of Peru, with correspondence in the case, the decree of Grand Master Christian Dam, who says:

"I decree, that on all Masonic altars the Bible shall be replaced by the Constitution of the Order of Freemasonry, and that in our rituals the word 'Bible' shall be struck out and the words 'the Constitution of the Grand Lodge of Peru' put in its place."

Now, here comes in a question in ethics. In every oath, vow, or obligation between two parties there must be some plane of reference higher in ethics as a referee by all of the parties.

In all Christian countries every legal oath is administered upon the "sacred writings" called the "Bible," because it is recognized as of divine inspiration, and its function in the "jurat" is to represent the "Divinity" who is thus invoked as a *witness* to the compact.

Take away this the sacred insignia of God and then substitute what? the very instrument itself, to which the party sworn is to be conformable in his acts, which has no such ethical position therein as did the original medium, which always and everywhere is referred as emanating from the highest moral authority in the universe.

What a blunder was made by a Grand Master.

The Grand Lodge adopted the report of the Committee on Jurisprudence to whom the address of the Grand Master was referred, who recommended a resolution sustaining the act of ten Grand Masters in withdrawing from official relations with the Grand Lodge of Peru.

The report on correspondence, of 296 pages, was again presented by the committee, Bro. Josiah H. Drummond, chairmain, and this report keeps up the well-earned reputation of Bro. D. for preparing the most careful and critical reviews of all the "guild." Our own proceedings for 1897 are reviewed in over seven pages.

He reviews with some severity the report of our Committee on Jurisprudence on the subject of "rejected candidates."

We thank him for his expression of gratitude that we have so fully recovered from illness.

Joseph A. Locke was re-elected M. W. Grand Master.

Stephen Berry was re-elected R. W. Grand Secretary.

MANITOBA.

The twenty-third annual communication was held at the city of Winnipeg June 8, 1898.

Thomas Robinson, M. W. Grand Master.

William George Scott, R. W. Grand Secretary.

Over eighteen pages occupied with the address of the Grand Master.

The fraternal dead are remembered.

Reference is made to the diamond jubilee of Her Majesty Queen Victoria.

His circumstances had prevented him from making many official visitations, but he had visited twelve of the lodges.

Seven decisions are reported.

Our English brethren are more liberal than most of our United States Grand Lodges in the matter of physical disabilities. "An applicant for the degrees of Masonry was not debarred from admission to the craft though having lost his second, third, and fourth fingers of his right hand."

The other decisions conform to Masonic usage.

On the subject of "physical qualification" we make the following extract from his address.

"PHYSICAL QUALIFICATION.

"For some time past I have been trying to arrive at some conception upon which to form a judgment on this difficult question, and inquiry and correspondence have brought out the fact that there is a great difference between the views entertained by the Grand Lodges of England, Scotland, and Ireland, the American Grand Lodges, and the Grand Lodge of Canada. Our own Grand Lodge having been derived from the Grand Lodge of Canada has followed chiefly the views of the rulers of the craft of that grand body, and this Grand Lodge follows very closely the American views rather than the views of the British Grand Lodges, although in ritual it is practically the same as that of the Grand Lodge of England. The written law bearing on the subject is derived from clause 5 of the Fifteen Points of the old York Constitutions namely: 'A candidate must be without blemish and have the full use of his limbs, for a maimed man can do the craft no good.' There is also the provision in the regulations of 1663, under the grand mastership of the Earl of St. Albans, namely: 'No person hereafter would be accepted as a Freemason but such as are of able body.' Then again in the Ancient Charges of Makings brought about in 1686, 'That he that be made be able in all degrees, that is, freeborn, of good kindred, true and no bondsman, and that he have his right limbs as a man ought to have.' Lastly, in the fourth clause of 'Anderson's Charges' approved of on the revival of Freemasonry in the year 1722: 'No Master shall take an apprentice unless he has sufficient employment for him and unless he be a perfect youth, having no maim or defect in his body that may render him incapable of learning the art of serving his Master's Lord, and of being made a brother.'

"The above extracts from the written law of Freemasonry have been the guide for American jurists in enunciating the view which chiefly obtains in all the American Grand Lodges and also in the Grand Lodge of Canada, 'That no person should be initiated into Freemasonry who is incapable of complying literally with all the requirements of the degrees.' I communicated at length with Right Worshipful Bro. W. J. Hughan, the great English Masonic historian, and the following is his interesting reply to me, namely:

"'I have not traced any reference to physical qualification in the report of our Board of General Purposes to the Grand Lodge of

England, but I know the question was considered privately by them, so to speak, twice or more in 1860. It was decided by the Board that one who had lost his left foot was not unsuitable for initiation, as it was the moral and mental qualities that made fit and proper persons for initiation.

" ' In 1875 the then Grand Secretary wrote: "That the Board of General Purposes feel that it is impossible to lay down a hard and fast rule as to the initiation of a candidate not perfect in his body, as required in Article IV of the Ancient Charges." I am directed to say that the general rule in this country is to consider a candidate eligible for election who, although not perfect in his limbs, is sufficiently so to comply with and go through the various ceremonies required in the different degrees. Each case of this description must be defined on its own merits by the members of the lodge to whom the candidate is personally known, subject to the approval of the Master of the lodge, who is personally responsible that the candidate was in condition to comply with the above-named requirements.

" ' In 1877 it was also ruled "that having a cork leg did not render a member unfit to take the third degree."

" ' The fact is that ever since the first Grand Lodge of England (and of the world) was formed in 1717, any ordinary defect of a physical character has been no bar to initiation, because the rule as to physical completion or perfection was a prerequisite of the operative period, never has been a regulation in our Book of Constitution, 1723 to 1784, and from the " Union " laws of 1813 to now.

" ' The "Atholl" or "Ancient " Grand Lodge rather leaned to the physical rule and hence the later provincial Grand Lodges of the United States of America and so of Canada (from which the Grand Lodge originated) followed the same custom. I scarcely know what would be a bar physically to initiation in England. Certainly anyone wholly blind, or deaf, or dumb would be inadmissible with us, just as it is by Regulation Grand Lodge of Scotland, agreed to February 6, 1878, and in laws of that Grand Lodge for 1896, it was then agreed by the same body that " lodges are allowed to exercise their own discretion as to the initiation of candidates who are mutilated in, or minus a limb." Also February 6, 1878. In Ireland the rule is (Laws, 1875), "If a candidate proposed for admission be in any manner maimed, lame, or defective, he shall not be initiated without a dispensation from the Grand Master or the Deputy Grand Master, the application to be made by memorial, wherein the defect shall be clearly specified."

" ' Not that I apprehend there would be any difficulty in obtaining permission in the general way. If the operative laws are to be our guide, why not have seven years for the apprenticeship and be wholly Christian as to conditions of membership, besides many other conditions not observed since? There can be no fair justification to take the rule "upright in body and limbs" and exclude others just as needful, and the result of such arbitrary selection has been a series of rulings by Grand Masters that provoke one's amusement, if it were not for the important question underlying all as to the real moral conditions.'

" Personally, so far as I can humbly presume to form my own judgment on this difficult subject, I feel that, with great diffidence and respect to the American rulers of the craft and the rulers of the Grand Lodge of Canada, their conception is too strict; on the other hand, I share the opinion prevalent on this continent, that the advisers of the Grand Lodges of England, Ireland, and Scotland have not been as strict and careful as the best interests of Masonry might demand. I think that the clause in the Charges of 1722 is the proper guide for us to take, and that the words 'that render him incapable of learning the *art*' modifies the strict, literal, and physical perfection which the American view seeks to enforce. The question is a moral and ethical one, just as much as a physical, and I do not think that the former view should be absolutely merged in the latter. The 'art' of Masonry is not so much a question of physical perfection but rather of the moral upbuilding of a perfect character, and this consideration should make us careful not to let the spirit of our craft be enslaved by a too rigid subserviency to the letter of the law. Moreover, the strict conception of physical perfection is founded more particularly upon the York Constitutions. These Constitutions embodied at the time a digest of the Masonic code, the most important of which was number one of the Fifteen Points, namely: 'Every Mason shall cultivate brotherly love, the love of God, and frequent Holy Church.' This is certainly Christian in character, but those who adopt the strict view of physical perfection acknowledge that in the evolution of Masonry this particular rule was changed to the more universal or deistic rule embodied in the first paragraph of Anderson's Charges, approved of in 1722, viz:

"NO. I—CONCERNING GOD AND RELIGION.

"'A Mason is obliged by his tenure to obey the moral law, and if he rightly understands the art he will never be a stupid atheist nor an irreligious libertine. But, though in ancient times, Masons were charged in every country or nation, whatever it was, yet 'tis now thought more expedient to only oblige them to that religion in which all men agree, leaving their particular opinions to themselves; that is, to be good men and true, or men of honor and honesty, by whatever denominations or persuasion they may be distinguished; whereby Masonry becomes the center of union and the means of conciliating true friendship among persons that must have remained at a perpetual distance.'

"I cannot myself see why portions of the York Constitution should be strictly insisted on and other portions admitted to have lost their orignal character; hence, in the decisions which I have given upon the subject I have not followed the same strict line of thought adopted by my predecessors, who have apparently taken as their guide the American conception.

"I have written fully on this question from a desire to convey information and provoke interest and consideration by you all on this important subject. The more you think about it, the more will you realize the all-important lesson of your individual responsibility of safe-guarding the portals of Freemasonry. I do not altogether like the English rule of leaving the matter almost wholly to the discretion of the Masters of lodges. Our Constitution provides that 'every candidate shall submit to the Constitution and conform to all the useges and regulations of the craft.' There is a similar general provision in the Constitution of the Grand

Lodge of England. In many of the constitutions of Grand Lodges in the United States the provisions are very strict, while others are more general. With the Grand Lodge of Canada it is provided:

"'SEC. 218.—Every candidate must be free-born and his own master, and at the time of his initiation be known to be in reputable circumstances. He shall be a lover of the liberal arts and sciences and have made some progress in one or the other of them.

"'SEC. 220.—A candidate who can comply literally with all the ceremonies and work of the Grand Lodge, and is mentally and morally worthy of admission is a fit subject to become a Mason.'

"I prefer the provision of the Constitution of the Grand Lodge of Ireland, and by way of guidance would, therefore, rule that if a candidate for admission suffer from any physical defect he shall not be initiated without the permission of the Grand Master, the application for such dispensation to set out clearly the nature of the defect. No definite rule can be laid down, and each case must be judged upon its own peculiar merits; without departing altogether from the idea of physical perfection, we should seek to admit persons whose lives and character indicate a natural affinity with our conception of what should constitute a fit and proper person to be made a Mason."

We call attention of the officers, particularly the secretaries of our lodges, to the following extracts relating to the clandestine Grand Lodge of Ontario, for their guidance in regard to visitors from Canada (Province of Ontario).

"THE LATE CLANDESTINE OR IRREGULAR GRAND LODGE OF ONTARIO.

"As there seems to be quite a number of members of this body in our jurisdiction, I deem it advisable by way of information for Masters of various lodges to give the following copy of a letter, containing an extract from the proceedings of the Grand Lodge of Canada, 1896, which I directed the Grand Secretary to write in connection with the healing of a member of the above body, viz:

"'That as the Grand Master of the Grand Lodge of Canada (in Ontario) in his address at the session held July 16, 1896, reported that such arrangements had been made with the members of this organization as to effectually sweep this body out of existence for all time to come, their charter (granted by the Provincial Government) had been transferred to myself and the Grand Secretary, as trustees for this Grand Lodge, all warrants issued to subordinate lodges, the seal and all other books and property of this so-called body, have been, or are being, delivered up and are now in possession of this Grand Lodge. All members of this so-called grand body who have applied have been healed, and declare their allegiance to this Grand Lodge. Many of them have applied for affiliation to our lodges and are now active and useful members of this grand body. The surrender is voluntary and complete, the only concession granted being that members of the extinct body holding the rank of Past Master therein are conceded that rank in any of our lodges with which they may affiliate or to which they may be admitted.'

" He thinks 'that the proper course for members of this late organization to pursue is to take advantage of the arrangements made, and make application to the Grand Lodge of Canada to be healed, and upon presentation of a certificate from the Grand Secretary of that jurisdiction they can present their application and be received into membership in any lodge in this jurisdiction willing to receive them.' "

" I concluded that the above course was the wise one to adopt. *First*, as a matter of courtesy to the Grand Lodge of Canada, and, secondly, because it would materially assist the Committee on Character as to whether such a person was a proper subject for affiliation. A certificate from the Grand Lodge of Canada will throw upon the proper parties the responsibility of stating whether such persons are entitled to be received as Masons and are in good standing.

" This awkward matter was brought before the Board of General Purposes on the 7th of October, 1895, when a resolution was passed as follows:—' That the procedure adopted by the Grand Lodge of Canada in the matter of healing members of the lodges formerly working under the jurisdiction of the so-called Grand Lodge of Ontario, be adopted in this jurisdiction.' This was prior to the surrender of all the property of this irregular body, and upon further consideration I felt that the Board would have acted differently if the surrender as above mentioned had then taken place.

" Moreover, there has been a conflict in the acts of my predecessors when dealing with this question. Some allowing such a man to be healed, and others refusing. This to me was a further reason for relegating the question to the quarter where it appeared to me to properly belong."

There was no report on correspondence.

George B. Murphy was elected M. W. Grand Master.

William George Scott was re-elected R. W. Grand Secretary.

NEVADA.

The thirty-fourth annual communication was held at Carson City June 14–15, 1898.

Albert Lackey, M. W. Grand Master.

Chauncey N. Noteware, V. W. Grand Secretary.

Twenty pages are occupied by the address of the Grand Master.

Reference is made to the difference in this country in the twelve months since the Grand Lodge met.

"Then all was peace but now the tramp of the soldier is heard from one end of the land to the other.

"The United States has a right to be proud of the fact that its sailors have successfully braved the perils of a great battle eight thousand miles from home. Not for the acquisition of territory, but as a means for the protection of a downtrodden and defenseless people in Cuba and to put an end to the oppressive tyranny imposed upon that people by Spain.

"This war is the final outcome of a great historic conflict; it is a part of the struggle for freedom which has been going on in the world for centuries; it is the final act in the great drama which began when the Armada sailed for England; and on that lovely Sunday morning when the church bells in the mother country summoned her sons, not to worship, but to fight a foe which was the enemy of their religion as well as of their freedom."

This reminds us of what occurred after the destruction of that Armada.

A medal was struck in the reign of Queen Elizabeth on the dispersion and destruction of the vaunted Spanish Armada with this inscription, *Afflavit Deus et dissipantur* (the breath of God has issued and they are dispersed).

He refers to the appointment by our Grand Master of Bro. Joseph A. Miller as Grand Representative of our Grand Lodge near that of Nevada, and his appointment of Past Grand Master George W. Baird as the Representative of his Grand Lodge near that of the District of Columbia.

He is able to state, from personal inspection and good information, that the lodges in that jurisdiction are in fairly prosperous condition.

He had made a few decisions, which are in conformity to Masonic usage.

He had issued a decree in the matter of the course pursued by the Grand Lodge of Peru—forbidding intercourse, &c., with that Grand Lodge and members thereof.

The Report on Correspondence, of eighty-three pages, including statistical tables, reviewing the proceedings of fifty-four Grand Lodge proceedings, was submitted by Bro. A. D. Bird. Our own for 1897 received about a page of extracts and fraternal comments.

Thanks, Bro. Bird, for your kind reference to ourself.

Matthew Kyle was elected M. W. Grand Master.

Chauncey N. Noteware was re-elected V. W. Grand Secretary.

NEW HAMPSHIRE.

The semi-annual communication was held at Manchester December 28, 1897.

Henry A. Marsh, M. W. Grand Master.

George P. Cleaves, R. W. Grand Secretary.

After organization the Grand Master announced that the exemplification of the work of the three degrees would be by lodges Nos. 64, 42, and 41. The Grand Lodge was then called from labor to refreshment, until 2 o'clock p. m.

Labor was resumed at 2 o'clock p. m., and the exemplification of the first and second degrees took place as above arranged.

In the evening the Grand Lodge was called to labor at eight o'clock and the work of the third degree was exemplified.

The one hundred and ninth annual communication was held at Concord May 18, 1898.

The same Grand Officers present.

Bro. Past Grand Master John F. Webster, Grand Representative of the Grand Lodge of the District of Columbia.

Fifty-eight lodges were represented.

The address of the Grand Master, of eighteen pages, gives an account of official acts and the condition of Masonry in that jurisdiction. Over six pages are devoted to obituary notices, and at his suggestion memorial pages are inscribed in an appropriate manner.

Many dispensations were granted to lodges to appear in Masonic clothing to attend religious services and also to publicly install their officers.

Several decisions are reported, all of which are conformable to Masonic law and usage.

He recommends that the Grand Lodge change its law upon trials to conform to the method adopted in many Grand Lodges where trials are conducted by a commission regulated by constitutional provision. In this we concur, and would like to have the same in our own jurisdiction, as in States where it has been in use the fraternity are satisfied with the change.

The District Deputy Grand Masters presented their reports of the condition of Masonry in their several districts.

The report on correspondence, of 152 pages, was again presented by Bro. A. S. Wait, reviewing the proceedings of fifty-five Grand Lodges, those of the District of Columbia not being among them. What was the matter? Our proceedings for 1897 were regularly mailed when all the others were.

John McLane was elected M. W. Grand Master.

George P. Cleaves was re-elected R. W. Grand Secretary.

NEW YORK.

The one hundred and seventeenth annual communication was held at New York City June 7, 1898.

William A. Sutherland, M. W. Grand Master.

Edward M. L. Ehlers, R. W. Grand Secretary.

John H. Cunningham, Grand Representative of the Grand Lodge of the District of Columbia, was excused from attendance at this session of the Grand Lodge.

The address of the Grand Master fills thirty-two pages. As usual, he mentions the deaths of those brethren who had departed during the year.

Referring to the death of Bro. J. Q. A. Fellows, Past Grand Master of Louisiana, he says:

"M. W. John Q. A. Fellows, Past Grand Master of Masons in Louisiana, died at New Orleans November 28, 1897.

"In the dark days of our civil war M. W. Bro. Fellows extended a fraternal hand to brethren of obedience of the Grand Lodge of New York under circumstances of extraordinary interest and ever grateful remembrance.

"Bro. Edwin Cole, a private in the 71st Regiment of New York Volunteers, and a member of Hope Lodge, No. 244, was, on the 21st day of July, 1861, severely wounded at the battle of Bull Run and taken prisoner. After a brief imprisonment at Richmond he was removed to the city of New Orleans, when M. W. Bro. Fellows, then Grand Master of Masons in Louisiana, provided Bro. Cole and eight of his fellow-prisoners, who were craftsmen, with clothing, with medical attendance, and with every needful comfort in the hour of their extremity. This exhibition of fraternal consideration, under such embarrassing and distressing circumstances, evoked a storm of criticism throughout the State of Louisiana, which was subsequently met by the formal action of the Grand Lodge of Louisiana approving the course of its Grand Master, and in June, 1862, the Grand Lodge of New York, by duly engrossed and certified resolutions, made its formal acknowledgments to the Grand Master of Louisiana for this most gracious evidence of his Masonic charity."

He had laid the corner-stones of eight public buildings, and had dedicated nine Masonic halls, and new rooms for Masonic purposes, and a monument of Roundout Lodge at Kingston.

No questions of sufficient importance had been passed upon to bring to the notice of the Grand Lodge.

But few complaints had come to him respecting the conduct of the officers of the 743 lodges in that great jurisdiction.

The well-nigh universal record of the lodges for the year is that prosperity has attended them, and that their officers have been faithful in every particular.

Two new lodges had been granted dispensations.

Several pages of the address are devoted to the discussion of the management of the Masonic Home.

On the subject of Mexico, we make the following extract from this address, which, we are sure, will be of much interest to our readers :

"MEXICO.

" When from the deeds of Spanish cruelty in Cuba the smoke of conflict was rising to touch our flag, whisperings were heard of European encouragement to Spain. But our neighbor on the south, the Republic of Mexico, extended her hand of friendship to the United States with most delicately expressed, but nevertheless emphatic, assurance that Spanish troops would not harass us from Mexican soil, nor Spanish men-of-war make of Mexican harbors a rendezvous. When the *Maine* was destroyed in Havana harbor, Mexico spoke; and this Grand Lodge was selected as the medium through which the people of the United States should hear her voice.

" The President of our sister Republic is also the Grand Master of Masons in Mexico. On the 15th day of February last, eighty-three Freemasons were among the two hundred and sixty-six American sailors who went down to their death with the battle-ship *Maine*.

" Five days afterwards the President and the Grand Master of Masons in Mexico directed his Grand Secretary, under the seal of the Grand Lodge, to issue an edict commanding all Masonic lodges within his jurisdiction to be draped in mourning on account of these our dead.

" The Grand Master and President also directed the Grand Secretary to make known to the Grand Lodge of New York this extremely significant evidence of his most valuable friendship.

" Accordingly the following communication, under the seal of the Grand Lodge of Mexico, was by due course of mail received by our Grand Secretary :

"'LA GRAN DIETA SIMBOLICA, &C.,
"'ORIENT OF MEXICO, 20 *February,* 1898.
"'*To the Grand Secretary of the Grand Lodge of Free and Accepted Masons of the State of New York.*
"'HON. BROTHER EHLERS : The Gran Dieta Simbolica of Mexico shakes with most terrible sorrow over the frightful explosion of the U. S. battle-ship *Maine* in Cuban waters, and the terrible loss of the lives of so many American citizens, and has ordered all the lodges in the Republic of Mexico under its jurisdiction to drape their altars in testimony of sorrow for such a calamity, and has ordered me to communicate it to you, and beg of you to transmit to the Grand Lodge of the State of New York the expression of our sincere sorrow at such a calamity which has happened to the citizens and Masons of the United States.

"'With best wishes and a fraternal embrace,
"'By order of the Grand Master,
"'ERMILO G. CANTON,
"'*Grand Secretary.*'

"In addition to this the representative of the Grand Lodge of New York near the Grand Lodge of Mexico transmitted to us his report, not only of the action of the Grand Master of Mexico, but of the subsequent assembling of various lodges in that jurisdiction in a lodge of sorrow on the 22d day of February, accompanying his report with translations of several of the speeches delivered on that occasion by the orators of the local lodges. These speeches breathed not only the most tender sentiments of fraternal sympathy with the United States, but they voiced profound horror at the character of the deed done in Havana harbor, severest reprobation of all who had a hand therein, and the warmest regard for our flag and for our country.

"Thus for the first time in the history of the world was the Masonic fraternity selected as the medium through which one nation should be made to feel the welcome handclasp of another, and the Grand Lodge of New York became, as it were, the cable by which the Republic of Mexico discovered to the United States that the pulsations of the one were responsive to the heart-beats of the other.

"Following an impulse most natural, and in accord with what seemed to me my duty as a citizen as well as a Mason, I promptly laid copies of these communications before the President of the United States, our Bro. William McKinley, which were acknowledged with the assurance of his 'deep appreciation and warmest thanks.' I do not need to recommend that this Grand Lodge take appropriate action in the premises, for I doubt not that ere these words had left my lips the resolution was formed in the breast of every member of the Grand Lodge to give prompt expression of our intense satisfaction at the signal honor conferred upon us as a Grand Lodge, and of our profound gratification as American citizens at these unprecedented evidences of the friendship of the Chief Magistrate and of the people of our sister Republic.

We also copy his remarks on Cuba and Porto Rico, and state that no action has been taken by our Grand Master in regard to these two Grand Lodges, for the very reasons assigned by the Grand Master of New York.

"Cuba and Porto Rico.

"Although we long have been, and theoretically are, in fraternal correspondence with the Grand Lodges of Cuba and Porto Rico, the war in Cuba and the persecution of the Cubans by the Spanish Government have practically suspended the operations of the Grand Lodge of Cuba for some years.

"On the 15th day of December last I addressed a communication to the representative of the Grand Lodge of New York near the Grand Lodge of Porto Rico, the answer to which was dated April 12th of the present year and explained in terms which, for prudential reasons, it is better not to repeat, why there had been such long delay in answering my communication. My own letter of acknowledgment, dated April 22d last, was stopped in transit by the United States Government on account of the order about that time issued prohibiting the transmission of mail matter to the island of Porto Rico.

"We are, therefore, and for some time have been, cut off from actual communication, either fraternal or otherwise, with our brethren in Cuba and Porto Rico. The war now waging for the deliverance of these islands from Spanish tyranny will very soon, as we all most fervently hope, succeed in brushing the Spanish flag from the face of Cuba and Porto Rico, the redemption of those two islands from tyrannous misrule, the re-establishment of two Grand Lodges, the resurrection of many subordinate lodges, and the revival of genuine Masonic work.

"Certainly by the close of the war, and possibly before, the way will open for extending relief to the suffering inhabitants of those islands. It must be that many of the Masonic household are among those who are in actual need.

"In January last, before war was declared between Spain and the United States, application was made to me for leave to issue an appeal to the craft in this jurisdiction for aid to the destitute Freemasons in Cuba. I took immediate steps to inquire by correspondence with the President of the United States and the Department of State whether funds thus contributed could be surely placed within reach of the object of our charity. Without feeling at liberty to disclose the nature of the replies which I received, it is sufficient to say that I deemed it unwise to issue such an appeal.

"Susequently, and even after the declaration of war, zealous brethren from other jurisdictions sought my official endorsement to the circulation of appeals for contributions in aid of the Freemasons in Cuba. The absolute impossibility of reaching Cubans except by permission of their enemies, the Spaniards, or else by the assistance of the United States troops, was to my mind a sufficient answer to all such appeals.

"When the time comes for an exhibition of genuine and practical charity, there is no doubt that the Freemasons of New York will be, as they ever have been, in the foremost rank, eager to discharge their duty to the fullest.

"I present this subject for your fraternal consideration, with the suggestion that the Grand Lodge itself, out of the treasury of the Grand Lodge, may well make provision for such quick relief as may seem advisable, in advance of the contributions by the lodges, to be expended or not, and in such amounts and under such safeguard as the Grand Lodge may deem wise."

His remarks under the heading of Peru are so forcible that we copy as follows:

"PERU.

"One year ago we were in fraternal correspondence and interchange of representatives with the Grand Lodge of Peru.

"On the 13th day of June, 1897, one Christian Dam was Grand Master of Masons in Peru, acknowledged as such by the entire Masonic world. On that day he fell, as Lucifer fell from Heaven. The light departed from a star in the Masonic firmament, and the law which had held it in the course of the majestic sweep of the constellation of Grand Lodges was set at naught as Peru plunged into the fathomless abyss of infidelity.

"On the 24th day of December last, there came to my notice, through Grand Secretary Ehlers, an edict of the said Christian

Dam, dated June 13, 1897, which is herewith submitted, wherein it directed that thereafter the altars in the lodges in Peru should no longer support the holy Bible, and all reference to the Great Light in Masonry should be excluded from their ritual.

"Before the sun had gone down that day, your Grand Master had penned an edict, which was addressed to all the lodges within this jurisdiction, announcing this Masonic suicide of the Grand Lodge of Peru, dismissing her representative as such from the presence of the Grand Lodge of New York, recalling the commission theretofore issued to our representative near the Grand Lodge of Peru, and interdicting Masonic intercourse with all persons thereafter claiming allegiance to the Grand Lodge of Peru, unless and until the said edict of the said Christian Dam should be revoked.

"The performance of my official duty began with the promulgation of this decree, and it ends when I herewith submit the same for your consideration; but our duty as Freemasons is still upon us, and that duty will not be discharged while life shall last.

"The waves of infidelity which broke upon the shores of Peru had already submerged the Grand Lodge of France, and it is for us to see that they do not lap the coast of our jurisdiction.

"The hand that snatches at the Bible upon our altars is the hand of an assassin, plucking at the heart of the fraternity; and the action of the Grand Lodge of Peru should awaken us to alertness as sentinels on guard.

"While Freemasonry is not a religion, and the doors of the lodge are freely open to devout and God-fearing men of whatsoever religious belief, nevertheless Freemasonry is the handmaid of religion, and teaches its votaries to give even closer allegiance to the faith of their acceptance.

"There stands in the city of Chester, England, and near its eastern wall, a venerable cathedral, in and out of which have passed generations of worshipers. The pulpit of that cathedral is adorned with Masonic emblems of richest carving. Before that pulpit and its altar have been brought little children for baptism. In the presence of that pulpit have stood young men and maidens to be united in the holy bonds of matrimony; and the solemn requiem for the dead has sounded over heads bowed before that pulpit in the bereavement brought by the hand of death. From one of its octagonal faces that pulpit shows to the visitor and the worshiper the square and the compass and the well-known sunburst. Upon another are carved representations of those twin patrons of Freemasonry, the Saints John. While upon a third are carved three figures: one, the entered apprentice, clothed as such, bringing forward a rough ashlar for the use of the fellow-craft; by his side the fellow-craft, clothed as such, engaged with the working tools of the craft in transforming a rough into a perfect ashlar; by their side, and standing erect, the unmistakable figure of the Master Mason, clothed as such, pointing the fellow-craft to the designs upon the trestle-board, and giving him proper instructions for his labors. On the right and left of these three figures stand the two Masonic columns just as we see them in every lodge room, except that upon one is carved the name Jachin, and upon the other the name Boaz. Standing in this cathedral a few years since, and looking upon the Holy Bible resting on the pulpit thus adorned, I could but exclaim: 'What mighty support does Freemasonry give to all religious teachers who open the Bible for the instruction of their people!'

"The entered apprentice is taught on his first entrance to the lodge room that the holy Bible is the Great Light in Masonry. He is commanded to take that Bible as the rule and guide for his faith and practice, and it becomes his duty to guard that Bible as the lover of his country would defend its flag.

"Many a widow has found it a pillow for her head in the hour of her affliction. It has been the solace of countless aching hearts, and has brought consolation to myriads of dying men. Without it there is neither light nor civilization nor Freemasonry; whereas we who gather about Masonic altars and drink in its teachings do learn therefrom the way to everlasting life.

"Sitting in this Grand Lodge under the official religious ministrations of the Jewish Rabbi, our Grand Chaplain, Doctor Rudolph Grossman, and of the Bishop of New York, our Grand Chaplain, the Right Rev. Henry C. Potter, let us as do they, clasp hands with fraternal grip, renewing our allegiance to the craft, increasing our devotion to its Great Light, and redoubling our faithful service to the Grand Master of the heavens and the earth.

"May our labors be guided by some measure of His wisdom, and be crowned with the smile of His approval.

"Brethren, the work of the one hundred and seventeenth annual communication of the Grand Lodge of Free and Accepted Masons of the State of New York is now in your hands."

(Before pronouncing the closing paragraph of the foregoing address, the Grand Master said:)

"Since the foregoing was put in print, and on Saturday evening last, a letter reached me from Lima, Peru, which I am delighted to lay before you.

"It so happened that the Rev. Henry W. Warren, a Bishop of the Methodist Episcopal Church, was about sailing upon a tour of inspection of the Methodist missions in South America as my edict relating to Peru was issued. A copy of that edict was carried by the Bishop to Peru and placed in the hands of Francis L. Crosby, of Lima.

"February 8th last, the Bishop wrote me from Callao, Peru, stating that Bro. Crosby, who is a past Grand Master of Peru, had already prophesied the action which would be taken by other Grand Lodges, and was, therefore, greatly pleased to receive a copy of my edict. The Bishop also wrote of the resignation of Senor Dam as Grand Master, of the great excitement which prevailed, and predicted great good as the result.

"I immediately wrote Most Worshipful Francis L. Crosby, Past Grand Master, for further particulars, and his reply, dated April 4, was not as reassuring as I had hoped.

"Subsequently I received from our Grand Secretary a translation of a communication over the signature of J. A. Ego Aguirre, Past Grand Secretary of the Grand Lodge of Peru, strongly opposing the action of the said Christian Dam.

"Saturday evening last I received the following welcome communication from Most Worshipful Francis L. Crosby:

"'LIMA, *May* 9, 1898.

"'W. A. SUTHERLAND, Esq., Rochester, N. Y.

"'VERY DEAR SIR AND BROTHER: I am most happy to advise you that at the quarterly session of the Grand Lodge of Peru, held three days ago, the Dam party was defeated and Bro. J. A. Ego Aguirre, a true Mason, was elected and installed as Grand Master. With this change, which your prompt and energetic action, together with that of other American Grand Masters, evidently aided very much to produce, the Bible will again occupy its honored place on our altars and true Masonry will be practiced.

"'With much respect, I am, dear sir and brother,

"'Sincerely and fraternally yours,

"'F. L. CROSBY, P. G. M.'

"It is said no joy in heaven equals that which is caused by the tears of the penitent.

"In the 'Lalla Rookh' of Thomas Moore the story of 'Paradise and the Peri' describes the priceless value attaching to the penitential tear in words of matchless beauty.

"The Peri, as you remember, standing before the gates of heaven and gazing with wistful eyes at the crystal bar which held them closed against her, asked the guardian angel if perchance she might not by some means atone for the past and gain admittance to Paradise.

"The angel bade her seek throughout the universe for that which would prove most precious in the sight of heaven, bringing which, the bar would fall and the gates open wide to receive her.

"You remember the story of her wanderings; how she brought back the last drop of blood that issued from the heart of the last survivor of the brave defenders of his native land against a conquering host of invasion. You remember how next she carried to the gates of Paradise the last sigh that escaped the lips of the dying maiden who gave up her life because of her love for another. You remember how each of these gifts proved unavailing and that for the third time the Peri visited the earth. She descended by the side of a playing boy, who had ceased his prattle and his games to fall upon his knees by the wayside and lisp his childish prayers. Passing by was a man of many sins, whose face was seamed with care and trouble. His hands were steeped in crime, his heart had been closed against pity, and his visage spoke the ferocity of the beasts of the jungle. The prayers of the child falling upon his ears awakened memories of his own youth, the teachings of his father and the prayers of his mother. Flinging himself upon the grass by the wayside these trooping memories opened the fountains of his heart, and penitential tears swept down his cheeks. Then it was that a light streamed upon the scene from the heavens above. The Peri knew it to be the approving smile of the guardian angel, and catching a tear from the sinner's cheek, she winged her way to the gates whose crystal bar had fallen, and which, swinging wide open before her, gave her abundant and joyful entrance into Paradise forever.

"Brethren, let us thank God that the tear of penitence has glistened upon the swarthy cheek of the Peruvian Freemason. Let us stand with wide-extended arms to welcome his return to the fold."

The report on correspondence was the tenth of the present committee, signed by Jesse B. Anthony, chairman, the other members being Emanuel Loewenstein and Emil Frenkel, the latter having made the translations of the proceedings of Grand Bodies in foreign countries.

This report covers 198 pages, including statistical tables, which are of great value to the Masonic student. The committee says, in concluding:

"It is with sadness we are again called to announce the death of a valued associate member of this committee—Bro. Ernest Ringer—whose sudden and unexpected death occurred January 8, 1898.

"The translations of foreign grand bodies were under his direction, and his two reports evinced eminent ability for the duties of that position. He was preeminently a student, and with a student's love and enthusiasm he entered upon a congenial labor, discharging it with great credit to himself and to the honor of the Grand Lodge of the State of New York. Of him it may be truly said, 'his death was untimely.'

"At an unlooked-for hour
The boatman came, and with his dripping oar
Conveyed him to the other shore."

William A. Sutherland was re-elected M. W. Grand Master.
Edward M. L. Ehlers was re-elected R. W. Grand Secretary.

OKLAHOMA.

The sixth annual communication was held at El Reno February 8-9, 1898.

Albert W. Fisher, M. W. Grand Master.
James S. Hunt, R. W. Grand Secretary.

The address of the Grand Master, of over eight pages, gives an account of his official acts and the state of the craft in that jurisdiction.

The usual attention is paid to the deaths of distinguished brethren abroad. He had not been notified of any deaths in his own jurisdiction.

He had made official visitations to some of the lodges, at all of which "he had been most kindly received and entertained, as only Masons entertain a brother."

Four new lodges had been constituted under charters.

One new lodge had been formed by dispensation.

Nine decisions rendered are reported, all of which appear to be in accordance with Masonic usage.

The reports of the Grand Secretary and Grand Treasurer show a favorable condition of work and finances.

The Maine resolutions as to rejected candidates were referred to the Committee on Law and Usage.

A communication from the M. W. Grand Master of the Grand Lodge of New York on the matter of the Grand Lodge of Pennsylvania was received, and the following resolutions were adopted by a rising vote:

WHEREAS, the circular letter of the M. W. Grand Master, William A. Sutherland, of the Grand Lodge of New York was read to this Grand Lodge; and,

"WHEREAS, the sentiments therein contained are such as ought to meet the hearty approval of all good men and Masons; therefore, be it

"*Resolved*, That this Grand Lodge, by a rising vote, express its full concurrence in the sentiments and actions of Grand Master Sutherland; and,

"*Resolved*, That the said letter be spread in full upon the proceedings of this Grand Lodge; and,

"*Resolved*, That our Grand Secretary be instructed to notify the Grand Lodge of New York of the action of this Grand Lodge in reference thereto."

An address was delivered by the R. W. Grand Orator, D. D. Leach.

There is no report on correspondence, but a resolution was adopted requiring one for the year 1899.

For the information of our own brethren who enjoy the reading of our annual proceedings we copy the following:

"*Resolved*, That the Grand Secretary be instructed to mail five copies of the Grand Lodge proceedings of each year to the secretary of each subordinate lodge in the jurisdiction.

"*Resolved*, That any member of the Grand Lodge be entitled to one copy of the proceedings of the last Grand Lodge by making application to the Grand Secretary and paying the cost price of the same.

"Amended, requiring application to be made prior to April 1st next."

Enoch M. Bradford was elected M. W. Grand Master.

James S. Hunt was re-elected R. W. Grand Secretary.

OREGON.

The forty-eighth annual communication was held in Portland June 15, 1898.

W. H. Hobson, M. W. Grand Master.

James F. Robinson, R. W. Grand Secretary.

Thomas A. McBride, Grand Representative of the Grand Lodge of the District of Columbia.

Eleven Past Grand Masters present, and Grand Representatives of thirty-eight Grand Lodges. The Grand Master delivered his address, which occupies over ten pages, with due and fraternal mention of the distinguished brethren who had died, among them being the Past Junior Grand Warden of his own jurisdiction, Bro. Samuel Hughes, and many others of sister jurisdictions.

He had laid the corner-stone of a Masonic Temple at Corvallis.

Two dispensations to form new lodges had been issued.

Authority had been given to the Deputy Grand Master and Junior Grand Warden each to institute a new lodge under charter and install their officers.

He had rendered six decisions, all of which are in accordance with Masonic usage.

The reports of the Grand Secretary and Grand Treasurer show a fair condition of finances and other matters in their departments.

Gross receipts, $5,428.53; number of lodges, 101; making returns, 98. After paying all expenses the Grand Treasurer reports a balance of $5,583.32. Of the educational fund there is reported a balance of $12,517.14. The Grand Orator, William T. Williamson, delivered an address.

The report on correspondence, of 176 pages, was presented by Bro. Robert Clow, in which he reviews the proceedings of fifty Grand Lodges, our own for 1897 receiving a fraternal notice of two pages, and we return our sincere thanks for his personal attention to this writer in his congratulations upon restoration to health and *activity.*

John B. Cleland was elected M. W. Grand Master.

James F. Robinson was re-elected R. W. Grand Secretary.

RHODE ISLAND.

A special communication was held in Providence October 15, 1896, for the purpose of laying the corner-stone of the new state-house being erected by the State of Rhode Island. A perspective view of the building appears in the volume of the proceedings.

The semi-annual communication was held in Providence November 16, 1896.

William H. Crawley, M. W. Grand Master.

Edwin Baker, R. W. Grand Secretary.

The regular business was transacted.

The first degree was exemplified.

A special communication was held April 15, 1898, for the purpose of laying the foundation-stone of the new Masonic Temple in Pawtucket. A picture of the building appears in the volume of proceedings.

The one hundred and seventh annual communication was held in Providence May 17, 1897.

William H. Crawley, M. W. Grand Master.

William H. Smythe, R. W. Grand Secretary.

The address of the Grand Master, of seven pages, as usual, gives an account of official acts and condition of the craft for the year.

Under necrology he mentions the names and history of thirteen Past Masters and a Past Deputy Grand Master who had died during the years of 1896 and 1897.

He had made sixteen official visitations to lodges.

We notice in his decisions that an applicant for a release of jurisdiction must himself make it to the lodge holding the jurisdiction. This has been the law of the Grand Lodge of the District of Columbia for many years, and in that time we have had no trouble on the score of invasion of jurisdiction. A lodge should never *receive* the application of a candidate, unless perfect in all particulars, so that it may be referred to a committee, and in due time be acted upon by the ballot.

The reports of the several Grand Officers show a favorable condition of Masonry in that jurisdiction.

The Grand Secretary shows a net gain of 130, against 219 last year. Total membership in the State, 5,018; the largest lodge has 523; smallest, 33.

This Grand Lodge has "Commissioners of Trials." Why cannot our own Grand Lodge adopt the same system?

Receipts were $4,591.45; expenditures, $5,405.98.

There is no report on correspondence in this volume; it is held over for the next.

Cyrus M. Van Slyck was elected M. W. Grand Master.

Edwin Baker was re-elected R. W. Grand Secretary.

The proceedings during the one hundred and seventh year received. The semi-annual communication was held in Providence November 15, 1897.

Cyrus M. Van Slyck, M. W. Grand Master.

Edwin Baker, R. W. Grand Secretary.

Twenty-eight lodges represented.

The address, of four pages, of the Grand Master refers altogether to the jurisdiction of one of its lodges.

Local business was transacted.

An emergent communication was held in Bristol February 4, 1898, for the purpose of burying Bro. Orrin Wilson, Past Master of Saint Alban's Lodge, No. 6.

A special communication was held in Pawtucket May 9, 1898, to dedicate a new Masonic Temple in that place.

The annual communication (the one hundred and eighth) was held in Providence May 16, 1898.

The grand officers as before.

Twelve pages are given to the address of the Grand Master; over two pages are devoted to memorials of deceased brethren.

Dispensations had been issued to many lodges for various purposes.

He had approved amendments to by-laws of several of the lodges.

He had officially visited quite a number of the lodges.

Under "decisions," we quote as follows:

"In this connection, there have arisen two cognate questions, upon which I have felt obliged to express an opinion.

"The first is in reference to the use of the stereopticon as an adjunct to the lessons of the several degrees. While I am aware that upon this subject there is room for an honest difference of opinion, to me the use of such an arrangement has seemed undesirable.

"It seems quite superfluous to attempt to paint the lily by adding to the beautiful word pictures of the several degrees, and with the most careful management there is a possibility, so near as to approach probability, that some error of the operator will excite one's sense of the ludicrous and lessen, if not destroy, the solemnity and impressiveness of the lessons taught by the lectures. In some jurisdictions the use of stereopticons and similar devices is specially prohibited, and at this time, when the only large collection of slides in the jurisdiction has been destroyed, it seemed to me wise to prohibit the use of the device until Grand Lodge should express an opinion upon the subject. If permitted at all, the use of the stereopticon should be allowed only within lines carefully and strictly marked.

"The second question arose from inquiries made by the Master of one of the lodges, and was, in my opinion, of sufficient importance to warrant the issuance of a circular letter to the Masters of the several lodges. It is as to the use of robes or costumes in the work.

"I think that I can no better express my views than by quoting from the above-mentioned circular letter:

" 'In reply to your request that I give my opinion as to the propriety of the use of robes or costumes in the work of the third degree, I deem it inexpedient to express my personal views until I shall present this subject to Grand Lodge at its next annual communication.

" 'For your present guidance, however, I think it proper to suggest that Grand Lodge has constantly expressed itself in favor of uniformity in the work, and in this direction has caused the ritual to be carefully revised and put in a form for permanent preservation. In that ritual no provision is made for any special costumes to be worn by officers or members during any portion of the work, and as it is the custom in this jurisdiction that, except in case of candidates, the dress should be the ordinary attire of a gentleman suitable to the time and place, it is reasonable to suppose that if Grand Lodge had intended to authorize any innovation in this particular, we would find regulations to that effect.

" 'I consider, also, that the adoption of special costumes of any kind by a portion of the lodges in the jurisdiction is inconsistent with the spirit of the strong and unvarying expressions in Grand Lodge in favor of strict uniformity in the work.

" 'Consequently, until Grand Lodge shall expressly authorize the use of such costumes, I deem it my duty to consider such use prohibited, and to require that the lodges in this jurisdiction omit the employment of any special costumes for the purpose of theatrical or dramatic effect in the work of the degrees.'

"In the circular I simply expressed the opinion that the use was prohibited because not expressly authorized.

"It seems proper that I should state now that my personal opinion is that the use of robes or special costumes is extremely inappropriate in a symbolic lodge. Bro. Mackey says: 'A proposition was made in the Grand Lodge of England, on April 8, 1778, that the Grand Master and his officers should be distinguished in future at all public meetings by robes.' 'This measure,' Preston says, 'was at first favorably received, but it was, on investigation, found to be so diametrically opposed to the original plan of the institution that it was very properly laid aside. In no jurisdiction are robes used in symbolic Masonry.'

" It would be unfortunate and a great mistake to depart from the uniform simplicity which has characterized Freemasonry in New England, and in seeking after theatrical display to an innovation likely to result in jealous contention between lodges of unequal financial ability.

"In a recent case, when a lodge received the petition and conferred the first degree upon a profane resident within the jurisdiction of a neighboring lodge, upon complaint I interdicted the Master of the lodge complained against proceeding further in conferring the degrees until investigation of the complaint should be made.

" Upon investigation, finding that the application on its face showed jurisdiction in the lodge to whom the petition was preferred, although the applicant resided out of the jurisdiction of that lodge, and finding no evidence of bad faith, but that the committee of investigation had been less careful in inquiring into the question of residence than it should have been, I authorized the Master of the lodge to proceed in conferring the degrees, provided his lodge should first pay to the lodge rightfully having jurisdiction the amount which that lodge would have received if the application had been properly made."

There is no report on correspondence, which is to be regretted.
Cyrus M. Van Slyck was re-elected M. W. Grand Master.
Edwin Baker was re-elected R. W. Grand Secretary.

SOUTH DAKOTA.

The twenty-fourth annual communication was held in Sioux Falls June 14-15, 1898.
Albert W. Coe, M. W. Grand Master.
George A. Pettigrew, R. W. Grand Secretary.
Sixty-nine lodges were represented.
Twelve and a half pages contain the address of the Grand Master, who renders an account of his stewardship for the past year.
After suitable reference to the distinguished dead, he states that charters were granted to three new lodges, which were duly constituted.
One dispensation had been issued to form a new lodge.
He had granted dispensations to several lodges to confer the several degrees on soldiers who were ordered to the front. He had refused to authorize a traveling lodge in the First Regiment of South Dakota Infantry, referring the matter to the Grand Lodge.
The report on correspondence, of 126 pages, was made by Past Grand Master William Blatt, reviewing the proceedings of sixty Grand Lodges. Our own for 1897 has two and a half pages of fraternal notice.
In regard to the "funeral" resolution, he says:

"A resolution was presented, providing, that in case where a sufficient number of brethren do not assemble to perform a respectable procession at the funeral of a deceased brother, *the Master is authorized to designate a committee, which may conduct the Masonic funeral service, wearing Masonic clothing.* The writer is wholly responsible for the *italics*. Shades of George Washington's monument! Where are you going? Or is it possible we are a back number, or too far West?"

We do not know what the *shades* of the monument have to do with this resolution, but we think that the Grand Lodge of the District of Columbia will dispose of it in a proper manner.

If Bro. Blatt will refer to pages sixty-six and sixty-seven of our last report, he will not require leather spectacles to find our review of his own proceedings.

Louis G. Levoy was elected M. W. Grand Master.

George A. Pettigrew was re-elected R. W. Grand Secretary.

VERMONT.

The one hundred and fifth annual communication was held in Burlington June 15–16, 1898.

Daniel N. Nicholson, M. W. Grand Master.

Warren G. Reynolds, R. W. Grand Secretary.

William H. Kingsley, Grand Representative of the Grand Lodge of the District of Columbia.

Ninety-seven lodges represented of 102 on the register.

The Grand Master presented a very lengthy address of thirty-five pages, over ten of which are devoted to memorials of the deceased brethren.

A special communication of the Grand Lodge had been held October 20, 1897, to lay the corner-stone of a new Masonic Temple in Burlington, and also a special in West Fairlee October 7, 1897, to dedicate the new Masonic Hall at that place.

At Sharon a special was held to constitute Sharon Lodge.

Five decisions rendered, all strictly conformable to law and usage.

At three o'clock p. m. the Grand Lodge proceeded to dedicate the new Masonic Temple, which in future is to be the place for holding the meetings of the Grand Lodge in all time to come.

The Grand Secretary's report shows number initiated, 388; number raised, 377; number admitted, 27; number reinstated, 14; total gain, 418; total loss, 385; present membership, 9,886.

The report on correspondence, of 132 pages, was presented by M. W. Marsh O. Perkins, P. G. M., reviewing the proceedings of fifty-two Grand Lodges, and in the regular alphabetical order we find three pages given to the proceedings of our own Grand Lodge for 1897, the present writer being highly honored by a lengthy extract from our review of Vermont for 1896, for which accept our thanks.

It was fully our intention to have attended the Grand Lodge of Vermont at the session for 1898, but it was not convenient to do so this year. If our life be continued to 1899, and health and strength should permit, we hope to do so at that time.

Daniel N. Nicholson was re-elected M. W. Grand Master.

Warren G. Reynolds was re-elected R. W. Grand Secretary.

WISCONSIN.

The fifty-fourth annual communication was held June 14-16, 1898, in Milwaukee.

Nathan C. Griffin, M. W. Grand Master.
John W. Laflin, R. W. Grand Secretary.

The address of the Grand Master occupies twenty-five pages. He says :

"During our fifty-four years of existence we have had twenty-eight Grand Masters, seventeen of whom are still living. There have been forty-four Deputy Grand Masters, thirty-three of whom are living, and twenty-one have occupied the Grand East. Out of forty-five Grand Senior Wardens, twenty-five are living, and eight have been permitted to fill the office of Grand Master. Out of forty-two who have been made permanent members during the last eighteen years, only four have died ; and we now have sixty-three living Past Grand Officers who are permanent members of this Grand body. * * *

"Between 1878 and 1897 I find that Wisconsin initiated, passed, and raised about 14,000 Masons. We lost by death during that time about 8,000. Our net increase for the twenty years was only about 6,000."

We notice this in one of his decisions :

"Can a new charge for un-Masonic conduct be made against a brother who is under suspension for a limited time before such sentence expires?

"A. Yes. It is doubtful, however, whether he can be tried under the new charge until his sentence of suspension has expired."

If a man be in prison for one year for robbery, and kills his jailer, what then ?

Eight special communications had been held to constitute lodges, lay corner-stones, and dedicate Masonic halls.

Reference is made, with suitable memorials, of the fraternal dead in his and sister jurisdictions.

The reports of the Grand Secretary and Grand Treasurer show a good financial condition, and from the report of the Committee on Returns we learn that there were raised, 802 ; admitted, 241 ; reinstated, 90 ; otherwise gained, 10 ; by new lodges, 19 ; total, 1,162 ; lost by various items, 882 ; net gain, 280 ; members last year, 16,946 ; present membership, 17,226.

The report on correspondence, of 113 pages, was prepared by Bro. Aldro Jenks, reviewing the proceedings of fifty-seven Grand Jurisdictions. Our proceedings for 1897 received a fraternal notice of about one page.

James G. Monahan was elected M. W. Grand Master.
John W. Laflin was re-elected R. W. Grand Secretary.

ILLINOIS.

The fifty-ninth annual communication was held in Chicago October 4–6, 1898.

Edward Cook, M. W. Grand Master.

George A. Stadler, W. Deputy Grand Secretary.

"The Grand Master read the following letter from M. W. Bro. Dewitt C. Cregier, and the chair was instructed to appoint a committee to call on the M. W. Brother and express the regret of the Grand Lodge at his illness and inability to attend the meeting:

"'St. Charles, Ill., *September* 27, 1898.
"'*M. W. Edward Cook, Grand Master, State of Illinois.*

"'Dear Sir and Brother: I am in receipt of your notice of appointment as chairman of Committee on Masonic Jurisprudence for the fifty-ninth annual communication of the Grand Lodge, with order to attend on 3d instant.

"'In the first place I am obliged to ask you to excuse this pencil writing, but be assured that the honor conferred by you is fully appreciated by the writer. I had delayed reply until now, hoping my health, after four months' sojourn in the country, would permit me to respond in person at least once more to one of those delightful annual meetings of the royal craft of Illinois, but at the present moment I feel that I must forego the pleasure of mingling with my brethren on their fifty-ninth general assembly; and I may be pardoned for adding my profound regret in being obliged to experience the first break in my attendance to the duties assigned me for more than a third of a century, and thus miss the warm grasp and fraternal greeting of those with whom I have long been associated in promoting the true principles of the ancient fraternity.

"'My dear Grand Master, this is penciled while quite sick, and in bed. Will you kindly convey to my colleagues of committee assurances of my high regard, and accept for yourself that full measure of personal and official esteem that long years intimate acquaintance have merited from,
"'Yours fraternally,
"'DEWITT C. CREGIER.'"

We copy this letter because Bro. Cregier *was* the Grand Representative of the Grand Lodge of the District of Columbia. With great regret we learn from the Masonic press that our esteemed brother died November last, although we have not yet received official notice of that sad event.

The address of the Grand Master is quite lengthy, being twenty-six pages long.

Three lodges had been authorized during the year.

Three lodge-halls had been dedicated.

Three corner-stones of public buildings had been laid.

In the matter of the observance of the centennial anniversary of the death of Bro. George Washington, December 14, 1899, the Grand Master reports all the correspondence, both from Colorado and Virginia, and says:

"The 'report' referred to in the foregoing letter from R. W. Bro. Carrington, and the 'program' mentioned in the communication from the committee, are herewith submitted for the inspection of brethren interested.

"It will be observed that the invitation to participate in the ceremonies is limited to the Grand Master or such alternate as he may designate, though there probably would be no objection to sending with him such escort or committee as might be considered advisable.

"It will also be noticed that the privilege is very courteously extended us to contribute such sum as we may think prudent to assist in making the occasion the complete success anticipated by its projectors.

"These thoughtful provisions do much to simplify the question, and will be of great assistance in shaping appropriate action on our part. The whole subject is respectfully submitted to the Grand Lodge for its further will and pleasure."

This was referred to the Committee on Finance, which reported:

"In the matter of the commemoration of the one hundredth anniversary of the death of Bro. George Washington, your committee fraternally refers the same to the Grand Lodge without recommendation."

We have searched the proceedings and do not find any action of the Grand Lodge on the report of that committee.

A special report was made by Bro. Robbins, chairman of the Committee on Correspondence, as follows:

"M. W. Bro. Robbins read his 'special report' upon 'Recognized, Recognizable, and Other Governing Bodies,' as printed on pages 125-143, Appendix, part 1, of this volume, and closing as follows, viz.:

"'In submitting the following lists we have had reference to the originally lawful character of the bodies named, and also to the question whether they have since set up any conditions or distinctions as tests of admission thereto not recognized by the charges of a Freemason, and which would consequently prevent the Masons of Illinois from meeting them upon the level of a perfect equality, whether in the governing or constituent lodges.

"'*Recognized Grand Lodges:* Alabama, Arizona, Arkansas, British Columbia, California, Canada, Colorado, Connecticut, Cuba, Delaware, District of Columbia, England, Florida, Georgia, Idaho, Indiana, Indian Territory, Iowa, Ireland, Kansas, Kentucky, Louisiana, Maine, Manitoba, Maryland, Massachusetts, Michigan, Minnesota, Mississippi, Missouri, Montana, Nebraska, Nevada, New Brunswick, New Hampshire, New Jersey, New Mexico, New South Wales, New York, New Zealand, North Carolina, North Dakota, Nova Scotia, Ohio, Oklahoma, Oregon, Pennsylvania, Prince Edward Island, Quebec, Rhode Island, Scotland, South Australia, South Carolina, South Dakota, Tennessee, Texas, Utah, Vermont, Victoria, Virginia, Washington, West Virginia, Wisconsin, Wyoming.

"'To this list should be added Tasmania, the conditions having long been ripe for the recognition of that Grand Lodge. Recognition has only waited upon their formal request therefor, and is herewith recommended.

"'The English District Grand Lodges and the Scotch and Irish Provincial Grand Lodges existing in the British colonies, or other open territory, are included in the recognition of the parent bodies.

"'*Grand Lodges known to have originally derived their Masonry, wholly or in part, from lawful sources, and which, in the present state of our knowledge, it is deemed expedient neither to accept nor reject as lawful members of the Masonic body:* The three Prussian Grand Lodges—The Three Globes, the Grand National Lodge of Germany, and the Royal York of Friendship, at Berlin; and the Grand Lodges of Concord (Zur Eintracht), at Darmstadt; Eclectic Union, Frankfort; Saxony, Dresden; The Sun (Zur Sonne), Bayreuth; The Netherlands, The Hague; National, of Egypt, Cairo. Also the lodges composing "The Free Association of Five Independent Lodges in Germany," viz.: Minerva of the Three Palms, and Baldwin of the Linden, both at Leipsic: Archimedes of the Three Tracing Boards, Altenberg; Carl of the Wreath of Rue, Hildburghausen; Archimedes of the Eternal Union, Gera.

"'*The following bodies are deemed to be without authority in Symbolic or Craft Masonry and the members of their obedience ineligible to visit lodges in Illinois:* Grand Lodge of Alpina, St. Galleen, Switzerland; Grand Orient of Argentine Republic, Buenos Ayres; Grand Orient of Belgium, Brussels; Grand Orient of Brazil, Rio Janeiro; Grand Orient of Chili, Valparaiso; National Grand Lodge of Denmark, Copenhagen; Grand Orient of France, Paris (*interdict*); Grand Orient of Greece, Athens; Symbolic Grand Lodge of Hungary, Budapest; Grand Lodge of Hamburg, Hamburg (*interdict*); Grand Orient of Italy, Rome; Grand Lodge of Luxemberg; Grand Symbolic Diet of Mexico, its constituent Grand Lodges and all other Grand Lodges in that country; Grand Lodge of Norway, Christiana; United Grand Orient of Lusitania (Portugal), Lisbon; Grand Lodge of Peru, Lima; Independent Grand Lodge of the Dominican Republic, San Domingo; Grand Orient of Spain, Madrid; Grand Lodge of Spain, Cadiz; Grand Lodge of Sweden, Stockholm; Grand Orient of Uruguay, Montivideo; Grand Orient of Venezuela, Caracas; *and all supreme councils, or sovereign sanctuaries, or other powers, however named, wherever situated, of whatever rite—excepting Grand Lodges of Free and Accepted Masons—assuming to erect lodges with authority to confer the degrees of Symbolic Masonry.*

"'Your committee recommends the adoption of the resolutions appended to this report. Fraternally submitted,
"'JOSEPH ROBBINS,
"'*Committee on Correspondence.*

"'*Resolved*, That the Grand Lodge of Tasmania, having been regularly formed by the concurrent action of the lodges having rightful authority in the premises, is hereby recognized as possessed of exclusive jurisdiction in that colony and cordially welcomed into the great family of Grand Lodges.

"'*Resolved*, That inasmuch as the Grand Lodges composing the German Grand Lodge League (*Grosslogen Bund*) have abdicated the authority to control their relations with other Grand Lodges, and therefore can no longer treat with them upon an equal footing, it is hereby directed that the recognition heretofore accorded to the said German Grand Bodies, or any of them, as independent Grand Lodges, be withdrawn without prejudice to their authority within the circumscribed domain in which they still maintain the right of separate action, and that all correspondence heretofore existing and based upon such recognition be discontinued.'

"M. W. Bro. Robbins moved the adoption of the foregoing resolutions.

"M. W. Bro. John C. Smith moved to amend the first resolution, as follows:

"'Insert after the word Tasmania, in the first line, the words "and Grand Lodge of Egypt;" also strike out the words "that Colony" in the fourth line, and insert the words "their respective countries.'"

"R. W. Bro. C. M. Forman moved to postpone the consideration of the amendment till next annual communication. This motion was lost. The amendment proposed by M. W. Bro. Smith was also lost. M. W. Bro. Robbins' motion to adopt the resolutions was then carried."

Bro. Robbins again prepared the report on correspondence.

He says in his introduction:

"*To the Most Worshipful Grand Lodge of Illinois, Free and Accepted Masons:*

"At the earnest solicitation of Grand Master Cook we have reluctantly determined to essay a report in the topical form. Only those who have had some experience in reviewing can appreciate how a busy man prosecuting for a livlihood a profession that is exacting both of time and endurance, and who has lived long enough to get tangled up with many other interests that may not be neglected without a guilty sense of having failed in duty to the community, the country, and the time in which he lives, might well hesitate before attempting a labor far in excess of that which has heretofore taxed his powers to the utmost—that of condensing the results of a survey of the Masonic field into one-half or one-third of the customary space.

"In determining the lines and scope of a report under this new departure we have before us two conspicuous examples; that of the lamented Past Grand Master Fellows, of Louisiana, who has just laid down the burden of life, and that of Grand Master Upton, of Washington. The former followed the topical plan for several years before his death, and the latter gave us a single example of it in his last report submitted one year before succeeding to the grand east."

As in the cases of Bros. Fellows and Upton referred to, we must decline any review of Bro. Robbins' report. We have neither time, patience, nor space to do justice to such reports, which are admirable, indeed, and we must add "*mirabile dictu.*"

Edward Cook was re-elected M. W. Grand Master.

George A. Stadler was re-elected W. Deputy Grand Secretary.

IOWA.

The fifty-fifth annual communication was held in Council Bluffs June 7, 1898.

Almon Ralph Dewey, M. W. Grand Master.

Theodore Sutton Parvin, R. W. Grand Secretary.

We are indebted to the Grand Secretary for advance sheets of the Grand Master's address and Grand Secretary's report; also the report on correspondence.

The address of the Grand Master occupies forty pages, and is a thorough "State paper."

We are a little suprised at the following:

"The earliest pages of history are too dim to acquaint us with the origin or the original powers of a Grand Lodge."

Now, the consensus of opinion of all Masons at the present day is that the very first Grand Lodge was organized in London in 1717, and the general regulations adopted by that very Grand Lodge in 1721 very distinctly set forth "the origin or original powers" of a Grand Lodge; and by those then adopted all Grand Lodges have been guided in the constitutions formed by them to a greater or less degree. It is possible, however, that in Iowa these "old regulations" may not be so faithfully observed as in most other Grand Lodges.

The Grand Master continues:

"But when first appearing with sufficient intelligence to be comprehended, it gives us the unmistakable evidence that a Grand Lodge was ever clothed with high authority, and at all times conceded to be the height of Masonic prerogative.

"Indeed, a Grand Lodge is clothed with all the attributes of government, and with a system of government complete within itself and peculiar to itself, and contains the elements of all forms of civil government. A civil government professes to contain the functions of the legislative, judicial, and executive. The first declaration of our laws—the preamble of the Constitution—is a declaration that contains all these elements of civil government. 'A Grand Lodge is the sovereign, legislative, judicial, and executive power of a territorial jurisdiction of Ancient, Free, and Accepted Masons.'

"Hence, within a Grand Lodge may be brought all these issues:
As a legislative body it may make laws; as a judicial body it may
construe them; as an executive body it may enforce them. No
higher authority exists to traverse or review its legislation; no
other tribunal can question the determination of its judicial functions, it being, for Masonic purposes, a court of last resort. Its
executive authority is conclusive and may be rigidly enforced."

    *   *   *   *   *   *   *   *

"The events of the past few months have awakened and astonished the whole civilized world at the conservatism manifested
by American statesmanship and the corresponding sentiment of
the American people. The warlike disposition, ever potent in all
arbitrary or despotic forms of government, has been found absent
in ours. The desire to grasp at grievances, either real or imag-
inary, for the purpose of conveying to the world that we possess
an ambition to retaliate on our neighbor without first appealing
to them to set all wrongs right by peaceful methods, has been fully
demonstrated to be no part of our disposition.

"And, my brethren, may we not justly and honorably attribute
this, or a great part of this noble American inclination of character, to the teachings and influences of Ancient, Free, and Accepted
Masonry?

"Masonry, with its peculiar yet silent aggressiveness, ingratiates
its teachings of humanity, beneficence, and conciliation into the
minds and hearts of its membership and through them to a whole
people. Yet Masonry, with all its army of followers; with its vast
influence, power, and greatness, can only continue where peace
reigns—that is, when and where war and contention commences,
Masonry ceases. Masonry never waged war; Masonry never mar-
shaled an army; Masonry never fought a battle.

"With a membership of over twenty-seven thousand in our
own fair State, with a roll of about eight hundred thousand in the
United States, each and all hearing and teaching the noble principles of our order, Masonry can well be claimed to exert an influence on the character of our people, and in its 'good way and
time' carry with it an influence that must tend to temper the disposition of a whole people."

Over thirteen pages are devoted to obituary notices of the distinguished brethren who had died during the year.

He refers to the decree of the Grand Master of Peru, and states
that when it came to his knowledge he issued on May 11th last an
edict of the usual form dissolving all relations with the Grand
Lodge of Peru.

Several corner-stones of public buildings were laid.

Three dispensations had been issued to form new lodges, several
having been refused because judged by him to be of doubtful propriety.

Necrology receives due attention, and reference is made to those
brethren in his own jurisdiction who had died and mention made
of them by name.

Two corner-stones of public buildings had been laid by him.

The jewel of one Worshipful Master had been arrested for irregular conduct as Worshipful Master.

Dispensations had been issued to organize three new lodges.

Charters had been granted to four new lodges, and deputies commissioned to constitute the same.

We copy the following extracts from the Grand Master's address:

"WASHINGTON MEMORIAL OBSERVANCES.

"At our last annual communication your Grand Master Ball reported fully the plan being prepared for observing 'the one hundredth anniversary of the death of Bro. George Washington,' which would occur on December 14, 1899.

"The sentiments and purposes set forth were received by this Grand Lodge with a fraternal and loyal spirit fittingly appropriate for so great a character and so distinguished a soldier, citizen, and Mason; so much so as to direct 'that a standing committee of five be appointed by this Most Worshipful Grand Lodge, to be known as the Washington Memorial Committee, and whose duty it shall be to correspond with other Grand Lodges and assist in formulating plans and arranging details for the proper observance of said anniversary; to propose a plan and program for the guidance of the several subordinate lodges in said observance, and to collate a brief history of George Washington's connection with and work in the Masonic fraternity, all of which shall be by said committee reported to this Most Worshipful Grand Lodge at the next annual communication for its action.'

"In obedience to said resolution and direction of this Grand Lodge, I appointed the following:

"Brother L. C. Blanchard (18), Oskaloosa.

"Brother Albert Head (159), Jefferson.

"Brother J. H. Trewin (144), Lansing.

"Brother J. F. Grote (349), West Side.

"Brother C. A. Carpenter (107), Columbus Junction.

"This committee, composed of distinguished citizens and Masons, have been active in considering the subject, and will submit to you their report at this session."

* * * * * * * * *

"The 'Order of the Eastern Star,' composed of Masons, their wives, widows, sisters, and daughters, has become a formidable organization in our State, being at this time composed of over two hundred chapters, with a membership exceeding eleven thousand, and officered and controlled by the 'fairest among ten thousand.'

"The character of its membership ought to have a tendency to attract the attention of this Grand Lodge, and, as far as consistent, receive our moral sympathy and support.

"My observation is, that where the chapters of the Order of the Eastern Star have been established, it has added a new zest to Masonry, stimulating its social features, and indeed proving itself an active auxiliary to our Order.

"If this be true, it would follow that it is little for us to do to so far extend our good wishes and fraternal sympathy as shall afford encouragement. That we may do so, I suggest the adoption of the following or some like enactment as a

"STANDING REGULATION:

"That the organization known and designated as the 'Order of the Eastern Star,' when composed of Masons, their wives, widows, sisters, and daughters, may occupy Masonic halls for festival and ceremonial purposes."

We fully concur in the above remarks from our own observation of the workings of the Order in this jurisdiction.

"In my years of devotion to and service in and for Masonry I have drank in my full share of the sweets of life; I have learned with greater force and power the meaning of the terms, 'Fraternity to all, charity unbounded, and brotherly love unrestrained.' Beautiful indeed are those sentiments; and grand are they to contemplate, cultivate, and exemplify. The lesson comes direct from Holy Writ, and finds sympathy and response in our better nature. To study and to know our Masonry is but a higher and more rigid cultivation of those principles—to them I commend you; to know them I encourage you; to practice them I entreat you.
"So, brethren—

> "'Press on! for it is Godlike to unloose
> The spirit, and forget yourself in thought;
> Bending a pinion for the deeper sky,
> And, in the very fetters of your flesh,
> Mating with the pure essences of heaven.'"

All active Masons devoted to the cause of humanity can heartily agree to this concluding paragraph of Grand Master Dewey.

The very excellent reports of Grand Secretary and Librarian Theo. S. Parvin are well worthy of perusal—quite too lengthy for us to take in hand.

The report on correspondence is again from the pen of that fearless brother, Rev. J. C. W. Coxe. It does ample justice to all interesting subject-matters, which are well handled. He gives our proceedings for 1897 over two pages.

Bro. Coxe gave us a friendly call on his return from the Grand Conclave at Pittsburg, which pleased us very much, and would wish to have more of them, but as it is not convenient, owing to the distance, we must cherish in our memory the *one*, hoping for a renewal at an early day.

We quote from his conclusions, viz.:

"In closing our report last year we renewed our dissent as to the wisdom of recognizing the Gran Dieta, as we did also when the report on that subject was presented to the Grand Lodge by the special committee. For reasons which were conclusive to our own mind, we refrained from setting forth in detail the ground of our reluctance to advise or consent to the proposed action, which we deemed premature, and, hence, unwise. Suffice it now to say that the chief of those reasons was the obligation of courtesy which we then deemed to be due, and which induced us to withhold much that was quite fully prepared for publication. That courtesy was not appreciated; at least, it was not reciprocated; and when, without the slightest previous intimation to us of the intention, the subject of recognition was presented to the Grand Lodge, there was no adequate opportunity for a fair and candid presentation of the reasons for delay. We therefore deem it but just to our brethren—to say nothing of ourself—that the considerations which influenced our judgment in urging the policy of prudent and cautious delay should be presented.

"Passing the inaccuracies of record and of action in our own Grand Lodge, to which we have elsewhere referred (under California); and also passing the questions of the regularity and the legitimacy of some of the Mexican lodges, concerning which not all intelligent investigators are agreed; and further passing the fact that there is no evidence of record of the healing by any competent authority of irregularly-made Masons within the jurisdiction of any of the Grand Lodges which composed the Gran Dieta, the Gran Dieta itself violated universal Masonic law and usage in several particulars."

Under head of California, he says:

"He quotes from Grand Master Ball on the Gran Dieta, and says that his 'recommendation was approved by the Committee on the address of the Grand Master, who reported as follows,' quoting then the resolution of recognition. It is singular how tangled are the threads of that record. The Committee on Grand Master's Address recommended the reference of the question of the recognition of the Gran Dieta 'to the Committee on Jurisprudence, to determine whether recognition of said Gran Dieta Symbolica is at this time feasible,' and their report was adopted. In the minutes of the second day, morning session, appears the record: 'In accordance with the order of yesterday the Grand Master announced the following special committees:

"'Mexican Masonry.—Matt Parrott (105); J. N. McClenahan (63), Past Grand Master; A. C. Dailey (108).'

"And it was this special committee (which, so far as the record shows, the Grand Lodge did not order) which made the report quoted by Bro. Davis; while the Committee on Jurisprudence, to whom the subject was referred, made no report."

Crom. Bowen was elected M. W. Grand Master.

Theodore Sutton Parvin was re-elected R. W. Grand Secretary.

MISSOURI.

The seventy-eighth annual communication was held in St. Louis October 18, 1898.

F. J. Tygard, M. W. Grand Master.

John D. Vincil, R. W. Grand Secretary.

The annual address of the Grand Master, consisting of thirteen pages, under distinct sub-headings, sets forth the condition of the craft and gives an account of his acts during the year. In his account of the dedication of the chapel at the Masonic Home on October 21 1897, which was his official duty, he refers to Mrs. Rosa L. Harris, Grand Worthy Matron, as being present, and who, in a most interesting manner, gave an account of the labors of the Eastern Star in accomplishing that work. Mrs. Sallie E. Dillon, the Grand Secretary, also gave valuable information in reference to details of efforts made by the Eastern Star in that connection.

He says:

"In view of the magnificent result attained, standing as it does, a monument to the labors and liberality of the ladies of the Order of Eastern Star, and without cost to the Masonic Home, I suggest that a vote of thanks be tendered to the Eastern Star for this evidence of their generosity and interest in the Masonic Home of Missouri."

We may add, just here, that in our reviews of the various Grand Jurisdictions we have, with great pleasure, observed that in all the Masonic enterprises started for Masonic purposes, wherever the ladies of the Eastern Star have been invited or permitted to assist, these enterprises have been eminently successful; and wherever we have become personally acquainted with these efforts, we have found that, without their aid, success would not have followed. We confess that we were greatly mortified when we learned of the unfavorable comments by ignorant brethren in regard to the establishment of their chapters and in the allowed use of our lodge-rooms for their meetings.

He had issued dispensations to form eight new lodges, declined issuing dispensation for one, and refused an application to organize an Army lodge.

He had rendered quite a number of decisions, all in accordance with general usage and the laws of his jurisdiction.

Several corner-stones of public buildings had been laid Masonically.

He had received the invitation to the Grand Lodge to authorize the Grand Master to attend and participate in the ceremonies at the Centennial Anniversary in honor of Bro. George Washington at Mt. Vernon, on December 14, 1899.

Those portions of the address not referred to were strictly local in character.

A voluminous report was made by the Grand Secretary, which comprises all the business transactions of the year.

In finances: Total received, $72,237.83; total expended, $28,-982.18; balance of assets, cash and bonds, $43,255.65.

The Committee on Jurisprudence did not sustain all the decisions of the Grand Master. Out of sixteen, four were not approved.

Rev. Bro. John D. Vincil, the Grand Secretary, as usual for several years, presented his report on correspondence, of 180 pages, reviewing therein the proceedings of fifty-four Grand Lodges, our own for 1897 receiving a fraternal review of four pages.

Bro. Vincil paid Washington City a visit during the summer, and it was a great pleasure and a high privilege to introduce him in his official capacity to Federal Lodge, No. 1, where he witnessed the conferring of the third degree upon three candidates.

We copy what he has to say on the visit.

"I record, with sincere pleasure, the ability of Bro. Singleton to resume his labors in this important field of duty. For a man of his years, the amount of labor performed is little short of marvelous. When tired Nature craves repose, and home claims the presence of the head of the family, this brother is found, nearly every night, for a given period of the year, visiting lodges, examining records, making official reports of work done, and meeting all other requirements incident to his office. Taking into account the fact of his illness, and the hindrance caused thereby, the wonder is that he was able to furnish any report on correspondence at all; but he has done so, to the credit of his Grand Lodge, and to the edification of all who will take the pains to read his twenty-eighth annual review. From a careful reading of his treatment of Mexican Masonry, I conclude that he is not in particular favor of the Gran Dieta.

"His Grand Lodge, in other years, had recognized a number of Grand Lodges in the Republic of Mexico, but he says that 'such Grand Lodges as have become members of the Gran Dieta should be erased from our list of correspondents.' He bases this view upon the sound principle that the Grand Lodges in the United States will remain as independent bodies, and never agree to enter into any league or union, by any other name, whereby any General Grand Body over all the Grand Lodges should become the supreme governing body of the rite. Placing himself upon the foregoing unanswerable principle, he asks: 'How, then, can any one of such Grand Lodges recognize and enter into official relations with the Gran Dieta of Mexico, which accomplishes the very purpose for that country which they decline doing in our own?'

"It affords this writer supreme satisfaction to find a member of the guild, possessing the experience and erudition of Bro. Singleton, declaring against a General Grand Lodge, and thereby refusing to recognize the Gran Dieta of Mexico. This has been the ground occupied by myself through the present controversy concerning the legitimacy of that body. The Grand Lodge of Missouri at its last session referred the subject of recognition to a special committee. Being assigned to a place on said committee, I shall never agree to the recognition of the Gran

Dieta, for the reasons so forcibly set forth by Bro. Singleton. I have made and reiterated the statement that recognition of a Grand Body in Mexico, that holds in subordination to itself independent Grand Lodges, is a clear and unequivocal surrender of the doctrine so long held among American Grand Lodges, as against a supreme governing body.

"Bro. Singleton's report contained many and extended extracts from proceedings reviewed, accompanied by terse and pertinent comments. Our Missouri proceedings for the years 1896 and 1897 were most fraternally and courteously treated. Hoping in the near future to meet Bro. Singleton in his own home in the Capital City of the Nation, I take leave of him with kindest personal and fraternal assurances of good will."

*   *   *   *   *   *   *

"Since the foregoing pages, I have been permitted to visit the Capital of our Nation. 'See Rome and die.' Not to 'see' Washington is to 'die' without having taken in the 'Eighth Wonder of the World.' There are many things to 'see' in Washington City that will cause 'wonder' to stir the thoughts of the beholder, whether he be an American or foreigner. For a Mason to visit the city named for him who founded the Great American Republic—himself a Mason—and not 'see' Bro. William R. Singleton, the Grand Secretary of the Grand Lodge of Masons in the District of Columbia, would be to evidence dereliction and indifference as unpardonable as surprising.

"Spending a time in sight-seeing about the Capital City of my country, I made bold to walk into the 'den' of my veteran brother and friend. To hand him my card was to evoke a welcome as warm as it was sincere. I was introduced to those present as 'Grand Secretary of the grandest State in the Union.' Bro. Singleton spoke feelingly and from experience, as he was once a resident citizen of this great commonwealth. It was in this Grand Jurisdiction that he first saw the light by which Masons work. From Missouri, he went out to labor and study as a 'wise and learned craftsman.' His mother jurisdiction holds him in tender remembrance and sincere reverence. Venerable in years and advanced in knowledge, he is held in great veneration by all who know him. I desire to join with thousands in doing honor to a veteran. Hence this addendum to my report.

"I am under many obligations for personal attention and courtesies received while in the 'city of magnificent distances.' Through him, I enjoyed the opportunity of greatly enlarging the number of acquaintances among the craft in the city of Washington. The visit with him to Federal Lodge, No. 1, the reception received there, with associations with Grand Master Palmer and others. all combined to render life perpetual sunshine for a whole week. May Bro. Singleton long be spared to go in and out among his admiring associates and co-workers."

E. F. Allen was elected M. W. Grand Master.
John D. Vincil was re-elected R. W. Grand Secretary.

NEW SOUTH WALES.

The proceedings from June, 1896, to June, 1897, were received November 22, 1897.

A special communication was held August 21, 1896.

A quarterly communication was held September 9, 1896.

The current business was transacted.

A quarterly communication was held December 9, 1896.

A quarterly communication was held March 10, 1897.

A special communication was held June 8, 1897.

At this communication the nomination of Grand Officers was proceeded with.

A quarterly communication was held June 9, 1897.

At these quarterly communications the regular current business of the Grand Lodge is transacted.

A special communication was held June 28, 1897.

Proclamation of the election of the Grand Officers was made. W. Bro. A. J. Scott, grand director of ceremonies, proclaimed M. W. Bro. Sir Joseph Palmer Abbott, K. C. M. G., speaker of the legislative assembly of New South Wales, as Grand Master.

The Grand Master then delivered a brief address.

The report on correspondence was presented at the communication of June 9, 1897, and is signed by John B. Trivett, chairman, and five others as members. Ninety-one pages are occupied. More than two pages are devoted to a friendly review of our proceedings for 1896.

We are indebted to the committee for their kind and complimentary notice of the present writer. As their Grand Representative since the death of our distinguished brother Albert G. Mackey we have taken a great interest in their rapid progress, since, by persistent efforts, they have succeeded in coming to the front as a prosperous Grand Lodge, and we feel assured that they will continue to exert a great influence for good in the Australian world.

Sir Joseph Palmer Abbott, M. W. Grand Master.

Arthur H. Bray, R. W. Grand Secretary.

KENTUCKY.

The ninety-ninth annual communication was held in Louisville October 18-20, 1898.

Reginald Heber Thompson, M. W. Grand Master.

Henry Bannister Grant, R. W. Grand Secretary.

Seventeen Past Grand Masters present.

Over twenty pages devoted to the address of the Grand Master, the most important part of which is given to the subject of "Negro Masonry," as developed in the action of the Grand Lodge of Washington at its last annual communication, held June 14, 1898, and which we shall give in our review of that Grand Lodge, should it be received in time for this report.

He says:

"By these resolutions the Grand Lodge of Washington recognizes as regular and legitimate Negroes who have been initiated in lodges which can trace their origin to Prince Hall Lodge, No. 459, which, with the First African Grand Lodge of North America, in and for the State of Pennsylvania, organized in 1815, and the Hiram Grand Lodge of Pennsylvania, are declared to be legitimate Grand Lodges, and by the third resolution the colored brethren are informed that, as 'both the white and colored races have shown a preference to remain, in purely social matters, separate and apart,' they are at liberty to establish lodges within the State of Washington, confined wholly or chiefly to brethren of their race, and in like manner to erect a Grand Lodge for the better administration of their affairs.

"Masonic charity would seem to demand that we should regard the illogical, unnecessary, and lame conclusion at which the Grand Lodge of Washington has arrived to a lack of information as to the recognized laws of the Masonic institution and of the facts of history rather than to a deliberate purpose to destroy the peace and harmony of American Freemasonry, which for more than a century has so gloriously fulfilled its mission of peace and good will among men. But whatever may have been the motive, this action has thrown an apple of discord into the peaceful ranks of our American brotherhood, which no motive can justify or excuse. Its effect is to abrogate the whole system of American Masonic jurisprudence, and must inevitably produce confusion and anarchy.

"I believe the Grand Lodge of Washington has been misled and deceived by the disingenuous report of its committee. 'The recognized laws of the Masonic institution and the facts of history' are absolutely at variance with the conclusions arrived at by that committee. It is pretended that Prince Hall was made a Mason in an English traveling lodge in 1775. There is no evidence of the fact but his own assertion; and it is a well authenticated fact that the Provincial Grand Lodge of Massachusetts, October 1, 1773, passed a vote that 'no traveling lodge has the right, in this jurisdiction, to make Masons of any citizens.' 'There is no pretense that he or any of his associates ever sat in a local lodge, and if they were citizens no British army lodge had a right to make them; consequently, if made at all, they were irregular and clandestine under the Provincial Grand Lodge rule.' (See Sir Woodbury's report, Grand Lodge Massachusetts, 1876.) Prince Hall himself professed that they had been working as a lodge for eight years prior to 1784. If so, they were certainly irregular and clandestine during that period. The English charter of 1787 conferred no authority, and was itself illegally and wrongfully issued ten years after the declaration of independence and eight years after the establishment of the Grand Lodge of Massachusetts; and even if they could derive any title from that charter, it is a well-authenticated fact that the African Lodge of Boston became dormant for many years, and was stricken from the roll of English lodges in 1813, thereby depriving them of the only possible title to regularity. There is no evidence that African Lodge, No. 459, ever worked after Prince Hall's death, in 1807. These are 'facts of history, well authenticated and worthy of full credit,' as ascertained by the Grand Lodge of Massachusetts after a candid and impartial review of all the evidence which could be adduced in regard to the origin and establishment of Negro Masonry, and upon these facts and others of like effect too numerous to mention that intelligent and justly esteemed Grand Lodge adjudged these Negro lodges illegal and clandestine, and they have been so held throughout the United States for more than one hundred years. There never was any such lodge as Prince Hall Lodge, No. 459, organized under the charter granted by Thomas Howard, Earl of Effingham. The lodge organized under that charter was African Lodge, No. 459, Boston, which became moribund after Prince Hall's death in 1807, and was stricken from the roll of English lodges in 1813. In 1827 parties calling themselves African Lodge, No. 459, for whose Masonry none can vouch, issued a manifesto, in which they repudiated the authority of the Grand Lodge of England, and declared themselves independent of any and all Masonic authority except their own sweet will.

"From this bastard progeny of an illegitimate and spurious body sprung the Prince Hall Grand Lodge. As to the two Pennsylvania Grand Lodges, no evidence of any fact in history, well authenticated or otherwise, has ever been adduced to show their legitimacy. From 1776 until 1813 the African Lodge was clearly clandestine by the 'recognized law of the Masonic Institution,' and in 1827 they declared themselves independent of the Grand Lodge of England and free from all Masonic authority, and from that day to this they have enjoyed the freedom of the wild ass and rejoiced in the liberty of an unbridled and unrecognized existence— a freedom which the committee of Washington Lodge seem anxious to emulate, when, in order to convince the outside world of the catholicity of their Masonry, they take unto their embrace the unctuous and unwilling African, ignore the facts of history, and insult the intelligence and challenge the honesty of the Grand Lodge of Massachusetts—in fact, the whole body of American Masonry—by denouncing the candid judgment of impartial men, acting under the sanction of Masonic obligation, as the unworthy result of race prejudice and cowardly prudence.

"It is 'a recognized law of the Masonic Institution,' first proclaimed in this very connection by the Grand Lodge of Massachusetts in 1782, and recognized and religiously observed by every Grand Lodge in America from that day to this, that 'no Masonic body can admit a rival upon its own territory, and the organization that commits encroachment upon territory previously appropriated and already held by another does, by so doing, invite repudiation, and places itself under the ban of Masonic interdiction;' that 'by the erection of a Grand Lodge in a State, all Masonic powers over what is called Blue Masonry are merged in it, and henceforth it exists therein supreme and sovereign over a jurisdiction which it can neither divide nor share with any other Masonic Grand Body in the world.' This is the fundamental principle of the American system. Without it, that system cannot exist. It is 'a recognized law of the Masonic Institution.' This principle, the violation of which disturbs the peace and threatens the existence of every Grand Lodge in the United States, the Washington committee sets aside with the flippant remark, 'What of it!' 'It's not a landmark,' and therefore not immutable, and the Grand Lodge of Washington, misled by its rash committee, abrogates and annuls.

"The Grand Lodge of Kentucky has always claimed and exercises the supreme right of determining who are and who are not Masons within its territorial bounds. It never has and does not now admit that two supreme bodies of legitimate Masons can exist at the same time in the same territory. It holds itself to be the true fountain and source of all Masonic life in Kentucky. If a Negro Grand Lodge can be erected in the State of Washington, co-ordinate in power and equal in legitimacy with the white Grand Lodge, then each should seek recognition of the other. We have no information that either has done so."

We have copied these remarks, because they coincide more or less with our own ideas, after a critical examination of this subject ever since the publication by the Grand Lodge of Massachusetts in 1870, which all should read if they desire to know the facts in this matter.

From the Masonic press we learned of the action taken by the Washington Grand Lodge, and in anticipation of our duty to our own Grand Lodge in the premises we corresponded with our distinguished brother William James Hughan, of England, upon the subject of charters of "army lodges" in England of the last century, requesting, if possible, that he send us a copy of one of the army lodge charters, our object being to show that such charters could not authorize any army lodge, or, as Bro. Gould calls them in his history of Masonry, "field" lodges to make Masons of citizens of any country where regular lodges under any constitutions already existed.

It is a canon of law that parties acting under chartered privileges are bound to conform to the specific purposes of such charters and cannot transact any other business or affairs except as specified in the very terms of said charter.

The following is copied from the Constitution of the Grand Lodge of England, page 40:

" It being essential to the interests of the craft that all military lodges should be strictly confined to the purposes for which their warrants were originally obtained; *and very great abuses having arisen from the improper initiation of Masons by such lodges,* every warrant, therefore, which is held by a military lodge shall be forfeited unless the following laws be complied with, in addition to those specified under the head of Private Lodges:

" ' 1. No warrant shall be granted for the establishment of a military lodge without the consent of the commanding officer of the regiment, battalion, or company to which it is to be attached.

" ' 2. No military lodge shall, on any pretense, initiate into Masonry any inhabitant or sojourner in any town or place at which its members may be stationed or through which it may be marching, nor any person who does not at the time belong to the military profession, nor any military person below the rank of corporal, except as serving brethren, or by dispensation from the Grand Master or Provincial Grand Master.

" ' 3. When any military lodge under the Constitution of England shall be out of England it shall conduct itself so as not to give offense to the Masonic authorities of the country or place in which it may sojourn, never losing sight of the duties it owes to the Grand Lodge of England, to which communication is ever to be made and all fees and dues regularly transmitted.' "

Bro. Gould says, Vol. VI, page 464:

" The black Masons, whose initiation in 1775 has been recorded under that year in the preceding chapter, page 415, applied to England for a charter, their lodge having then existed for eight years, in 1784. Their request was granted September 29, 1784, but the warrant did not arrive in Boston until 1787. It bore the number 459 and the title 'African Lodge.' Prince Hall, born 1748, died 1807, who was the first Master, established a lodge by *his own authority* at Philadelphia in 1797, and a second at Providence, R. I., shortly afterwards. The three lodges formed a Grand Lodge in 1808. The 'African Lodge' was not shown in the English lists after 1813, but it did not formally declare its independence of foreign control until 1827. In 1847 there were three colored Grand Lodges—one at Boston and two in Pennsylvania. These met in convention and organized a National Grand Lodge, which has met since triennially."

English Constitution, page 38, section 28:

" If the warrant of a lodge be sold or procured by any other means than through the regular channel of petition to the Grand Master or a provincial Grand Master, such warrant shall be forfeited and the lodge erased."

After the close of our Grand Lodge, at its communication held December 27, 1898, we received two pamphlets from the Grand Lodge of Arkansas on the subject, with a reference to the Constitution of the United Grand Lodge of England, quoted from Dr. Oliver; one of these we sent to Bro. Hughan, and recently received the following answer:

"I have again looked into the matter since the receipt of Grand Lodge of Arkansas *re* Grand Lodge of Washington, and have once more to report that no such regulation, as referred to by Dr. Oliver in his Dictionary of Symbolic Masons *re* Military Lodges, appears in any * * * * * of Courts of Grand Lodge of England until the year 1815. Dr. Oliver gives no date, and he was simply quoting laws in operation when his work was published.
"Yours fraternally,
"WM. J. HUGHAN."

In response to this we have to say that the irregularities like that case of Prince Hall, where military lodges had repeatedly violated their charters, impelled the Grand Lodge of England to place their interdict *formally* upon their statutes to show that no chartered privileges ever existed beyond the "*wording*" of the charter.

It seems that sentiment controls our distinguished brother, and he evidently inclines to be in favor of the regularity of the Prince Hall organization, which we greatly regret. Our view, as above expressed, as to the powers conveyed by a charter, must prevail in the minds of all who know what a charter of any kind is designed to accomplish, viz., its *specific declarations*.

We have always viewed the matter in this light, viz :

A military lodge never had any authority whatever to act outside of its chartered privileges in any locality. In Boston at that time, March 6, 1775, there were lodges in full operation under three distinct constitutions, viz., the modern Grand Lodge, the Ancients, and Scotland.

Prince Hall and his compeers were distinctly instructed that a charter was *necessary* from England. If they applied for one *immediately*, which is doubtful, they did not receive one before 1787. In the meantime, they had been making Masons.

We find this in Gould, "Sea or Field Lodges" (p. 419, vol. VI):

"In nearly all cases, the army lodges, in the event of removal from one State to another, were authorized to continue working *unless there was in existence a Grand or Provincial Grand Lodge, when the sanction of the presiding officer had to be obtained.*"

In this way we may possibly discern the first germ of the principle of "exclusive (State) jurisdiction."

Did the army lodge, in 1775, comply with the above and obtain the *sanction* of either of the Provincial Grand Masters of Masons of Massachusetts? No, they did not; for if so, there was no necessity for seeking a charter from the Grand Lodge of England.

In view of the foregoing remarks, we are constrained to believe that not a single impartial examiner into this question can for a moment believe that there ever was or ever could be any legitimate Masonry derived from the unauthorized action of the military lodge in 1775.

First, the conferring of the degrees was an irregular proceeding. The Grand Lodge of England would *at this day* decide it to have been such.

Second, these irregularly-made Masons proceeded, without a charter or any other kind of a warrant, to make other Masons for more than ten years before they received their charter.

We now quote section VIII, second paragraph, of the General Regulations of 1721, *from an original copy of 1723*, before us:

"If any set or number of *Masons* shall take upon themselves to form a *lodge* without the *Grand Master's* warrant, the *regular lodges* are not to countenance them as *fair brethren* and duly formed, nor approve of their acts and deeds, but must treat them as *rebels* until they humble themselves as the *Grand Master* shall in his prudence direct, and until he approves of them by his warrant, which must be signified to the other lodges, as the custom is when a *new lodge* is to be registered in the *List of Lodges*."

Secondly, we quote also from the same book, page 71:

"The manner of constituting a *new lodge* practiced by his Grace the DUKE WHARTON, the present RIGHT WORSHIPFUL GRAND MASTER, according to the *ancient usages of Masons.* A *new lodge*, for avoiding many irregularities, should be solemnly constituted by the *Grand Master*, with his Deputy and Wardens, or, in the Grand Master's absence, the *Deputy* shall act for his *Worship*, and shall choose some *Master* of a *lodge* to assist him," &c.

This has always been considered as *mandatory* and never omitted, and no lodge has ever been permitted to do any Masonic work until the constitution of the same by authority of a Grand Master.

We refer now, in this connection especially, to what occurred in Washington City in 1793, September 18th, when the corner-stone of the Capitol was laid by General Washington. Federal Lodge, No. 15, was chartered by the Grand Lodge of Maryland September 6, and the lodge was assembled on that occasion but took no part in the ceremonies, "*because it had not yet been regularly constituted.*"

We have no evidence that the officers of that famous *mob* of colored men were ever installed; for who was there to install them?

We must bear in mind that this was the invariable custom from the earliest date of our modern Masonry, since 1717.

Have we not shown the foulness of the fountain-head of this so-called *colored* Masonry? We firmly believe if they had been *white* men the whole affair would have passed away with that generation.

Now, the present writer has always duly *recognized* and *fraternized* with regularly-made Negro Masons, and he has met many such in the fifty-nine years of his Masonic career.

In 1843, in the city of St. Louis, Bro. Joab Bernard, Deputy Grand Master of the Grand Lodge of Missouri, laid the corner-stone of the Centennial Methodist Church.

Frank Johnson and his famous Negro band of minstrels were in St. Louis giving concerts. The present writer was Acting Grand Marshal, and engaged that band to furnish music for the occasion. When he arrived at our hall Frank Johnson proclaimed himself to be a Mason, with three others of the band. We examined Johnson and he vouched for the others. These four were admitted to the Grand Lodge room and were furnished with suitable regalia. They took their places in the band with regalia on, and St. Louis citizens for the first time beheld the white and colored Masons parading the streets together.

In Boston a great many colored men have been made Masons by the regular bodies, even to the Commandery.

In our position as Grand Secretary we have had many interviews in our office with colored Masons from foreign lodges, bearing regular diplomas, and we have invariably treated them just as we do our white brethren.

We do not recognize *color* in Masonry, hence the *color* question has nothing to do with this discussion, except with many *Negrophiles*, who seem to care more for the welfare of the Negro than for the peace and harmony of their white brethren; but we feel assured that if those two applicants in Washington had been white men the Grand Lodge of Washington would never have considered the question at all.

We think that it has been clearly shown, first, that the military lodge had no authority for conferring the degrees upon Prince Hall and others unless their charter shall be produced showing such authority; second, that if such authority did exist in that charter, that Hall and his crew, not being a regularly-chartered lodge by section VIII, Old Regulations, had not authority to work as a body; third, that although a charter had been granted and received by Hall, there was never a regularly *constituted* lodge, and therefore all work done under the presumption of a charter was irregular; and, finally, fourth, there has never been any regu. lar or Masonic authority since that time to legalize any act of theirs down to the present day.

We shall have more to say on this subject when we have an opportunity to review the proceedings of the Grand Lodge of Washington in reply, *seriatim*, to the *pretended* arguments of the committee.

James E. Wilhelm was elected M. W. Grand Master.

Henry B. Grant was re-elected R. W. Grand Secretary.

INDEX TO APPENDIX.

Number of Grand Lodges reviewed, 50.

Address of M. W. Grand Master:

JOHN H. SMALL, Jr.,

Corner Fourteenth and G Streets, N. W.

᙮ ᙮ ᙮

Address of R. W. Grand Secretary:

WM. R. SINGLETON,

909 F Street, N. W., Masonic Temple.

᙮ ᙮ ᙮

Address of R. W. Assistant Grand Secretary:

WILLIAM A. GATLEY,

1833 Fifth Street, Le Droit Park.

᙮ ᙮ ᙮

Communications of the Grand Lodge:

March 30 (special),
May 10,
November 8,
December 27,

at 6 o'clock P. M.

www.ingramcontent.com/pod-product-compliance
Lightning Source LLC
Chambersburg PA
CBHW060447280326
41933CB00014B/2690